CUSACK'S FREEHAND ORNAMENT

CUSACK'S FREEHAND ORNAMENT

A Text Book with Chapters on Elements, Principles, and Methods of Freehand Drawing,

FOR THE GENERAL USE OF

Teachers and Students of Public, Private and Elementary Schools; for Students in Training Colleges, and for ElementaryArt Students.

BY

CHARLES ARMSTRONG,

Art, Master, City of London School of Art; Late of the National Art Training School; Examiner to the Art Department.

Author of "Cusack's Shading" and "Cusack's Model Drawing.

KALPAZ

ISBN: 978-93-5128-720-9(PB)

First Published in 1895
Indian Reprint in 2017

Published by

Kalpaz Publications
C-30, Satyawati Nagar,
Delhi – 110052
E-mail: kalpaz@hotmail.com
Website: kalpazpublications.com
Ph.: +91-9212142040

Cataloging in Publication Data—DK
Courtesy: D.K. Agencies (P) Ltd. <docinfo@dkagencies.com>

Armstrong, Charles *(Art master)*, author.
Cusack's freehand ornament : a text book with chapters on elements, principles, and methods of freehand drawing, for the general use of teachers and students of public, private and elementary schools; for students in training colleges, and for elementary art students / by Charles Armstrong.
pages cm
"First published in 1895"—Title page verso.
ISBN 9789351287209

1. Design—Study and teaching. 2. Drawing—Study and teaching. I. Title.

NK1510.A76 2017 DDC 745.4071 23

PREFACE.

Twenty years ago it was generally believed that only a very small portion of the population were born with natural ability to draw, and that it was useless for the remainder to try.

Now, however, it is generally admitted that all can develop a certain amount of ability to draw. Drawing has become general in elementary schools, and is recognised as a help in almost every trade or profession.

This sudden popularity of the subject must make it very hard for teachers, who find a large proportion of their pupils with natural ability far below the average. To make headway at all with such pupils, definite method is essential. The object of this book is to teach definite methods, and to impress them on the mind by repetition.

The Plates are therefore numerous, tending to increase interest in the subject by constant change in the material to which method is applied. They are carefully graduated from a few elementary lines to a stage beyond the requirements of the usual elementary examinations.

An analysis of each Plate is given, and the different steps shown so that by working on the lines suggested the student acquires a definite method of procedure, which becomes so much a habit with him, by constant use, that he will naturally apply it to any drawing he may attempt, whether at an examination or elsewhere.

The preliminary chapters deal with Elements, Principles, and Methods, only so far as they are "to the point," or directly helpful in this subject. There are many other Elements, not so common as those used, and also many other Principles of Ornament, but they are for the designer, and not essential for the elementary student of drawing.

The Principles illustrated, however, are really helpful to the student who wishes to make an intelligent rendering of the Ornament.

Many of the Plates are taken from copies set at the examinations of the Art Department, and are placed as nearly as possible in order of difficulty, but the student must remember that the copies are no sure index to the difficulty of the examination, for if the copies of late are easier, the standard of examination may be increasing steadily year by year.

Many of the Plates have been designed to emphasise some particular principle, and have been used successfully in the large classes under the Author's supervision.

I am indebted to Professor Cusack for reading over the proofs, and for the encouragement given to my methods and ideas on this and other subjects, as also for many valuable hints in the preparation of this and previous works.

"Art is long," is true for everyone, but it is much longer for some than for others; the weak ones must not be discouraged, however, but must give the subject more time and more strenuous brain effort, by which in the end they will succeed. It is to be remembered that not the fact of being born clever makes a genius, but that "infinite trouble is the mother of genius." Those who are born clever do not need method, they can draw without it, but they are a very small minority.

If, therefore, the weak ones find help from the methods, and interesting fields for practice in the multiplicity of examples, the expectations of the Author will be realised.

C. ARMSTRONG.

CITY OF LONDON SCHOOL OF ART.

June 25th, 1895.

CHAPTER I.

ELEMENTS OF WHICH DRAWINGS OF ORNAMENT ARE MADE UP.

(*a*).—**Straight Lines** :—

A straight line, being the shortest distance between two points, can admit of no variation or irregularity. In attitude or position it may be (1) vertical, (2) horizontal, or (3) inclined.

(1) *Vertical* lines, in reality, are those which point to the centre of the earth. They are represented on paper upright, as in Fig. 1.

Fig. 1

(2) *Horizontal* lines are those which are level; that is, they take the same direction as the surface of water. They are represented on paper from side to side, as in Fig. 2.

Fig 2

(3) *Inclined* lines are those which are drawn in any other direction than those above named, as in Fig. 3.

Fig. 3

Ornament may be composed of mere repetition of either of these kinds, or by the combination of two, or of all three of them, as in fret patterns, as in Figs. 4, 5, 6, 7.

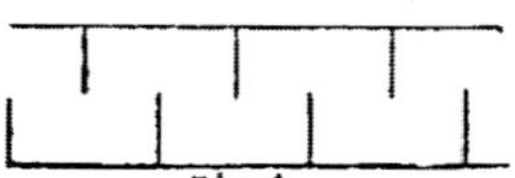

Fig. 4

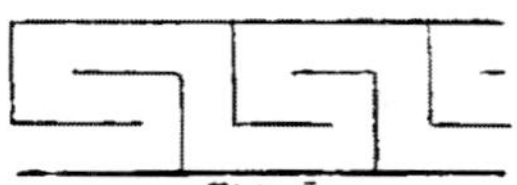

Fig. 5

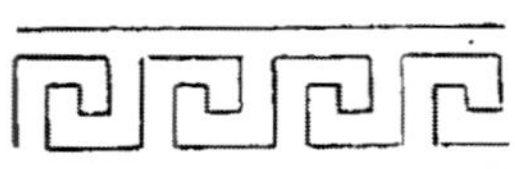

Fig. 6

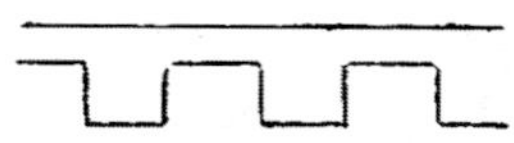

Fig. 7

and flutings, Fig. 8.

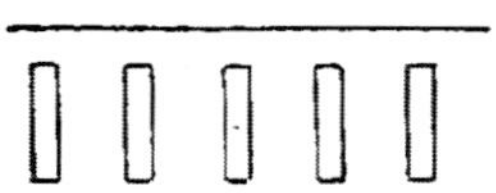

Fig. 8

the zigzag, Fig. 9.

Fig. 9

and plait, Fig. 10.

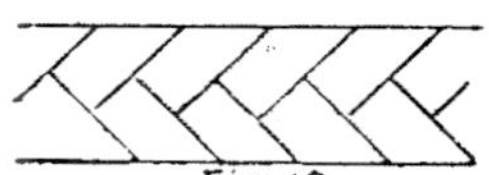

Fig. 10

(*b*).—**Simple Curves** :—

A simple curve is a line which is evenly bent in one direction only. Some of them may be classified thus :—

Spirals, or parts of them.
Volutes, „ „ „
Circles, or arcs of circles.
Ellipses, or parts of ellipses.
Catenary curves.

(1) *A spiral* is commonly represented as in Fig. 11., and the commonest illustration of it is a wire spring.

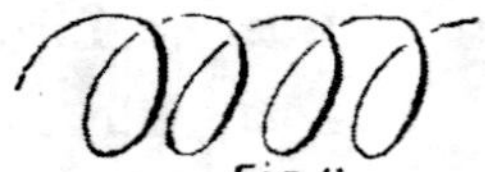
Fig. 11

(2) *A volute* is an evenly diminishing simple curve, or spiral, and is represented as in Fig. 12.

Fig 12

(3) *A circle* is the name commonly given to the boundary line (or circumference) of a plane figure whose edge is equally distant from one point, the centre. Properly speaking, the circle is the *figure contained* by the circumference.

(4) *An ellipse* is the name given to the shape of the appearance of a circle viewed at an angle, and is such that its upper and lower halves, its right and left halves, and its four quarters are in each case equal to one another, in every respect.

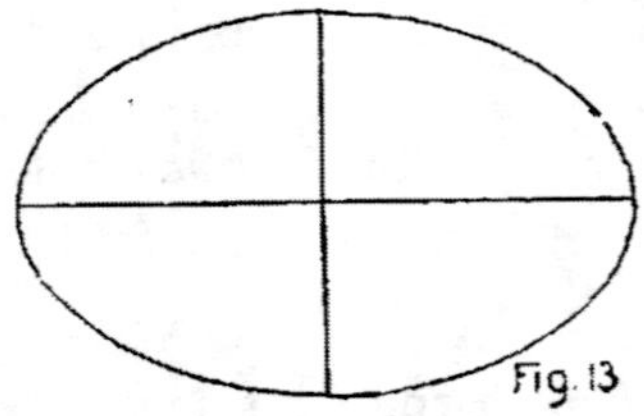
Fig. 13

(5) *Catenary curves* are those formed by suspending ropes, chains, drapery, garlands, &c., from two points, as in Figs. 14, 15, 16.

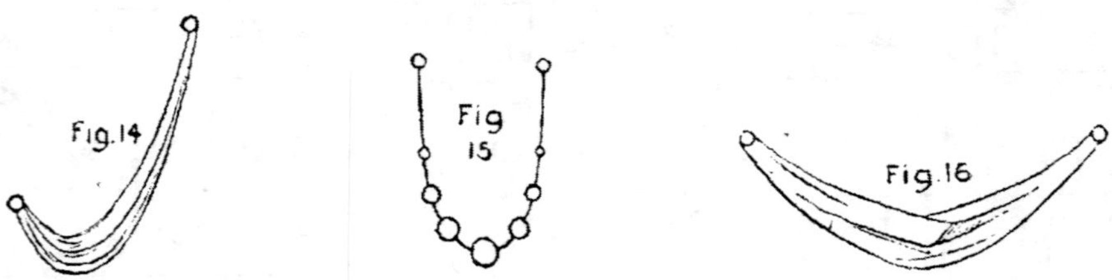

They are sometimes called *swags* or *festoons*.

(*c*).—**Double Curves:**—

A double curve bends first in one direction and then in another. They are sometimes called "lines of beauty." The following kinds of ornament are made up of double curves.

(1) *Waves.*—
Figs. 17, 18.

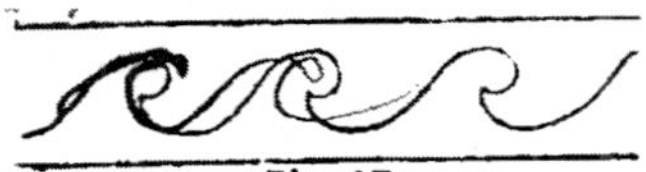
Fig. 17

and

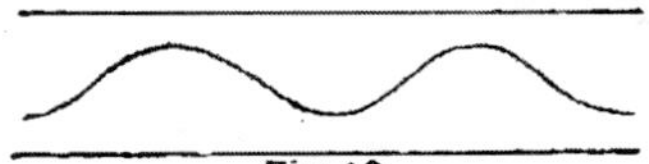
Fig. 18

(2) *Twists*—
Figs. 19, 20.

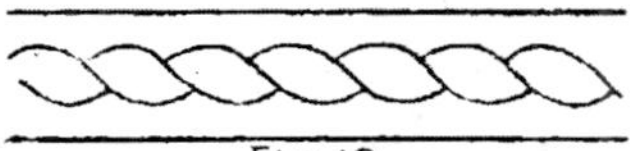
Fig. 19

and

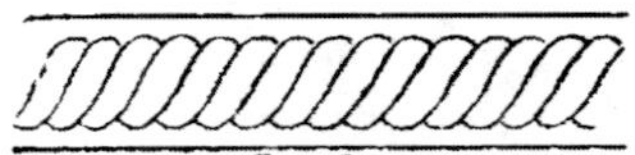
Fig. 20

(3) *Scrolls*—
Fig. 21.

Fig. 21

(4) *Reversed scroll borders*—
Figs. 22, 23.

Fig 22

and

Fig. 23

Having considered the various kinds of line that we are likely to meet with in drawings of ornament, we shall pass on to the details of them, such as leaves, stems, &c., complete in themselves in one sense, but yet being only elements in the complete drawing.

(*d*).—**Direct from nature** we get:—

Leaves.
Stems.
Tendrils.
Foliage nests.
Sheath leaves.
Buds.
Flowers.

(1) *Leaves.*—The leaves most commonly used in ornament are the water leaf, with a prominent midrib, and a wavy edge, as in Figs. 24 and 25.

Fig 24

and

Fig 25
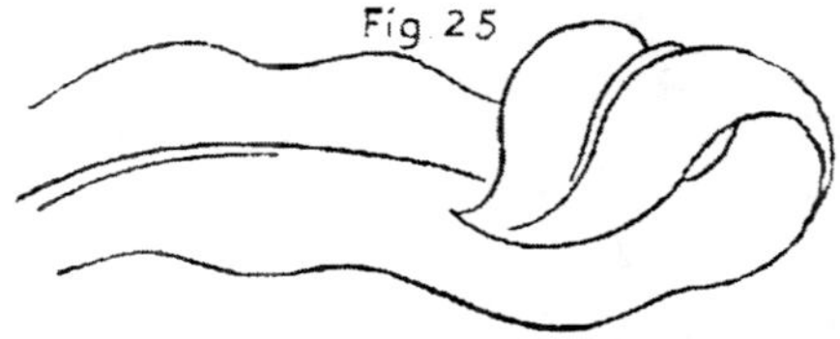

and the acanthus leaf, Fig. 26, which is divided up into lobes and sublobes. The loops or divisions between the lobes point in the direction of growth.

Fig. 26

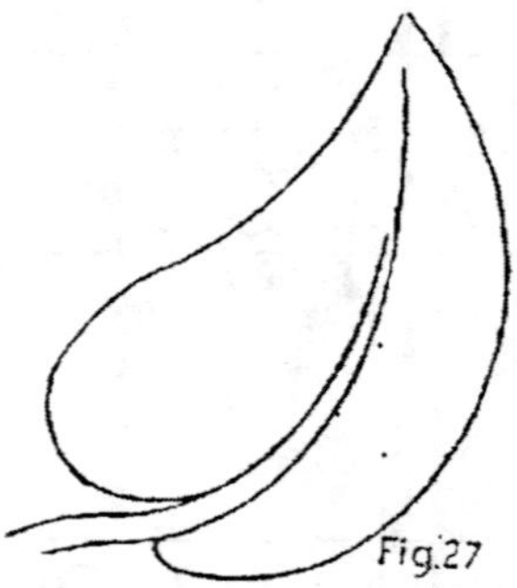

Fig. 27

Other leaves are used occasionally, and are generally based on some particular plant. Their edges are *serrated* or varied with saw like points or teeth, or merely curved, as in Fig. 27.

(2) *Stems.*—In nature the parts of stems generally grow at slight angles to one another, diminishing in length and thickness as they extend. This diminution is known as "*exhaustion.*" See Fig. 28.

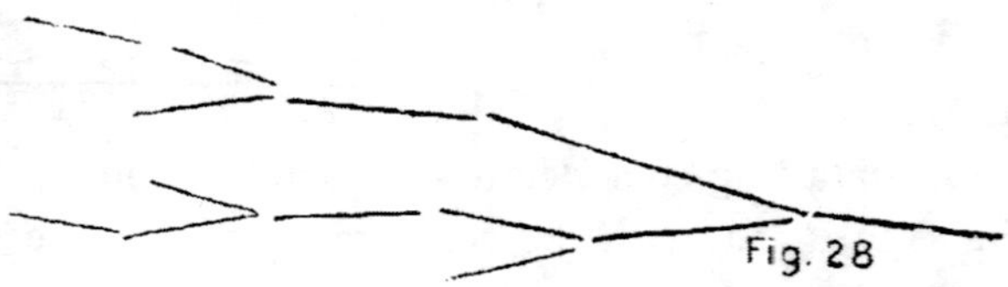

Fig. 28

Exhaustion is often shown in ornament by diminishing the thickness of stems gradually, but the angularity of growth is very seldom seen in ornament, although so general in nature. See Fig. 30. In most ornament the stems are evenly bent, and very often equally thick throughout. See Fig. 39.

Fig 29

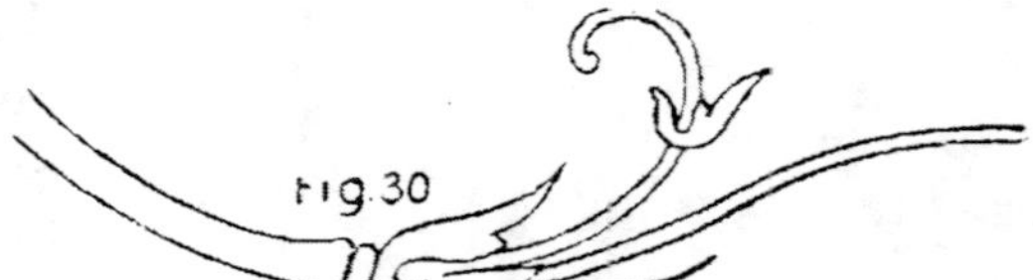

Fig. 30

(3) *Tendrils.*—These are generally in the form of spirals, or volutes; see Figs. 31, 32, 33; the best examples in nature are the vine, honeysuckle, &c.

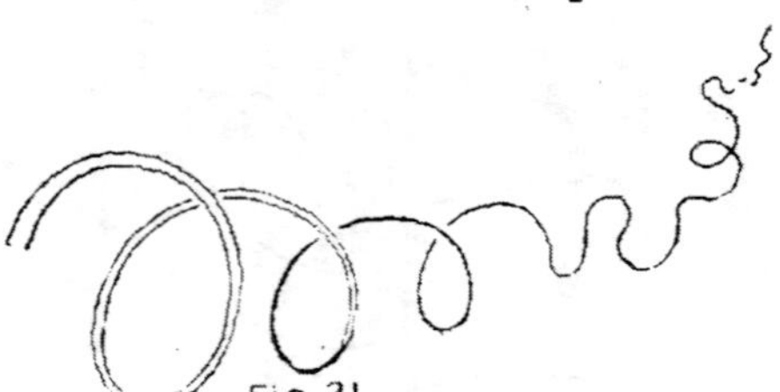

Fig. 31

Fig. 32

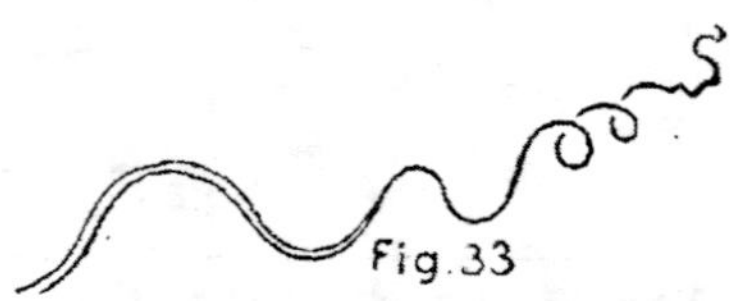

Fig. 33

(4) *Foliage Nests.*—The best illustrations of this element of ornament, in nature, are the cabbage and rhubarb, when running to seed. Fig. 34, 35.

Fig 34

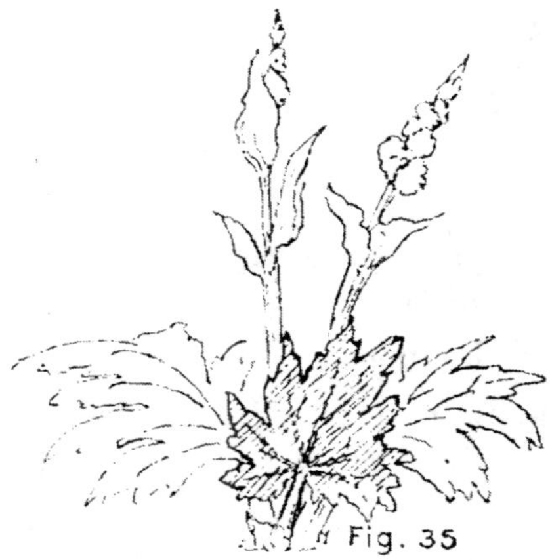

Fig. 35

In ornament they are generally made up of acanthus leaves.

(5) *Sheath-leaves.* — These are very common in both nature and ornament. They are plainer than the leaf bursting from them, and as the name implies, they protect the proper leaves whilst forming.

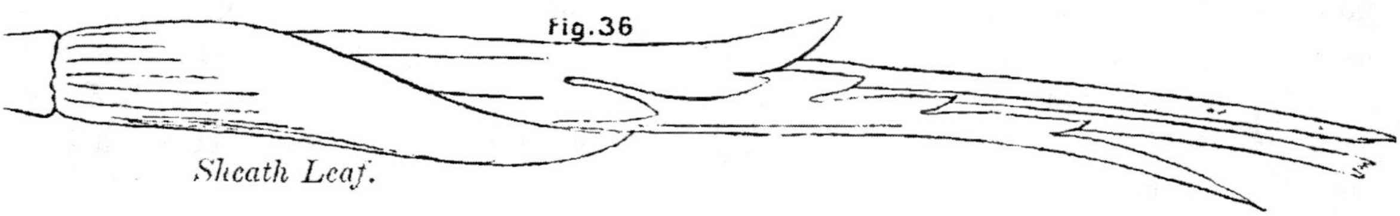

Fig. 36

Sheath Leaf.

(6) *Buds.*—The use of buds in ornament is somewhat limited, but they are generally very pleasing. See Figs. 37, 38, 39.

Fig. 37

Fig. 38

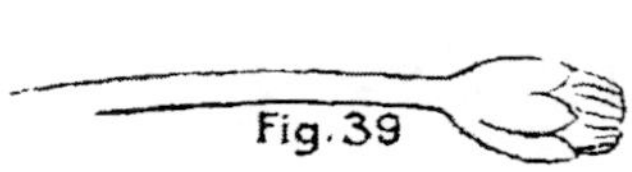

Fig. 39

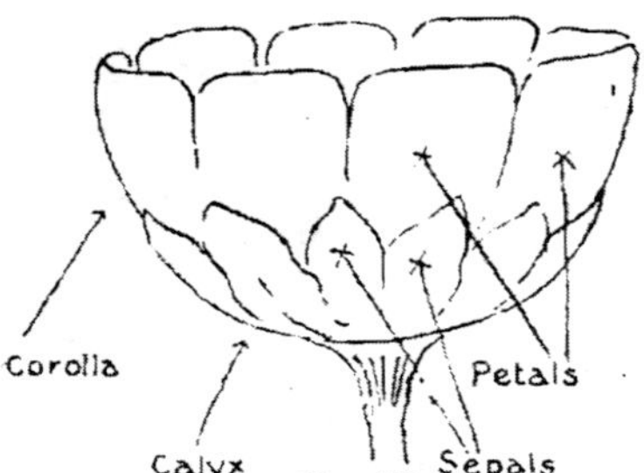

Fig. 40

(7) *Flowers.*—Ornament is very full of flowers, but often conventionalized into rosettes. The chief parts of the flower are the corolla and the calyx. The calyx forms a protection for the corolla whilst developing, and so corresponds to the sheath leaf. The corolla is made up of petals, or flower leaves. The calyx is made up of sepals. See Fig. 40.

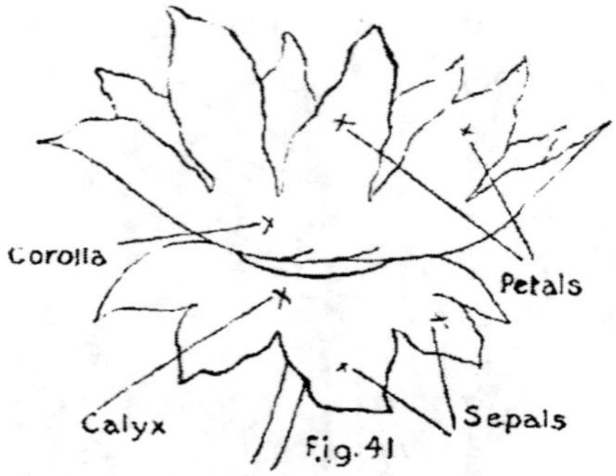

Fig. 41

Sometimes the calyx falls back and so gives the appearance of the two parts of the flower growing in opposite directions. See Fig. 41.

(*e*).—**Fixed Forms:—**

We now leave the elements which are derived from natural foliage, and pass on to those things which are more or less fixed and settled in shape, *e.g.*—

Rosettes.	Skulls.	Shields.
Basins.	Beads.	Pendants.
Shells.	Crowns.	Knobs.
Dolphins.	Straps and Ribands.	Loops and Folds.

(1) *Rosettes.*—If we look at such flowers as the daisy, buttercup, anemone, poppy, dahlia, &c., we see in nature the original whose counterpart we represent by what is commonly called a rosette. These rosettes may be made of ribbon, paper, wax, wood, clay, or any material, but yet the under-lying idea is to imitate one of nature's flowers in a simple way. Rosettes in ornament take their names from the number of leaves or sides they have, thus:—

Triangular = 3 angled = 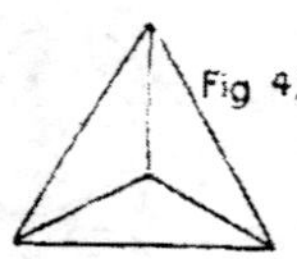 Fig 42 giving 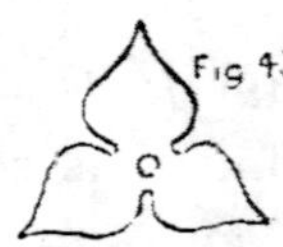 Fig 43.

Square = 4 sided =  Fig 44 giving 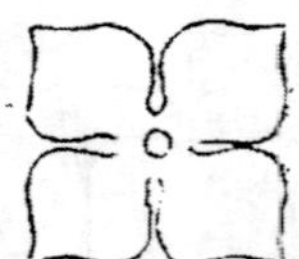 Fig 45

Pentagonal = 5 cornered = 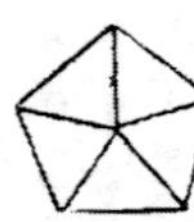 Fig. 46 giving  Fig 47

Hexagonal = 6 cornered = 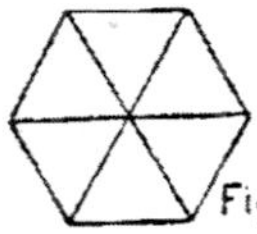 Fig. 48 giving  Fig 49

Heptagonal = 7 cornered = 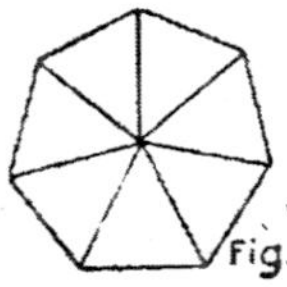 Fig. 50 giving  Fig. 51

Octagonal = 8 cornered = 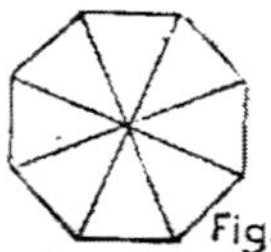 Fig. 52 giving  Fig. 53

Note.—(1) That the odd numbers have a point at the top, opposite the base, (2) that the even numbers have all their sides opposite and parallel, (3) that the rosettes are best formed by dividing the figure into triangles by joining the corners to the centres, and (4) that the lines thus drawn to the centre, if produced, each bisect a side, in the case of those with an odd number of sides.

(2) *Basins and Vases.*—When forming part of a piece of ornament, these generally occur on the central axis (see Figs. 54, 55, 56), either upheld by it (as in Plates 28, 32, 122, 127, 138, 154, 173, 190),

Fig 54

Fig. 55

Fig. 56

or with the central axis growing out of it, as commonly found in panel ornament, to give stability or a settled appearance to the ornament. See Figs. 57, 58, 59.

Fig 57

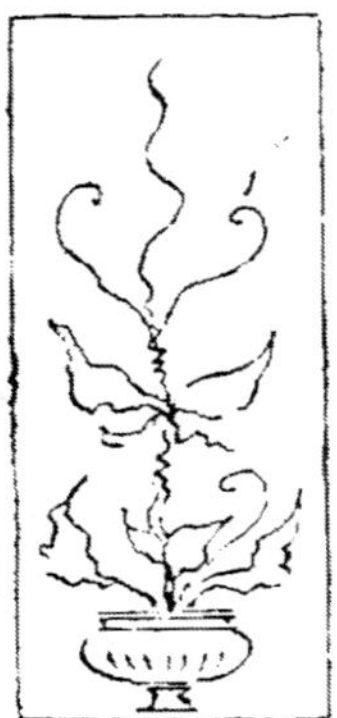
Fig. 58

Fig 59

(3) *Shells.*—These often occur as centre pieces for the starting of ornament, as in Plate 179, or reversed, as in Plate 32, or as the ornament itself, Plate 27. See Figs. 60, 61, 62.

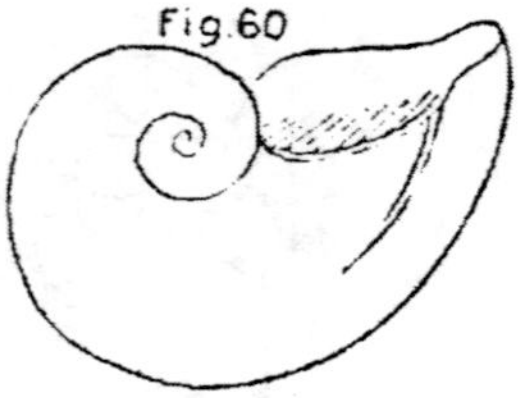

Fig.60

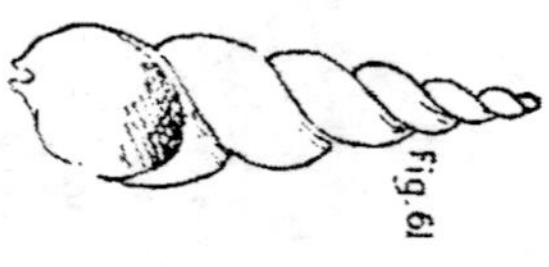

Fig.61

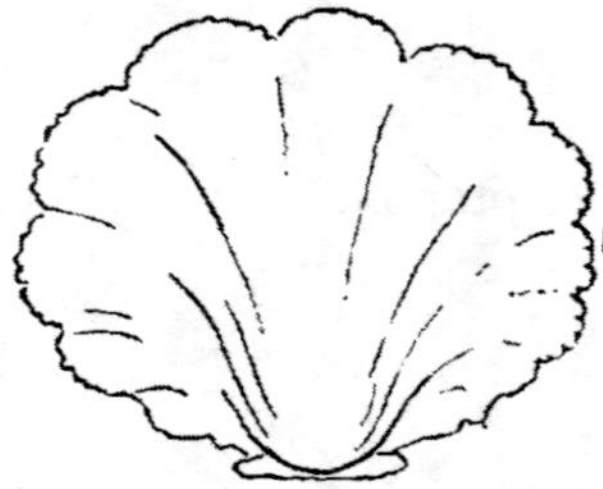

Fig 62

(4) *Dolphins* (Fig. 63) also are very much used as ornament, or as starts for ornament. See Plates 119, 188, 190, 191, 154 and 155.

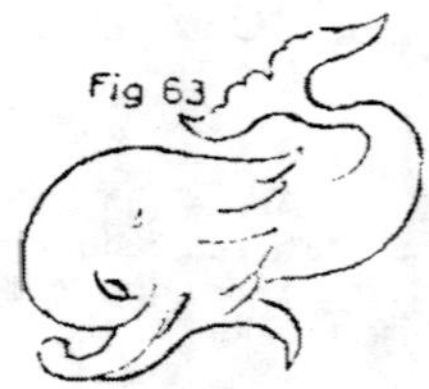

Fig 63

(5) *Skulls* of animals are often used as symbolic ornament, *e.g.*, that of the ox signifying sacrifice, see Plate 129, and the human skull and crossbones representing death.

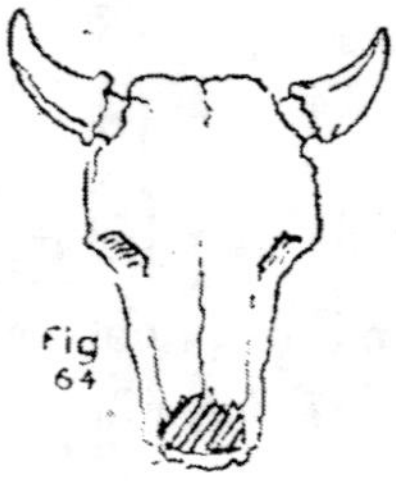

Fig 64

Fig 65

(6) *Loops and Folds* in leaves (see Figs. 66, 68, 69, 70), particularly in the acanthus leaf, are nearly always in conjunction with one another, the loop causing the fold,

Fig 66

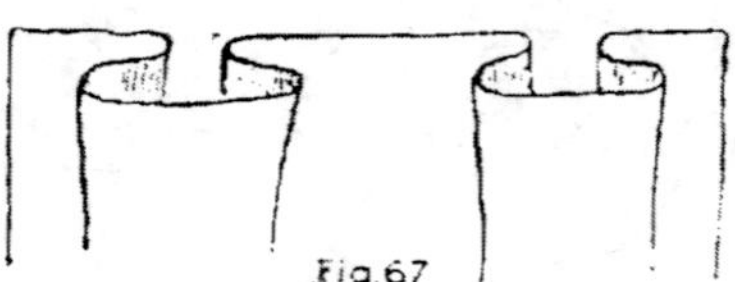

Fig.67

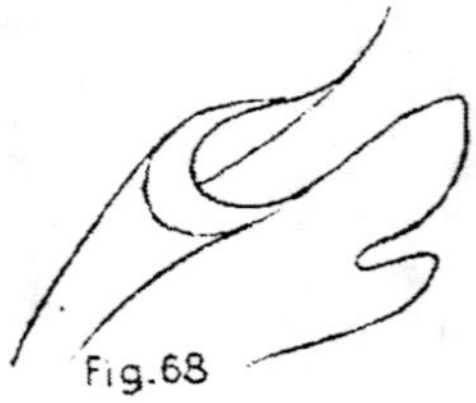

Fig.68

Fig 69

Fig.70

or the fold causing the loop. If we take a piece of paper and make folds in it, as in Fig. 67, and look at it anglewise, we see the folds forming the appearance of loops, and also that the sides of the folds, now standing out like pipes in front of the rest of the paper, can only be represented by straight or curved lines, according to the direction of the folds, and that these lines start from the sides of the loops, their distances apart being thus governed by the widths of the loops.

(7) *Beads* are very commonly used to break up the monotonous continuance of stems, or threaded in numbers on *swags* or *festoons.*

Their greatest width should be at right angles to the direction of stem or string, as in Figs. 72, 73.

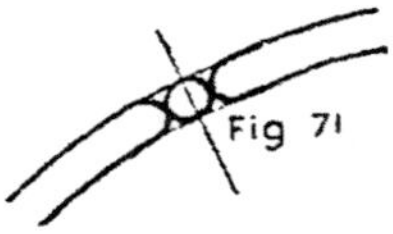

Fig 71

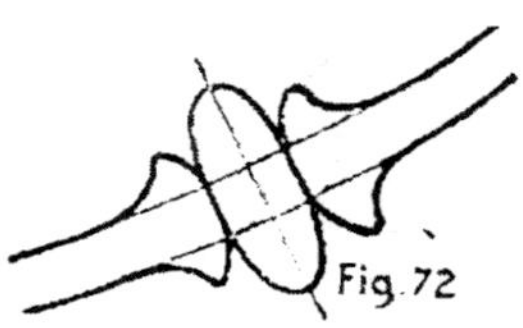

Fig. 72

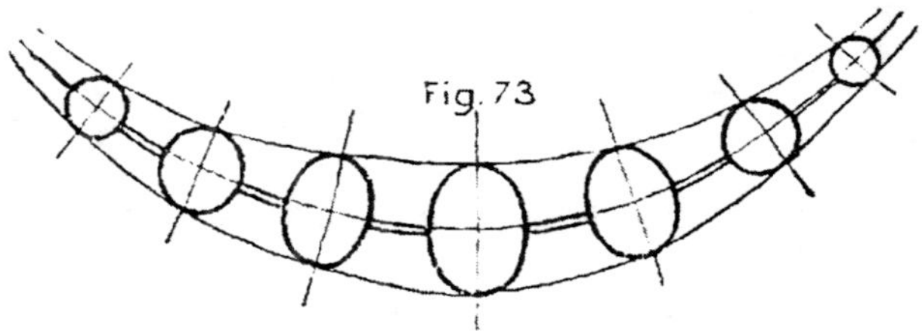

Fig. 73

(8) *Straps and ribands.* See Figs. 74, 75. These are used in great variety, especially in work done about the time of Queen Elizabeth. The riband lends itself to folding in every possible way, and the work shows overlapping and interlacing as a special feature. See Plates 12, 15, 49, 50 and 179.

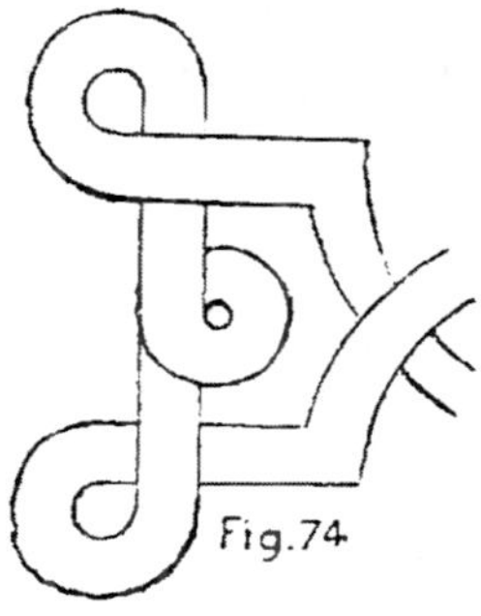

Fig. 74

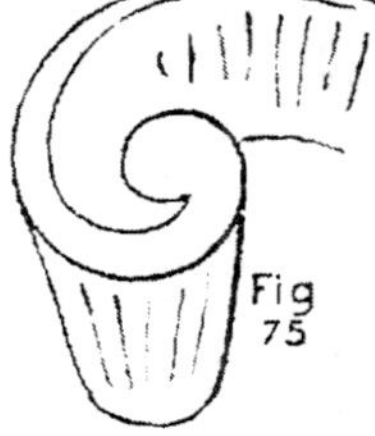

Fig 75

(9) *Shields* are used as centre pieces of ornament (see Plates 63, 134, 164, 172, 186), or as the ornament itself (see Plates, 25, 106), or repeated as ornament in a border or frieze. See Fig. 76.

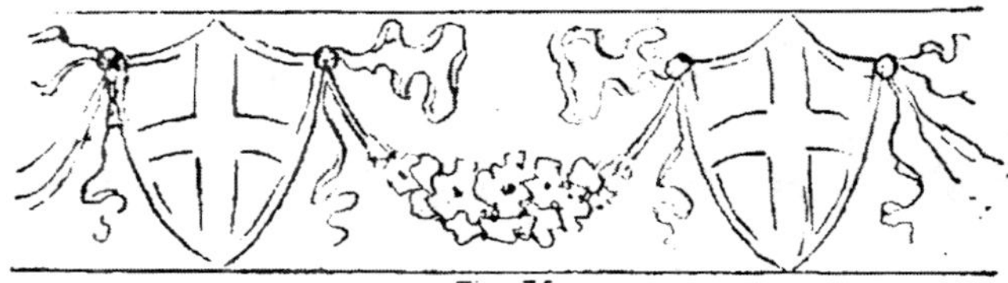

Fig. 76

(10) *Pendants, drops, or tassels* are occasionally used. See Plate 172.

Their centre lines should be vertical, as otherwise an appearance of wiry rigidity is given to the stem or string suspending them. See Figs. 77, 78, 79, 80.

Fig. 77

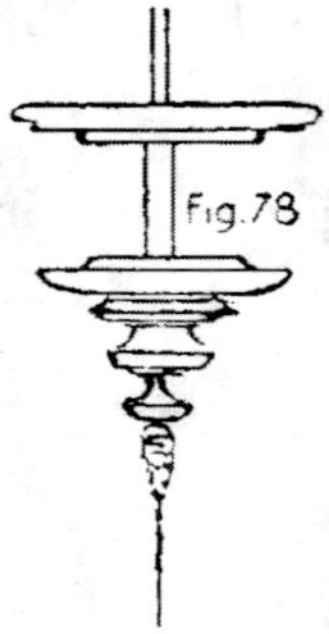
Fig. 78

Fig. 79

Fig. 80

(11) *Knobs* are very common (see Plates 4, 6, 11, 13, &c.). They are used as terminations to tendrils, stems, vase handles, &c. The outer and larger curve is best done first. See Figs. 81, 82.

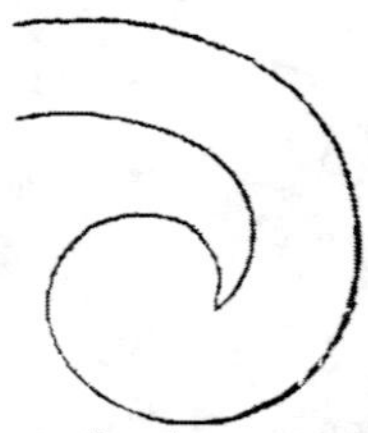
Fig. 81.

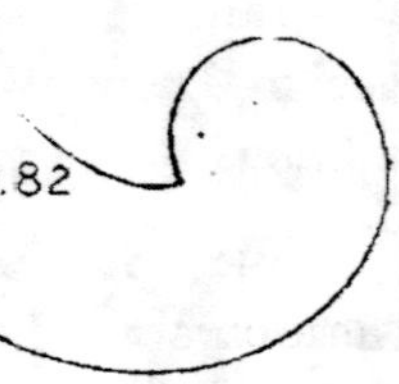
Fig. 82

CHAPTER II.

THE PRINCIPLES UNDERLYING THE COMBINATION OF ELEMENTS IN DRAWINGS OF ORNAMENT.

All good ornament is built up on certain principles of arrangement. Anyone who can use these principles successfully to the production of good and useful ornament is called a "designer."

A "design" is good or bad according to its suitability in filling the place for which it is intended, or in beautifying an object without detracting from its usefulness. "To design," therefore, requires a knowledge of manufactures and handicrafts, as well as a knowledge of elements and principles of ornament.

We will therefore leave out of consideration the subject of Design, as this is merely a work on Drawing. The drawings are in many cases only parts of designs, or perhaps in some cases not designs at all properly speaking, but merely exercises introducing, or giving practice in, the use of principles of ornament, with the object of enabling the student to sketch ornament intelligently.

Principle 1:—**Distribution.**—

This principle has for its sphere the spread or expansion of the ornament over surface. In a drawing there is the ornament itself, and the spaces between the parts of it. The student must take both into careful consideration, by observing the widths and shapes of spaces compared with one another and with the thicknesses of the ornament.

The ornament may be thin or sparse and the spaces large, see Fig. 1; or the reverse, *i.e.*, the spaces small, and the ornament profuse and covering the surface almost entirely, see Fig. 2.

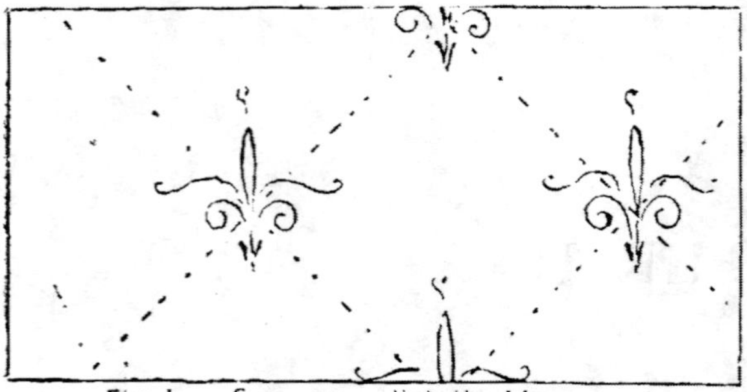

Fig. 1 Sparse distribution.

Fig. 2 Profuse distribution

See also Plates 43, 44, 72, 117, 148 for sparseness, and Plates 32, 38, 86, 108, 110, &c., for profuseness.

The *bases* or foundations of the drawing must be arranged with a view to carrying out this idea of distribution. Thus Figs. 1 and 2 are arranged on a series of diamond shapes, as in Fig. 3.

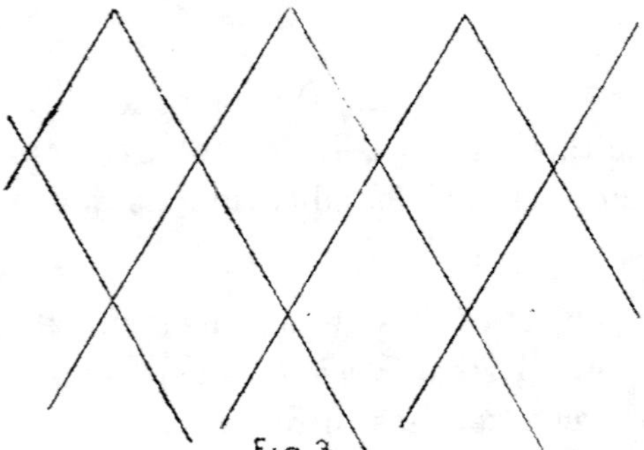

Fig. 3

These *base* lines, *foundations*, or *scaffoldings* may, or may not, form part of the drawing. In the example we have taken they do not, for they do not appear in the resultant drawing. It is evident, however, that they are necessary to make the designing, or the drawing of the design, easy and accurate. The base lines, or foundation of distribution is given in Fig. 1 of each plate. These lines in Fig. 2 of each plate are shown clothed with the ornament in a rough, lumpy form, called "*mapping out*," "*blocking in*," or "*blocking out*"; this mapping out determining at once whether the ornament is sparse or profuse in its distribution.

Principle 2:—**Composition of Line.**—

In the preceding paragraph we noted that sometimes the base lines remain as part of the ornament. In such case they must be the *leading lines* or chief lines of it, on which the smaller details depend.

If these leading lines are prominent, and as a rule they are so, they should be so harmoniously arranged with one another as to attract and carry the eye throughout their course, leading the sight into other principal lines, in the same way that a train is made to twist about by the lines upon which it runs.

This agreement of the lines and curves with one another to captivate the sight and lead it in a particular direction instead of allowing it to jump restlessly from one part to another, is called *Composition of line.* As good examples, take Plates 105, 110, 112, 116, 131, 153 and 155.

Composition of line includes :—

(*a*) Continuity of growth,
(*b*) Tangential junction, and
(*c*) Radiation.

(*a*) *Continuity of growth* means that parts growing out of others must be in the same leading line, as in Fig. 4, and not suggesting by their attitude any other source but the one intended, as is done in Fig. 5.

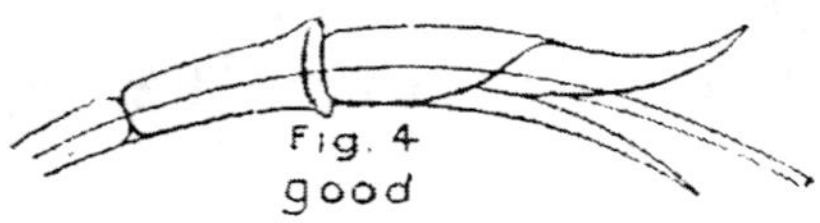
Fig. 4 good

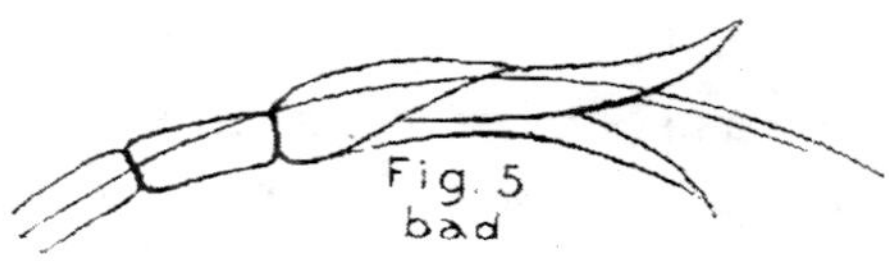
Fig. 5 bad

Another example of this would be when a leaf is crossing a stem, both parts of the stem must look as if they belonged to one another, and should be in the same line or curve of growth, as in Fig. 6. To obtain this effect it is necessary to draw the stem continuous at first, then the leaf across it (or *vice versâ*), and afterwards to rub out the parts of stem or leaf not wanted, as indicated by the dotted lines in Fig. 6. In Fig. 7 we have an example of what is bad, because the two parts of the stem do not appear in the same line of growth.

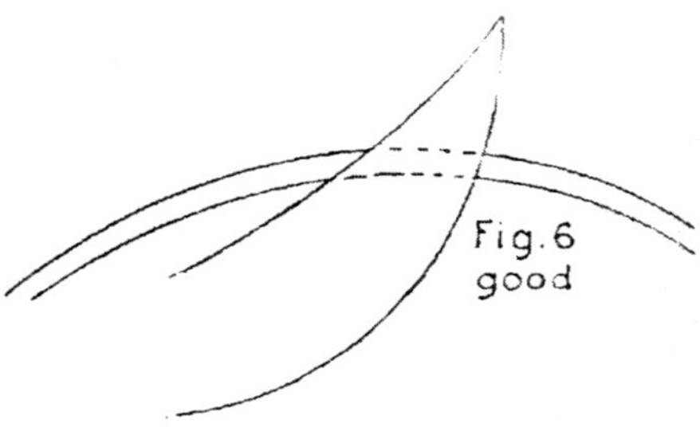
Fig. 6 good

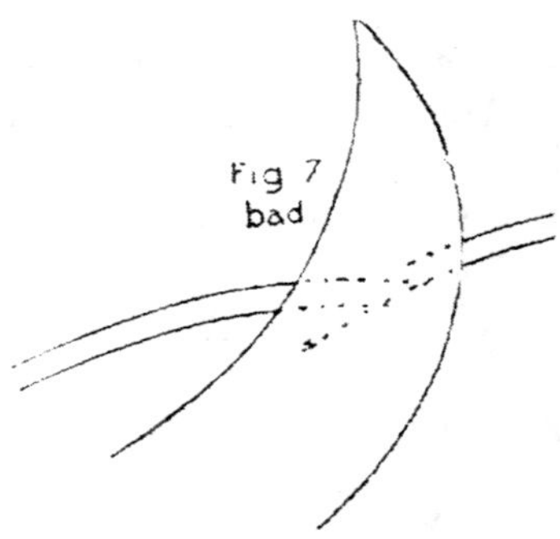
Fig. 7 bad

(*b*). *Tangential junction* means the joining of lines or curves with one another so gently and gradually that there will be no jerk or suddenness of turning or joining.

If the subtle curves of railway junctions be kept in mind there will be no difficulty in realising this principle. A tangent is a line or curve which, when meeting another, *does not cut it if produced,* as in Figs. 8, 9.

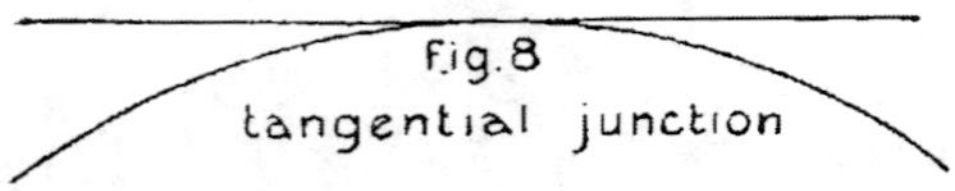

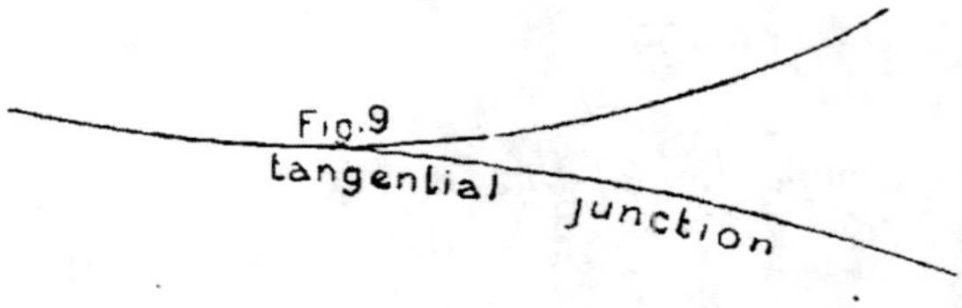

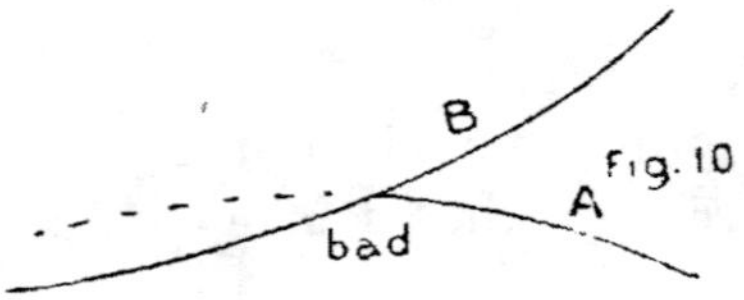

Fig. 10 is not a tangential junction, because A if produced, would cut through B, instead of gliding into it. There are examples of tangential junction in almost every drawing.

(*c*). *Radiation.*—Although we have examples of parallel radiation, and radiation from points on an axis, or branching, in Plates 1 and 2, yet the majority of radiation is from points, and wherever there is tangential junction there is radiation.

In the folds of drapery, the hair, the outspread fingers and toes, the waterfall, the dashing spray, the waving corn, the spreading branches, the reticulation or network in the leaves, and almost everywhere we look in nature, we find this radiation in some form.

If we suppose a point giving light, the light is said to be emitted in rays travelling in every direction. These rays must necessarily be diverging or getting wider apart. Hence any lines diverging as the rays of light are said to be radiating.

If the light-giving body be a large one, like the sun, there are a certain number of rays which must be parallel to one another, because coming from different points on the sun's surface. Hence there is such a thing in nature as parallel radiation.

For examples of good radiation, see Plates 1, 2, 3, 26, 27, 38, 39, 47, 48, 51, 52, &c.

Principle 3 :—**Parallelism.**—

This may be divided into three parts, viz. :

(1) Parallelism of straight lines to one another.
(2) Parallelism of curves to one another, and
(3) Parallelism of ornament to a boundary or shape.

(1) Parallel straight lines are those which being produced ever so far both ways will never meet. They must therefore be equally distant at all points.

(2) Parallel curves also are equally distant at all points.

(3) Parallelism of ornament to a bounding shape will be best understood by referring to Plates 15, 26, 61, 79, 110 and 156.

In the first three the inner ornament recognises the outer part by being parallel to it. In the fourth, the ornamental border recognises the bounding lines by keeping a certain distance at all points from it, *i.e.*, parallel. In the fifth and sixth examples, the ornament recognises the particular shape of the boundary lines by keeping its outer points equally distant from it.

Fig. 2, Plate 110, and Fig. 1, Plate 156, show how this result is obtained by sketching a line parallel to, and at the desired distance from, the boundary. The ornament is drawn to touch this line, and then the line after being so used can be rubbed out.

In almost every plate there are examples of parallel straight lines or parallel curves. In the case of parallel curves, the outer and larger one should be drawn first and very carefully trimmed and improved. It will then be very easy to add the inner parallel curve.

Principle 4:—**Symmetry and Balance.**—

Symmetry.—A drawing which has one side exactly the reverse of the other, as if the pattern were taken and turned over from one side to the other, like the leaf of a book, is said to be *symmetrical.*

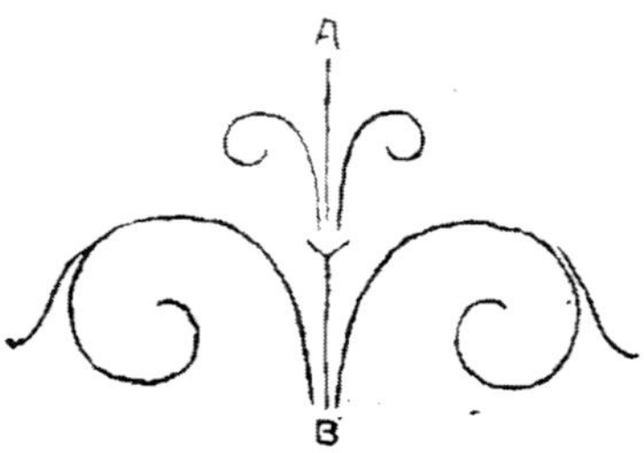

Fig. 11

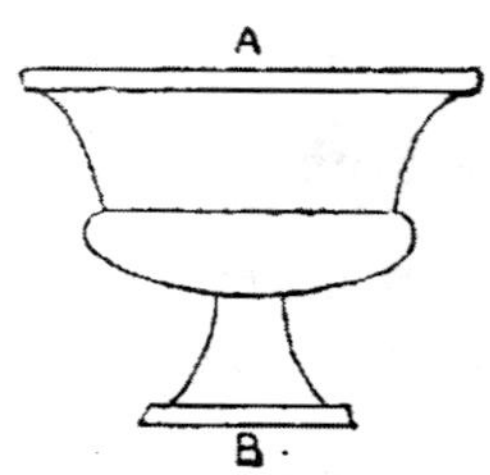

Fig. 12

In Figs. 11 and 12, A B is the axis or hinge on which the shape is turned from one side to the other.

Balance is similar to symmetry in that the apparent weight of the ornament on one side of the axis or centre line is equal to that on the other.

In balance, then, both sides are not alike, and are not the reverse of one another. Compare the balanced Figs. 13 and 14 with the symmetrical Figs. 11 and 12 to realise this.

Fig 13

Fig. 14

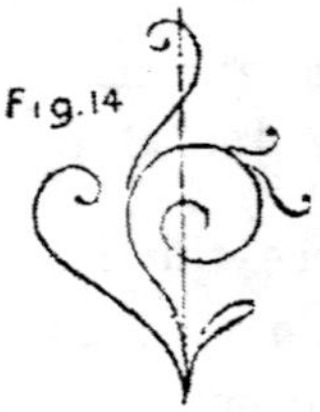

In symmetrical drawings the word *balance* is often used in speaking of a curve and its reverse, merely because it is a simpler word than symmetrical, although not so exacting.

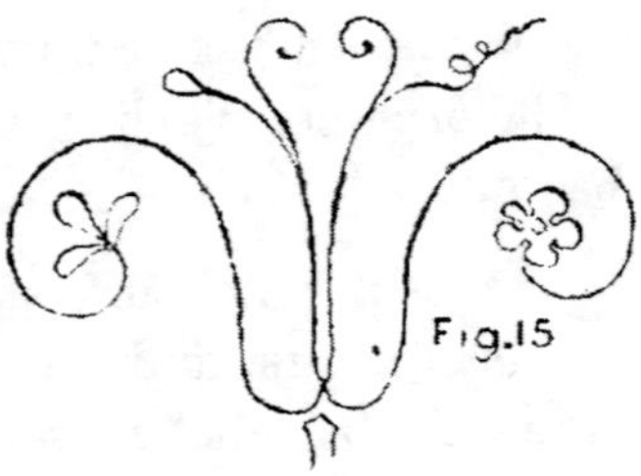

Fig. 15

A drawing may have symmetry in its principal parts, and only balance in its details, but seldom the reverse of this. Thus in Fig. 15 the principal curves are symmetrical, whilst the details are balanced.

The majority of the plates are symmetrical, not that symmetry is more common, nor yet that it is better, but because it is considered a proper step to balance. The student who can best obtain symmetry can most readily get subtle balance.

Balance in ornament is good, and, owing to its variety, gives interest.

Balance is much more common in nature than symmetry is.

For examples of balance see Plates 35, 96, 120, 139, 160, 165 and 186.

Principle 5 :—**Stability.**—

Stability means that appearance of steadiness which anything has when built up on a firm basis, and when that basis is visible.

The best example of stability or steadiness is a pyramid, for it has a spreading base, and its mass gradually diminishes upwards.

If ornament is depending on, or growing from, a centre line, that centre line should be evident, and bold enough to suggest that it is capable of carrying the ornament, if required to do so, in reality.

In Plates 20, 31, 41, 75, 82, 84 and 146, the vases are good as regards stability, having good broad bases compared with their size, whilst Plates 23, 67, 114 and 186 are wanting stability, because their bases are so small compared with their general size, and they look top-heavy in consequence, and would be easily overturned.

The stability of a drawing is greatly helped if the corresponding parts are on lines at right angles to the axis.

The regular curvature of stems gives an appearance of rigidity and freshness as compared with the limp and weak appearance of badly drawn stems.

Principle 6 :—**Repetition and Variety.**—

In many of the plates it will be noticed that a certain part of the ornament is repeated, and that this repetition is pleasing. See Plates 7 to 12; also 14, 15, 18, 26, 38, 52 and 56. In these cases it is necessary to become fully acquainted with the shape of one of these repeating parts, and then the remainder will be found easier.

Many of the drawings themselves will admit of repetition as a whole, some of them being so adapted for repetition that they do not look nearly so well by themselves. Take for instance, Plates 14, 47, 61, 79, 116, 117, 118 and 119, which are parts of borders.

Variety is found in the edges of the leaves, and is always interesting.

In Plate 76 the leaf edges are broken up by serrations or saw-like teeth, but as they are all alike, it is merely repetition, whilst in Plates 73 and 74 the edges are not only serrated, but every serration is different in shape and size, and every leaf is different also. These leaves are therefore good examples of variety.

Principle 6 :—**The Curvature of Ellipses in Vases.**—

As a rule, vases are circular in section when looking down on them from above. Every edge, rim, or line of any kind drawn round them is in reality a circle. But the common view of a vase is the side view, the vase being either on a level with the eye or a little below. We therefore commonly get side views of these rims and circles, and they take, in consequence, such an appearance as that shown in *c*, *d*, or *e*, Fig. 16.

These side views of circles are called ellipses, and as the circles themselves are curved at every part, so also the ellipses must be curved at every part.

It is impossible to have a pointed ellipse. Fig. 16 shows *a* and *b*, the extreme views of a circle.

At (*a*), when seen from the side, its surface entirely lost, it appears as a straight line.

The other extreme (*b*) shows it a full circle.

All the intermediate views of it are ellipses, and all contain a longest line and a shortest line. The shortest line is called the minor (less) axis, and the longest line is called the major (greater) axis.

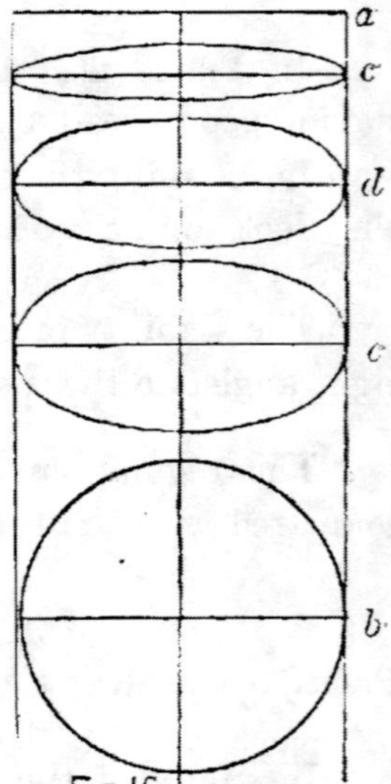

Fig. 16

These axes cross one another at right angles, and each divides the other into equal parts (or bisects it).

In drawing one of these ellipses, or half of one, it is necessary to commence with the major and minor axes, as these govern the proportion of its width to its length, and consequently the amount of curvature.

In Plate 31 the bottom rim of the vase is supposed on a level with the eye, and is therefore represented as a straight line, whilst the top rims and lines being above the eye are represented by elliptical curves.

In Plate 62 all are below the eye, and so are all represented by ellipses or parts of ellipses.

In Plate 67 the top is on the level of the eye and is represented straight, whilst the lower rims are represented by ellipses.

See also Plates 75, 82, 84 and 146.

Notice that starting from the straight line on the level of the eye the ellipses become wider, and consequently their curves rounder, the lower down the vase they are, so that in any one vase there must be a difference in the roundness of each curve.

CHAPTER III.

METHODS OF DRAWING.

The beginner who sits down to copy a drawing of ornament without method attempts an impossibility. He attempts what a clever man would not. The designer may not think of method, but he nevertheless has method of starting, and of building up his design in proper sequence.

Students sometimes start with one little part, thinking that if they get that right, they can add the next and so on, until they get through the drawing, but that sort of thing always ends in hopeless failure, and is bound to disgust the student and kill the interest he may have felt in the subject.

Necessity for method.—We have noticed that the designer of the ornament builds up his work "in proper sequence," or order, that is, he begins with a certain part or foundation, and finishes with other parts which he adds last in all his designs, and if he asked himself at each step or stage of the work the question "Why am I doing this next?" he would find that his method, or the habitual sequence which he always followed, had a reason at every step.

Now, the ordinary student, who has not natural ability for drawing exceptionally developed, but only a certain amount of it along with many other abilities, needs the ornament analysed, or taken to pieces and divided up into steps from foundation to finish, in order that he may make an intelligent copy or rendering of the ornament, and his road to success lies only through the help of practice in first analysing the ornament and then building it up step by step himself, in the way that he supposes the designer did in the first place.

Such a method in order to be of value to the student should become a habit, that is, it should be to the student a matter of course, and as ready as the alphabet, or the multiplication table. The method can only become a habit by constant practice and by applying it to every drawing, even if the drawing be so simple as to tempt the student to try it without method.

Results of Method.—The best method is that which gets the *right result* in the shortest time. The first aim, to which all else must give way, is correctness, or the right result. This having been attained, the student must practise obtaining that result at a gradually increasing speed, and if the method he has adopted helps in this respect, it is a good one.

The various examinations in drawing which are attempted by students, often as a proof to themselves of their ability or progress, often as an immediate aim to urge themselves on to improvement, and often, unfortunately, merely to gain the certificate (careless whether they have the real ability or not), combine these two things, correctness and speed. It is not sufficient for these examinations to merely be able to make a correct and intelligent rendering of the drawing, but to be able to make such a rendering in a limited time. Therefore, taking it from the lowest standpoint, viz., that of passing the examination, method is good, and is the way to that so-called success.

If drawing is studied with the object of acquiring real ability, then the ability which combines speed will get through the largest amount of drawing in a lifetime, and will make it pay when in competition with others who may not have acquired habitual method and speed.

Again, if the object of the student's efforts is the acquirement of sufficient ability and knowledge of the subject to be able to teach it to others, then speed becomes an essential, for the teacher who can make quick sketches, with only approximate correctness perhaps, can do infinitely more good than the teacher who must spend a large amount of the time of the class (as well as his own) in making an exact drawing or sketch slowly.

General Method.—The proper start for nearly every drawing of ornament is a vertical line, the object of which is to get the upright posture of the drawing. This vertical line is in most cases the centre line, but it may be in any other part across the drawing in such drawings as Plates 77, 115, 123.

When the vertical line is the centre line and the half drawing on the left of it exactly corresponds in every part to the half drawing on the right, *i.e.*, the one half is the reverse of the other half, then the drawing is called *symmetrical.*

If it has a centre line, but the two halves differing in details, then it is said to be *balanced.* (See Principle 4, Chapter II.)

Ornament like that in Plates 77, 115, 123, 139, is called "*free ornament.*"

Position of Paper.—The paper, when starting the drawing, and whilst mapping out its principal parts, proportions, and the masses of details, should be placed square with the desk or table as in Fig. 1.

Fig. 1

The paper should be such that a pencil mark will easily rub out, and should not be too rough so as to quickly blunt the pencil. Bad materials discourage the beginner.

How to Sit.—Having placed the paper square with the desk, it is necessary to sit exactly opposite it, and square with the desk also, the feet flat on the floor, and the body upright, the head and shoulders supported by the back and not by the elbows.

Note.—If the student sits sideways as in writing, the tendency will be to get a slanting drawing corresponding to the slanting writing when sitting sideways at that.

How to hold the Pencil.—In drawing the centre line the most natural way of holding the pencil is that suggested by Fig. 2, the pencil pointing upwards towards the right, and at an angle of about 45° (half a right angle) to the paper. In this position the point can be easily seen.

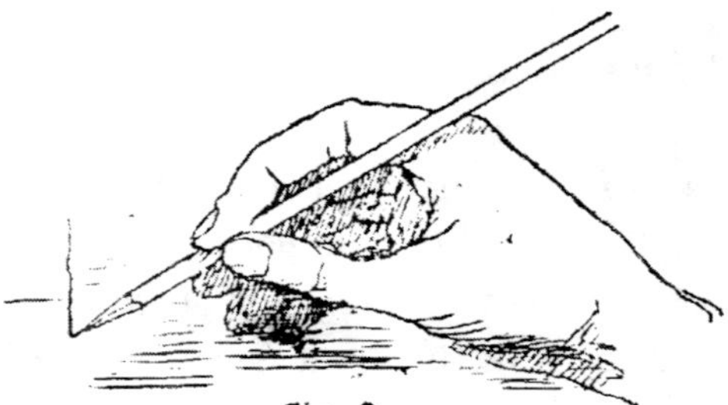

Fig. 2

The elbow should merely touch the desk so as to glide easily over it, but no weight should be allowed on it. In drawing straight lines, the hand may be steadied by allowing the second joint of the little finger to touch the paper (see the difference in drawing curves). The first two fingers and the thumb should be on the pencil about two inches from the end. By holding the pencil at an angle to the paper, a fainter and more delicate line can be drawn, which will admit of easy alteration.

Note.—In drawing at an easel the pencil, chalk, charcoal or brush, instead of passing over the band and pointing upwards, may pass entirely below the hand and point in any direction according to the direction of the line which is being drawn.

How to draw a straight line.—With the paper, body, and pencil held as above, commence at the upper part of the paper and draw the pencil towards you, thinking of the direction in which you want the line, rather than of its minute straightness. Direction is of first importance, straightness second, so a wavering line in the right direction is better than a straight line in the wrong direction. After making this first wavering line, take up your paper, and closing one eye, look down the line with the other, in the same way that you have seen a joiner or carpenter look down the edge of a piece of wood which he is trying to get straight. When looking down the line in this way the errors will at once be seen, and not only that it is bending to the right or left of the general direction, but the exact place can be touched with the pencil point and the amount of difference thus noted. Next place the paper on the desk again, and *without rubbing out the wrong part*, add the improvement, as in Figs. 3, 4, 5, which shows improvements marked A B added, and errors marked C ready for removal. *Never* rub out the bad attempt until you have improved upon it, because the faulty line helps you get the correct one, as you see what to avoid.

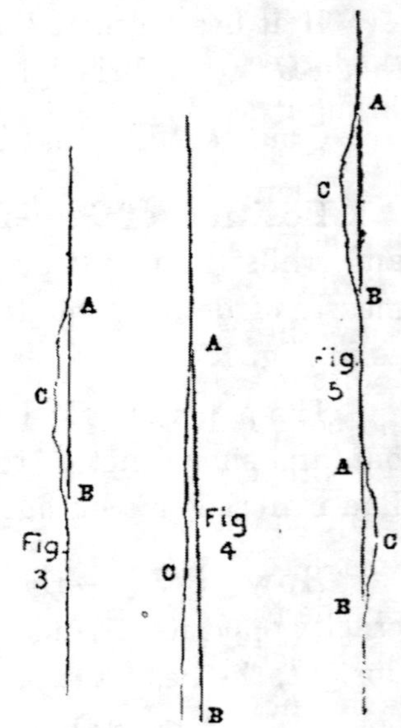

Fig. 3 Fig. 4 Fig. 5

If the first attempt be rubbed out, the second and third may be worse, but by retaining the first, improvement must be made (see Figs. 3, 4, and 5).

How to draw lines at right angles.—To draw the cross lines at right angles (Fig. 6), first mark the points on the centre-line through which they should pass, then start from these points and draw outwards right and left, taking care to judge with the eye if the angles, *e.g.*, X and Y are equal. Test the straightness of each new line by looking down it as before described.

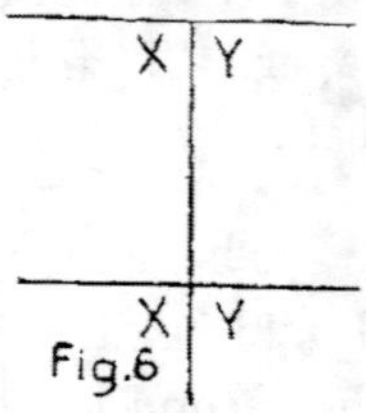

Fig. 6

Another way is to turn the paper until the first vertical line is horizontal, then to start drawing from the point on it downwards towards you, and turn the paper entirely round, so that the other half of the new line can be drawn downwards from the centre line in the same way. Test by looking down the entire line.

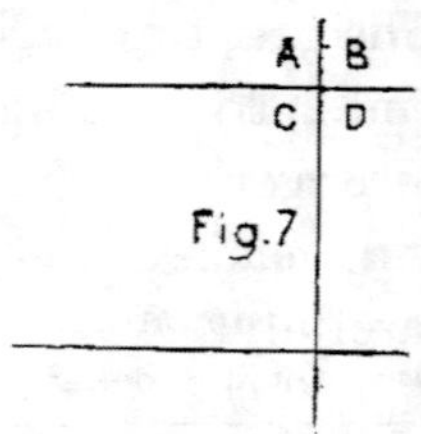

Fig. 7

To get the angles of a square, produce the sides a little as in Fig. 7, for then it is easier to judge if the four angles, A, B, C and D, are equal. If so, then required angle C is a right angle.

How to draw the principal curves.—The principal curves, generally only two or three in number (see Fig. 1 of each plate), should be selected after the cross lines are drawn, and should generally be commenced by examining carefully the nature of one curve, the largest on the left, then marking on the cross lines and one or two other places points through which the curve should pass.

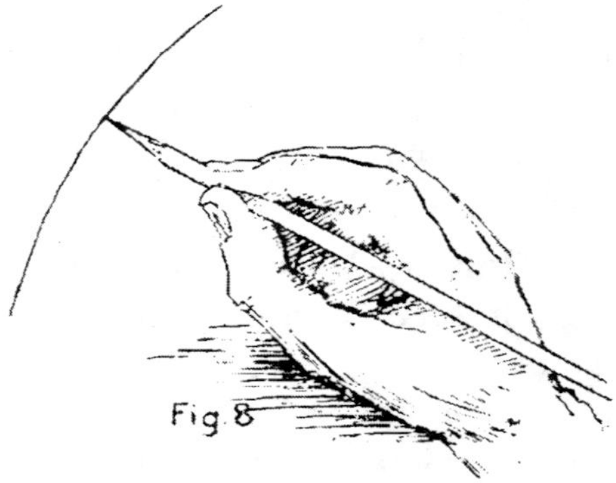

Fig 8

Then resting the hand lightly on the pivot bone of the wrist, and on the inside of the curve, so that the whole hand may be used like a compass (see Fig. 8), draw the curve lightly and delicately through the points marked for it. Then compare it carefully with the copy, and proceed to trim it into even curvature and proper shape, not by rubbing it out and trying again, but by adding the improvements as shown in Figs. 3, 4 and 5, taking the irregular first attempt as a guide to something better. This curve once correct on the left, the next step, viz., to reverse the same curve on the right, is somewhat easier, as no new shape has to be realised, but merely the same shape carefully turned over and balanced. Then proceed to the curve next in importance and draw it in the same way, carefully judging the spaces as well as the shape of the curve (see Chapter II, Principle I.)

Proceed to add curve by curve in order of their importance, taking each one on the left and then its reverse on the right, so that a succession of steps is adopted, and becomes a habit, left, right; left, right; left, right; as in marching.

Note.—1. In reference to these principal curves, see Chapter II., Principle II., on composition of line.

2. Lines or curves drawn through principal points by the student as helps are to be considered as important, and may be even more so than some of the actual lines of the drawing (see Plates 38, 39 and 40.)

3. The curve on the left is drawn first because it helps the drawing of the one on the right; whereas if the curve on the right be drawn first, it is no help because covered by the hand whilst drawing the one on the left.

Blocking in.—By referring to Fig. 2 of each of the Plates, and particularly to Fig. 2, Plate 71; Fig. 2, Plate 95; Fig. 3, Plate 111; Fig. 2, Plate 120; Fig. 2, Plate 141; Fig. 2, Plate 144; Fig. 2, Plate 147; Fig. 4, Plate 159; and so on, the student will at once get an idea of what is meant by "blocking in." The object of it is to get the size and general shape of the part taken "mapped out" (see Principle I, Chapter II), and carefully placed before spending any time over drawing it carefully. It is evident then that "*blocking in*" or "*mapping out*" is a saving in time, for if time be spent over drawing a leaf or a flower, and then it is found to be in the wrong place, or wrong posture, or the wrong size, it is very discouraging to have to rub it out and do it all over again. Therefore it is wise to invent lines enclosing the general shape, as in the Plates referred to at the beginning of this paragraph, and to draw them first as a foundation, which may be easily altered or adjusted, and then to fill in this enclosure or frame-work with the delicately drawn particular shape.

Details.—The parts so filled in, *i.e.*, the details or small parts, should be delicately drawn, each little part showing its dependence on the main lines, and showing a tender appreciation on the part of the student of the principles of growth and arrangement of the ornament, and of every little bend in the small curves.

Finish.—The drawing is now complete in one sense, viz., that every portion of it, large or small, is drawn, and therefore at this stage it should be carefully revised, by taking a sharply pointed piece of good india rubber and rubbing out all straggling lines, as well as the lines and curves that were drawn for mere construction. Then with a sharp H pencil re-draw all indefinite parts faintly, rub down and re-draw all thick parts also, glancing at the copy all the time with a view to improving every little curve.

The drawing should now present a faint, delicate, but definite appearance. Now take a sharp F pencil, or an H pencil, and "line in" the drawing with a clear crisp line. Firm and even curves are best obtained by turning the paper so that the hand is on the inside of each curve in succession.

The pencil may be raised as often as the student finds convenient, so long as the junctions are not evident in the drawing. Carelessness in this respect will result in the lines being lumpy and uneven in thickness.

Only two or three inches of line should be drawn with the same point, which should then be sharpened again before proceeding.

To avoid the point breaking with the pressure necessary to get crispness, hold the pencil nearly vertical while lining in.

Note.—In examinations much time is saved by having a number of pencils carefully sharpened beforehand. Sharp pencils should be used for making the first lines just as much as for lining in, as the work is then more likely to be careful and delicate.

Proportion.—The pencil can be used as a help to get the proportions of parts to one another, and the directions of lines, as well as to do the actual drawing. Such help or such a use of the pencil may be prohibited in some examinations, and the student allowed to depend on the eye only, but yet in every day work, from the practical and business point of view, all possible help which can be got from the pencil is allowable and legitimate.

Proportion in drawing, as in arithmetic, is the "equality of two ratios."

A ratio is the comparison of two things of the same kind, and which may be two parts of the same thing, or two quantities of a certain kind of thing.

The first ratio of the proportion is on the copy itself, viz., one part compared with another: the second ratio is on the student's drawing, the first term of which he gives himself, any convenient size, and from it by the help of the first ratio, finds the second term, or fourth of the whole proportion.

So that if the width of the copy divides into its length $1\frac{1}{4}$ times, and the length of the student's drawing is 15 inches, we have—

$$\text{As } \overbrace{1 : 1\tfrac{1}{4}}^{\text{ratio on copy}} :: \overbrace{x : 15 \text{ ins.}}^{\text{ratio on student's drawing}}$$

Therefore x = 12 inches = width student's drawing is to be when it is 15 inches long.

Or if the student starts with width 8 inches, then—

$$\text{As } \overbrace{1 : 1\tfrac{1}{4}}^{\text{ratio on copy}} :: \overbrace{8 \text{ ins.} : x}^{\text{ratio on student's drawing}}$$

Therefore x = 10 = length student's drawing is to be when its width is 8 inches.

This applies to every drawing, and every part of a drawing. There must be proportion of every part to every other part.

It is always best to find the large proportions first, viz., width to length. If these are right, the smaller parts are bound to fit in.

It is generally better to divide *large* parts into *larger* ones, rather than to compare large ones with small ones, or small ones with large ones, and it is more definite to divide the less into the greater, for then the result will be such as $1\frac{1}{4}$, $1\frac{1}{7}$, $2\frac{1}{3}$, $3\frac{1}{5}$, instead of being always a fraction, as $\frac{4}{5}$, $\frac{7}{8}$, $\frac{3}{7}$, $\frac{5}{16}$.

Direction.—Granted that both copy and drawing are square with the desk, the general direction of a line can be transferred from the copy to the drawing, irrespective of the size of the drawing, by laying the pencil on the copy so as to coincide with the part under consideration, and then taking it in the thumb and finger, without losing its particular direction, passing it to the corresponding part of the drawing, and after carefully noticing the direction in which it is lying, picking it up and drawing a line in that direction.

This method is quick and fairly accurate for practical purposes.

How to draw a circle.—It is frequently necessary to draw a circle in Freehand practice, either as construction for a drawing, or as part of the drawing. The method is briefly as follows:—Draw a centre line and a cross line, each any length, and taking the crossing point as the centre of the circle, draw through it any number of lines, at least as many as are given in Fig. 9. Then mark off on each of these lines a certain distance from the centre. The points so found, being equally distant from the centre, are points on the required circle, or through which it passes, and therefore, once correct, should not be altered, but the curve of the circle made to pass through them, and trimmed up to them. To start the curve draw short lines at right angles to the first lines, as shown in the diagram, and bend the curve gradually from these short beginnings. By so doing the common fault of points on the circle is avoided. Place the hand on the inside of the curve to draw easily.

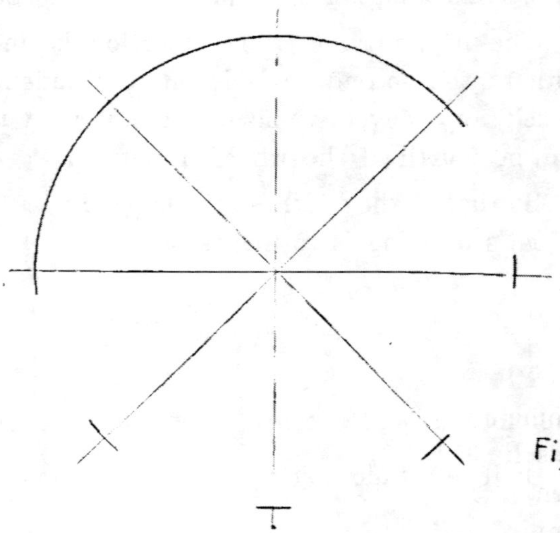

Fig. 9

How to draw an Ellipse.—Draw first the major, then the minor axis, each any length at first, having ascertained their due proportion, and marked them off accordingly, as previously directed, then through points in the major axis, equidistant from one another, draw a number of lines, the more the better, but at least as many as shown in Fig. 10, at right angles to the major axis, these will be parallel to the minor axis, and are to diminish gradually in length both to the right and left of the minor axis. By careful observation mark off their respective lengths, then the curve drawn as previously directed through the points thus obtained will be an ellipse.

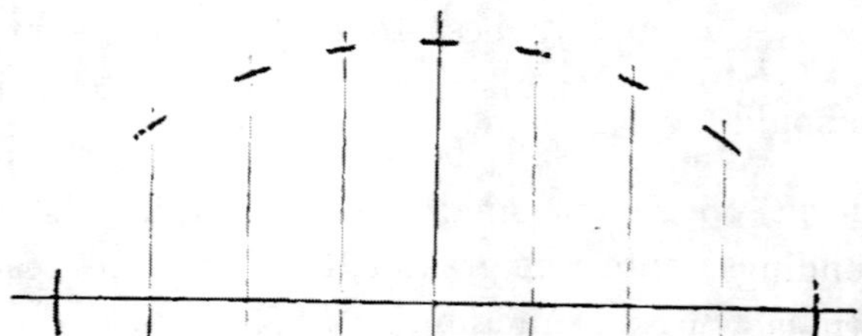

Fig 10

The curve is to be started as in the circle by short lines at the ends of the lines already drawn, but observe carefully that, except in the case of the major and minor axes, these short lines are not at right angles to the guide lines.

CHAPTER IV.

DESCRIPTION OF THE PLATES.

Plate 1.—Is a simple exercise on parallel straight lines, and parallel curves, arranged symmetrically on a central stem. The centre line should in each case be drawn first, then cross lines at the top and bottom, and finally the side lines as shown in Figs. 1, 3 and 5. Then, after marking the points on these lines, the drawing itself is made by connecting these points. In Figs. 4 and 6 the paper should be turned round, and the hand placed on the inside of the curve, and used as a compass, as explained in Chapter III., paragraph headed "How to draw the principal curves."

Plate 2—Is similar to Plate 1 in construction, but in this case the straight lines and curves are diverging (*i.e.* getting wider apart) as they extend. Notice that the upper and lower lines are drawn first, and the remaining ones fitted in.

Plate 3—Is an exercise on lines diverging from a point. In this case great care should be taken that they all meet evenly in the point, and that the divergence is equal.

Plate 4—This and Plates **5** and **6** are exercises in scrolls, or double curves, and their endings. Notice that Plates 4 and 6 have knob endings, whilst Plate 5 has point endings. In each case the outer curve should be drawn first partially, as shown in Figs. 1 and 2, and after drawing one little piece of curve on the left, that piece should be reversed at once before proceeding further, so that both sides of the drawing are kept going at the same rate. See Chapter III., paragraph headed "How to draw the principal curves."

Plate 7—Has for its basis a square, which is itself sub-divided into smaller squares by drawing the diagonals. The diagonals of the four smaller squares are divided equally, giving points through which the principal curves pass. Refer to Chapter III., paragraph headed "How to draw a straight line, and how to draw lines at right angles."

Plate 8—Introduces into the foundation lines a circle, which should be drawn next to the straight lines, as shown in Fig. 1. All the points and parts shown in Fig. 2 should then be added, so that in this, as in all other plates, all the lines in Fig. 1 are first drawn, then all in Fig. 2 are added before the resultant curves are put in.

Plate 9—In this plate the diagonals of the small squares may be drawn as in the previous plates, to get the four curves at the corners. Notice that the corner ornaments do not touch the other four leaves.

Plate 10—In this plate, to get the balance of the flowers, the paper should be turned, so as to bring each flower upright in succession, and a line may be drawn across the points of the flower to get them balanced. The tangential junction of curves is introduced, and is a very important principle. Refer to Chapter II., Principle 2.

Plate 11—Is also an exercise on tangential junction, and the centre part of it is an exercise on Plate 6.

Plate 12—This plate introduces strap work, the lines being parallel, or equally distant at all parts. In this kind of work the most important thing for the student to attend to is the interlacing and overlapping of the straps. To get this right, the lines should be drawn crossing one another at first, as in Fig. 2, then the finished drawing should be carefully studied, to get the interlacing, and the parts not wanted rubbed out. If this interlacing is not noticed, the benefit of this exercise will be lost.

Plate 13—In this plate we have parallel curves, the large outer curve being an exercise on Plate 6; the small inner curves at the bottom, an exercise on Plate 4, and the central horned part, an exercise on Plate 5. The outer curve should be drawn first, as shown in Fig. 2, and made as perfect as possible, before doing the inner curve; so that the hard work of the exercise is in getting the outer curve right, afterwards the inner curve is comparatively easy.

Plate 14—Introduces a bounding curve as construction, see Fig. 1; then the radiating lines should be added, as in Fig. 2, thus making divisions into which the semi-circular curves are fitted.

Plate 15—Notice that the foundation of this plate is made up of squares. The riband should be drawn continuous, as shown in Fig. 2, in order to get the continuity of line right where the overlapping occurs. All the curves in this are parallel.

Plate 16—In this plate the foundation is again squares, and the principal curve is hidden by the ornament, its use being to give direction to the ornament. The berries at the sides should be enclosed by curves, making three curves to get these berries right. Notice that the leaves at the lower part are drawn by a curve first, as in Fig. 2, then the leaf points marked on this curve. All leaves of this kind are drawn by a bounding curve containing the leaf points. The lines on the centre part of the drawing are radiating, and follow the shape of the ornament. If these are not carefully drawn, they are better left out, as they will spoil the rest.

Plate 17.—In this plate we have the centre line and one principal curve, the largest, which should be drawn first. This curve can be balanced by the help of a crossline at the top.

Plate 18—The foundation of this drawing is a circle divided up into eight equal parts. The straight lines forming these divisions should be drawn first, in the following order—the centre line, the cross line, the diagonal lines; then an equal distance is marked off on each of these lines from the centre, thus giving the eight points through which to draw the circle; then parallel lines should be drawn to these eight lines as shown in Fig. 2, and the semi-circular curves last. This plate introduces rosettes. See Chapter I., fixed forms, 1 (rosettes).

Plate 19—The centre part at the top of this drawing is an exercise on Plate 6. The side leaves are acanthus leaves, and are obtained by drawing the curve at the back first; then a guiding curve, passing through the leaf points, as shown in Fig. 2; next the loops are marked, and from these loops the secondary curves within the first guiding curve. All these are to be done before adding the leaf points. The folds or pipes from the loops follow the curve of the leaf. Notice that the double line at the loop shows the thickness of the leaf and should be carefully drawn. See Chapter I., Fixed Forms, 6 (loops and folds).

Plate 20—In Fig. 1, notice that the varied curves of the stem are first mapped out by two straight lines. Then in Fig. 2, the principal curves of the stem are drawn; lastly the smaller parts are added.

Plate 21—This is a five-sided rosette, and the chief difficulty is to get the five divisions of the circle equal. This is best done by drawing a centre line and a cross-line first, as shown in Fig. 1. Proceed as in Fig. 2. To balance the separate leaves, turn the paper round, so that you see each leaf upright in succession.

Plate 22—The foundation of this is made up of squares, and the circle in the centre contains a four-sided rosette, which is very easily filled in, after getting the construction as in Fig. 2.

Plate 23—Notice in this plate that the handles of the vase are slightly above the top of the vase, which is not shown in Figs. 1 or 2. Before doubling the curves of the handles, the single curve should be made as perfect as possible.

Plate 24—In this plate additional cross lines may be used to get the scrolls balanced. The radiating fan-like parts at the top and bottom should have their lines pointing to the centre of the plate.

Plate 25—The difficulty in this plate is to get the scroll-like twist nicely shown. Draw these as single curls as shown in Fig. 2, then from those curls, the little straight lines, passing behind the shield, should be parallel to the straight lines shown.

Plate 26—The important line in this drawing is the large outer curve, and no trouble should be spared to get it right before proceeding further.

Plate 27—The radiating curves in this are very important, because if they are not radiating equally, the drawing is at once spoilt. Notice that only one of these curves is continuous, and it should be drawn first. It is shown in Fig. 1.

Plate 28—In getting the hanging strings, or swags, as they are sometimes called, be careful to make them look as if they were really hanging down by their own weight, otherwise they will look like wires, instead of strings. The leaf points should be drawn last, after the bounding curve.

Plate 29—The most important curve in this drawing is the construction curve, or boundary curve, passing through the leaf points. After it is completed the inner curve, or back of the leaf, should be drawn, then the loops and leaf points marked, as shown in Fig. 2. The berries are in straight lines, therefore in addition to the straight line given in Fig. 2. passing through the lower three, three other straight lines should be drawn. This will simplify what would otherwise be a difficulty.

Plate 30—Is made up of serrated or saw-like leaves, all of which should be mapped out, as shown in Fig. 2, by construction curves, and the leaf points marked on them.

Plate 31—Be careful to get the principal curve of the vase right before adding the handles. Notice that the handles overlap the principal curve, therefore part of it must be rubbed out after the handles are put in. The decoration on the neck of the vase is radiating downwards, and great care should be taken that these radiating lines follow the shape of the vase. For the curves at the top, see Chapter II., Principle 6.

Plate 32—Notice that the large outer curve of the shell is continued to the cross line at the top, and encloses the ornament. The leaves growing out of the shell should be drawn farther than shown in the finished plate, see Fig. 2, in order to get their direction right, because the curves should suggest that they grow evenly from the inner part of the shell, diverging as they grow, in the same way that the shell itself enlarges gradually from its centre. Cross lines may be used to get the top points of the shell balanced, and to get the scrolls balanced.

Plate 33—Notice that this plate is based on squares, and that the acanthus leaves of which it is made up are first enclosed by a large bounding curve, then the sub-lobes are enclosed by other curves coming from the loops, and on these curves the small points of the leaves are marked. The loops and folds must be so drawn as to suggest the direction of growth, and the tendrils or flower stems should be drawn carefully as a single line, as shown in Fig. 2, and the position and size of the flowers mapped out as suggested. See Chapter III, paragraph headed " Blocking in."

Plate 34—Notice that the principal lines of this are only two in number, and that all the other lines depend on these two. The same method of mapping out the sub-lobes of the acanthus leaves, as in the last plate, is to be carried out in this and all such drawings. Notice that the lines radiating from the back of the leaves join the back of the leaf very gradually or tangentially.

Plate 35—This plate, although not necessarily based on squares, can be very conveniently started by a system of squares, It is the first case we have had of balanced ornament—that is, both sides equally heavy, but not symmetrical throughout. See Chapter II, Principle 4. In drawing the snakes draw them as a single line first, the start for which is suggested in Fig. 2.

Plate 36—This example affords a good exercise in blocking in, or spreading out the parts in masses, before filling in the details. Be careful to get all the loops and lines pointing to the bottom of the ornament, suggesting the direction of growth.

Plate 37—Is an example of a four-sided rosette. Draw the eight lines first, marking off points equally distant from the centre through which to draw the circle, then proceed as shown in Fig. 2.

Plate 38—The most important line in this is a bounding or containing line passing through the points, as shown in Fig. 1. After this curve is drawn and balanced with its reverse, the leaf points should be marked on it, and then the converging lines (*i.e.*, lines getting closer together) drawn from these points to the stem. If one leaf is carefully studied the remainder of the drawing will be found to be mere repetition.

Plate 39—This is a splendid example of radiation, but care should be taken to draw the principal leaves first, as shown in Fig. 2, overlapping at first, afterwards rubbing out parts.

Plate 40—This example shows very well how acanthus leaves are built up. The principal curves shown in Fig. 1 have the loops added to them in Fig. 2, and the sub-lobes of the leaf mapped out. The leaf points are then added to these sub-lobes, and the pipes or folds from the loops drawn. The lines on the leaves, and the pipes, are good examples of composition of line. See Chapter II., Principle 2.

Plate 41—Notice that the bowl of the vase is nearly circular, and that the principal divisions on the centre line are almost thirds. Do not attempt to draw the points on the handles without first drawing the curve, as shown in Fig. 2.

Plate 42—This drawing contains seven-sided rosettes; each should be started as suggested in Fig. 2, by dividing the circle carefully into seven equal parts. Be careful to start the drawing with the large curves, as shown in Fig. 1. Other cross lines may be used to balance the sides.

Plate 43—This copy was set at an examination by the Art Department, and is evidently simple, if methodically drawn by building up the drawing on the first flowing lines, as shown in Fig. 1, and then by blocking in or mapping out the smaller parts, as in Fig. 2, but if this method is neglected the drawing would prove difficult.

Plate 44—The flower in this plate is an example of an eight-sided rosette, the construction of which is similar to Fig. 1, Plate 37. The spaces between the leaves of this rosette are parallel and should be added before the small curves. Be careful to get the flow of line in the loops of the leaves, and the overlapping of the leaves and tendrils, which must be drawn continuous at first, and afterwards the parts not wanted rubbed out.

Plate 45—The scrolls in this are similar to those in Plate 6, with knob endings. The outer curves should be drawn first as shown in Fig. 1.

Plate 46—The foundation of this is made up of squares. The principal curve is shown in Fig. 1, and this curve is drawn by taking one little piece and reversing it all round the drawing, then another part of the curve, reversing it all round the drawing in the same way, so that only one curve is studied at a time and the drawing kept growing equally all round, as shown in Fig. 2. The overlapping of the ribands must be made by rubbing out the parts of the curves which pass underneath. If the drawing is attempted without making the curves continuous at first it will be a hopeless failure.

Plate 47—This is a similar piece of ornament to Plate 39, and is built up in the same way, drawing the curves overlapping at first in order to get their direction of growth, and afterwards rubbing out the parts not wanted.

Plate 48—Is an example of a six-sided rosette, and depends upon a careful foundation as shown in Fig. 1. Keep the drawing going at the same rate all round, sketching one little bit at a time and repeating it throughout as shown in Fig. 2.

Plate 49—Is an example of strap work, the essential point being the overlapping and interlacing of the ribands. All curves and lines to be drawn continuous at first.

Plate 50—Is another example of strap work, and should be carefully built up in the manner shown in Fig. 2. Notice in this and in plate 49, that the ribands are equal in width throughout, whether curved or straight.

Plate 51—Is an exercise on radiation and tangential junction, see Chap. II. on Principles. The leaves that are divided up into scale-like portions should have the distances between the scales marked by points, before drawing the curves. It is very important, in drawings of this kind, to leave the semi-circular curves at the ends of the leaves till last. Notice that the enclosing line is a circle.

Plate 52—Another example of diverging curves. Notice that the principal lines are the bounding curves, passing through the leaf points. Be very careful in this drawing to compare the space between the leaves with the width of the leaves themselves.

Plate 53—Is an exercise on Acanthus leaf ornament, which should be mapped out as in Fig. 2. The knob endings should have the outer curve drawn first.

Plate 54—A similar example to Plate 25. Draw the single curves first, as in Fig. 1, next the scrolls, starting from this curve, as in Fig. 2.

Plate 55—The difficult part of this exercise is to get the large outer scrolls correct; draw them as single curves first, trim them carefully, and balance them, before doubling the curve. Many students lose time by making the double curve before the first one is right.

Plate 56—It is very important in this one to draw the outer curves of the leaves first, and to notice the size of the spaces, compared with the width of the leaves. Additional cross lines may be used, as the student feels the necessity.

Plate 57—In this, the student should be very careful to get the smaller leaves to suggest that they are growing out of the trumpet-like sheaths at the sides. These small leaves should be drawn continuous at first. Be careful to get the loops on the central leaves tangential (*i.e.*, joining gradually).

Plate 58—This is an exercise on parallel curves; the single outer curve should be very carefully balanced and corrected before doing the inner curve, and the proportions of the circles to the whole drawing, very carefully ascertained.

Plate 59—This exercise requires great care to get the flow of line. The stems of the leaves should be drawn continuous at first, as shown in Figs. 1 and 2; and in making the curves even, the hand should be on the inner side of the curve, so as to use it as a compass.

Plate 60—The centre of this drawing is an example of an eight-sided rosette, and should be blocked in first, as shown in Fig. 1 on squares. The stems should be drawn continuous at first, single line as in Fig. 1, then double, as in Fig. 2, and lastly the parts not wanted rubbed out.

Plate 61—Is a kind of ornament intended for repetition, by taking the side lines as centre lines, and reversing in both directions. It is a good example of loops and folds, see Chapter I., "Fixed forms," paragraph 6, "Loops and Folds."

Plate 62—The rims of this vase should be drawn on a foundation of cross lines; refer to Chapter II., Principle 6.

Plate 63—Without method this drawing would be intricate and difficult, and if built up, as suggested in Figs. 1 and 2, then the additional lines added, as in the finished drawing, it will be found comparatively easy. All the curves in this should be drawn with the hand on the inside.

Plate 64—Is an example of a four-sided rosette. The leaves should be blocked in first by simple curves, as shown in Fig. 2, afterwards crenated, or sub-divided into the smaller curves.

Plate 65—Is an example of shell ornament, and if one of the curves in such a position as that shown in Fig. 2 be taken first, it is easier to fit the remainder, in making them converge with one another towards the centre.

Plate 66—Is based on squares, and the curves should be taken in parts, which should be repeated all round, so that the drawing is progressing at the same rate throughout as in Plate 46. Cross lines may be used in each corner to get the scrolls balanced.

Plate 67—All the large curves and proportions should be carefully corrected before adding the small parts for the lower part of the vase. See Chapter II., Principle 6.

Plate 68—This plate is based on squares, and is what might be called a revolving rosette. It depends on careful divisions.

Plate 69—Be careful to complete the foundation straight lines, as in Fig. 1, before attempting any curves. The drawing will then be simple. Notice the curves at the loops, which must be carefully drawn to suggest folds.

Plate 70—In this plate, besides the construction lines given, additional cross lines may be used to balance the large scrolls, or any other opposite points, but all students are not advised to use a large number of guiding lines, because it takes time and makes confusion. On the large curve enclosing the lower part the points of the leaves should be marked.

Plate 71—Is an example of free ornament, not symmetrical, nor yet in itself balanced. For this kind of ornament, although it has no centre line in itself, a vertical line may be taken through any part, and one or more cross lines at right angles. These vertical and horizontal lines govern the attitude or posture of the drawing, and make it possible to show the uprightness of it. Compare these lines with the lines of latitude and longitude on a map, and notice that all distances can be taken from these two lines; for instance, any point on the ornament is so much to the right or left of the vertical, and so much above or below the horizontal line. This drawing depends on the swing of the scroll, so that it is impossible to give too much attention to Fig. 1.

Plate 72—This drawing is suitable for a repeating border, by taking vertical lines at the ends and reversing the scrolls. It is very important to notice the shapes of the spaces between the leaves, as well as the leaves themselves.

Plate 73—The principal curve in this drawing is very evident, and should be drawn first, carefully keeping the proportions of its width to its length. The acanthus leaves are simplified by blocking them in as suggested in Fig. 2. When a number of leaves are diverging from one another like those in the centre, the upper lines of all the leaves should be taken first, and carefully spaced, as in Fig. 2, before attempting the lower line of any leaf.

Plate 74—This is another example of diverging leaves, and in this case again the upper curves or backs of the leaves are drawn by themselves, reversed, and balanced; then a curve passing through all the leaf points is drawn, and then the principal divisions of the leaves and loops.

Plate 75—After drawing the contour or curve of the side, all the other curves should be parts of ellipses. See Chapter II., Principle 6.

Plate 76—This drawing depends on careful blocking out of the masses of the leaves; and after drawing the two principal curves the serrations or leaf points are easy.

Plate 77—Is another example of free ornament, without any particular centre line of its own, but yet better managed by drawing a vertical and a horizontal line through any part of it. Notice in Fig. 1 the three principal curves drawn first; in Fig. 2 the masses of the foliage blocked out, and in Fig 3 the blocking in of the sub-lobes, so that there are three or four stages in the drawing.

Plate 78—This drawing depends for its success on the large elliptical curve, so that the majority of time and attention should be given to it. The details are much easier.

Plate 79—Notice that the principal curve taken in Fig. 1 is the outer curve in each scroll. This continued, forms the inner curve of the opposite scroll, which accounts for the break in the principal line. Fig. 2 shows these curves continued.

Plate 80—An example of free ornament, a scroll and rosette. Again vertical and horizontal lines are taken to get the attitude or pose of the ornament, then the principal curve is carefully drawn, and the remainder depends on the artistic feeling that the student may have acquired for delicately varying curves, because the curves forming the rosette are all different and yet each little variation in curvature has its meaning.

Plate 81—This drawing is based on squares and their subdivisions, and should be taken a curve at a time, and this curve repeated and reversed all round the drawing. This is a very good exercise, for the student draws each curve eight times before thinking of another shape ; it is a good exercise on knob endings, there being 24 of them contained in it.

Plate 82—The shape of this vase should be blocked in as suggested in Fig. 1, straight lines passing through the points of the upper part ; next, the large curves of the handles should be drawn. The subdivisions in the upper part should be attempted by picking out one central curve, as the one suggested in Fig. 2, then by dividing the two spaces thus obtained by taking other two about half way between the first, and so breaking up the space in that way ; that is, taking the largest divisions possible. If we commence by drawing one moulding, and then adding the next one to it, we may get the whole number of mouldings to take up considerably too much or too little of the space at our disposal. The top line is the only straight line, all the others are curved in an increasing degree towards the bottom. See Chapter II., Principle 6.

Plate 83—This is an example of a six-sided rosette, and depends on the accuracy with which the divisions are made, then the curves should be added as in Fig. 2, taking one part at a time and repeating it all round the ornament. See Chapter I. (rosettes).

Plate 84—Some parts of this vase would be difficult to draw without method. Notice the stem in Fig. 2, also the management of the wavy glass in Fig. 3, and the method of getting the tops of the flutings in Fig. 4.

Plate 85—This is an example of Arabic fan-work, and by referring to Figs. 1 and 2, it will be noticed that the divisions between the leaves all point to the same centre, excepting one or two at the bottom, which are horizontal. To get the semi-circular ends of the leaves regular, draw an additional construction line as in Fig. 4, Plate 84.

Plate 86—The principal lines of this drawing are rather difficult to pick out at first, but if those suggested in Fig. 1 are taken, and then an additional one in Fig. 2, the drawing after that is easy. It is essential that the interlacing of the ornament should be carefully followed out.

Plate 87—This is an example of "Fleur-de-lis" ornament, and as shown in Figs. 1 and 2, the backs of the leaves should be drawn first, giving the general shape and flow of line of the ornament. It will be noticed that the side leaves are similar leaves to the two upper ones, but owing to their being bent round, the lobes of the leaves must overlap one another. This makes it rather difficult unless a proper method be used. Fig. 3 shows how to start this inner portion; Fig. 4, how to build up the lobes from the loops; and then the finished effect depends on the student rubbing carefully out those parts of the curves not wanted, and so showing the overlapping.

Plate 88—In this drawing the principal lines are easily detected, and the blocking out of the masses of the foliagê is important. Notice that the ornament itself takes up more space than the ground, and is thus an example of profuse distribution.

Plate 89—Success in this drawing depends on the mapping out of the scrolls in single lines, as shown in Fig. 2. Notice that in every case the outer curve is taken. When these scrolls are corrected, as far as possible, the addition of the parallel curve is easy enough.

Plate 90—The containing lines of this must be at right angles to one another, so that the two lower ones produced would form a square with the two upper ones. This may be done as a test of correctness. In this case all the scrolls should be drawn in single curves, as in the last plate, first taking the principal curves, as shown in Fig. 1, and then developing these by adding the smaller parts as shown in Fig. 2. Notice that what forms the outer curve in one scroll, forms the inner curve of another.

Plate 91—The centre portion of this drawing should be fairly easy to the student, as there have been similar shapes in previous plates, but the difficulty introduced is the flowing leaves at the sides. These should be first drawn as a single curve, see Fig. 1, then carefully blocked in, as shown in Fig. 2.

Plate 92—Is an example of a hinge, the small circles on it being the holes for the screws. Draw the principal curve first, as in Fig. 1, and then be very careful to get the direction of the lines crossing this curve correct. Notice which part of the centre line these lines point to.

Plate 93—In this it is best to block in the entire ornament by straight lines, as in Fig. 1, and then to add the principal curves. The interlacing of the stems is rather difficult to make out, and requires careful study.

Plate 94—By taking single curves, and repeating them all round, as shown in Fig. 2, this drawing is made fairly simple.

Plate 95—Notice that, as shown in Fig. 1, one large curve is taken as the foundation line, then the varied curves are added to this, and the parts blocked in.

Plate 96—This is fairly easy if the principal curves be taken, and the smaller curves added, as they diminish in size. Notice that the flower cup is balanced and not symmetrical.

Plate 97—Is rather an intricate example of acanthus leaf ornament, and depends on the careful drawing of the principal curves. By adding the centre lines of the leaves, as shown in Fig. 2, the drawing can be very well mastered. Another way would be to block in the leaves by lines passing through the leaf points, but in this case the blocking in would be rather confusing, so that the method suggested in Fig. 2 is advisable.

Plate 98—Is an example of acanthus leaf ornament containing two four-sided rosettes. These rosettes should be started by the cross lines as shown in Fig. 2. The leaves themselves should be blocked in by drawing curves through the leaf points, as shown in Fig. 2.

Plate 99—Is what is called a nest of foliage, that is a sort of base or starting point for the growth of foliage. It affords good practice for blocking in, as shown in Fig. 2. If this blocking in is carefully done, the drawing will be found easy.

Plate 100—This depends upon the flow of the principal lines which are given in Fig. 1. To get the sides balanced with one another, two or three cross lines may be used.

Plate 101—An example of Greek ornament, the scrolls being the chief difficulty. These should be drawn singly as shown in Figs. 1 and 2, taking the outer curve of each scroll first. Notice that the spaces in the scroll diminish regularly.

Plate 102—This was an examination test which looks easy, but contains many points where the careless student may stumble, such as the joint in the stem, and the continuity of curvature in the scrolls. Each scroll must appear to belong to the main stem. The spaces contained in the scrolls diminish regularly; the distances of the scrolls should be carefully noticed from the other parts of the ornament. Notice the method suggested in Fig. 1 for getting continuity of curve.

Plate 103—After drawing the centre line, any large curve may be taken as principal and reversed. Notice that all the curves cross on the centre line, so that starting from any one of these points any curve and its reverse may be taken. All curves should be drawn continuous at first, and the parts not wanted rubbed out, in order to show the interlacing.

Plate 104—The principal curve in this, is that suggested in Fig. 1. Notice that part of the foliage overlaps this line. One or two additional cross lines may be used to get the symmetry of the drawing.

Plate 105—Notice in this that the outer curves of the scrolls are drawn first, and that what forms the outer curve of one, forms the inner curve of another. The drawing is based on squares. In drawing the bead-like processes or fruit, 2 more containing lines should be drawn, in addition to the one in Fig. 2, which only gives direction, see Plate 35.

Plate 106—The lines forming the scrolls in this should be drawn continuous at first, as in Fig. 2, then the small curls added at proper intervals, and from this the remainder developed. Additional cross lines may used, but not more than 2 or 3.

Plate 107—The fan-like central part is easy to the student who has been through the earlier plates, but the flowers at the sides require careful blocking in, in the manner suggested in Fig. 2. A curve must also be drawn through the leaf points, and the leaves started in the way suggested.

Plate 108—The blocking in of this is the most difficult. The curved midribs of the leaves should be drawn first, and then curves passing through the leaf points, as shown in Fig. 2. Be careful to get the folds from the loops all pointing to the centre of the ornament.

Plate 109—The rosette in this, is the most difficult part ; it is five-sided, and the student should refer to Plate 68, and to Chapter I., "Rosettes."

Plate 110—This is a case of the ornament filling a certain space or panel, and the student should read Chapter II., Principle 1, on Distribution. The spaces must be very carefully considered, as well as the shape of the ornament itself. The rosette is eight-sided, and the best method of getting it is suggested in Fig. 3. The overlapping of the leaves on the centre line, at the lower part, is rather difficult. The curves must be drawn continuous at first, in both leaves. Plate 44 is a similar case to which the student might refer, as the opposite leaf overlaps.

Plate 111—This plate is easily analysed, the principal lines being very evident; the blocking in of the flowers is shown in Fig. 3, and the management of the leaf points in Fig. 2.

Plate 112—The centre portion, and the two principal outer curves should be drawn first, then the branching curves, and the blocking in of the leaves as shown in Fig. 2.

Plate 113—The principal lines of this are very evident, and the details must be made to depend on the blocking in of the curves, Fig. 2.

Plate 114—This is a geometrical representation of a vase, the important part of the exercise being to get the curves of the decorations to recognise the shape of the vase. These curves should be drawn continuous at first, from the handles to the base, then the semi-circles and circles filled in.

Plate 115—This depends for its attitude on the comparison with the vertical line, which may be taken through any part. The details will be found easy, if Fig. 2 is carefully studied. A drawing of this kind depends largely on the artistic feeling of the student, for the gracefulness of its finish.

Plate 116—Great care should be taken to get the directions of the straight lines, blocking in the flowers, or leaf cups, in the right direction. Notice that the first curves taken, Fig. 1, overlap one another the exact amount required as thickness for the stems.

Plate 117—The principal curves in this are very evident; the small parts, the fork-like processes at the sides for instance, should be carefully blocked in.

Plate 118—This is a drawing of inlaid wood, accounting for the way in which the parts of it are detached. The student must draw them continuous at first, then rub the parts out to show these points of detachment. The rosettes are five-sided, and may be drawn by means of a circle, or if the student prefers, blocked in in straight lines, see Fig. 2.

Plate 119—This is the first example of dolphin ornament, the curves of the ornament being suggested by the graceful bending of the fish. It will be noticed that all curves are tangential with, or composing with, the curve of the back.

Plate 120—In this plate the rosettes are very uneven in shape, and this unevenness should be blocked in, in straight lines, as shown in Fig. 2. It will be noticed that they are nearly square. This plate forms a good test for the student's knowledge of continuity of growth, as will be noticed that at two or three parts the stem is hidden by sheath leaves. Of course it must be drawn continuous by the student, as in Fig. 2.

Plate 121—Is also an exercise on continuity of growth, the sheath leaves purposely hiding the stem in some parts to see if the student will be able to show the direction of growth of the remainder. Fig. 1 shows which is the first curve to draw.

Plate 122—Forms a good example to test the student's ability of drawing loops and folds; the swag or hanging drapery at the top should be carefully drawn and balanced.

Plate 123—This plate is an example of a foliage nest or a group of sheath leaves; the thick stem should be drawn continuous at first, as shown in Figs. 1 and 2. Vertical and horizontal lines should be used to get the posture of the ornament.

Plate 124—In this the principal curve is easily detected, all other curves appear to branch from this one.

Plate 125—This is a good example for practising blocking in. Notice that the leaves, although curved themselves, and their details curved, can yet be blocked in by straight lines. Fig. 1 shows this blocking in, Fig. 2 shows the blocking in of the sub-lobes, to which must be added the leaf points or serrations.

Plate 126—This plate is a good exercise on tangential growth, that is, curves branching gradually from one another, see Chapter II., Principle 2.

Plate 127—This plate depends for its gracefulness, on the composition of line, or the gradual branching of the smaller curves from the large ones.

Plate 128—In this the principal curves are very evident, the foliage in the centre at the bottom should be blocked in, marking the loops before putting in the details. The rosettes should be drawn in circles, an additional curve should be drawn inside the one at the top in Fig. 2, in order to get the semi-circular endings to the fan.

Plate 129—The curl in this is not difficult if drawn in straight lines as directed, but the direction of these lines must be carefully noticed. The loops should be marked before the details of the foliage are attempted, as shown in Fig. 2.

Plate 130—This is another example of acanthus leaf foliage, and depends on the careful blocking in of the masses.

Plate 131—This is a fine example of composition of line, and the student should refer to Chapter II., Principle 2.

Plate 132—Notice that the foundation curves of this drawing are similar to Plate 6, and that the foliage is merely added to this principal line.

Plate 133—The twisted ornament, passing behind the leaves, is best drawn by taking one or two of the lines, as shown in Fig. 2. Draw them first, then afterwards divide the spaces so formed, by other lines. In this way the student is certain to get the right number of twists in.

Plate 134—This drawing depends on starting the principal lines, and descending step by step to smaller curves.

Plate 135—Plan the work out, as shown in Fig. 2, marking the spaces and shapes of the masses first, afterwards fill in the details by starting with the loops, and drawing towards the leaf points.

Plate 136—This ornament depends on the flow of line, and the appreciation by the student of the curves.

Plate 137—This example contains very good five-sided rosettes, and it is evident from a glance at them, that they will be best drawn by enclosing them in straight lines, not in a circle, as sometimes happens. Notice the triangular shape of the drawing generally, and how this is mapped out in Fig. 2.

Plate 138—This is intended as an exercise on continuity of curve, the stems being broken up at intervals by joints and sheath leaves. They should, of course, be drawn continuous at first, as shown in Figs. 1 and 2.

Plate 139—This is an example of free ornament. Notice that the parts are detached, which is owing to the fact that the ornament is made up in little squares of differently coloured marble. Be careful to get the tendril gracefully bent, and correctly overlapping.

Plate 140—The scroll-work in this plate is rather difficult; the student should, therefore, take great care to get the single curves right, before attempting to double them. The straggling nature of the ornament also adds to the difficulty.

Plate 141—This example can only be successfully drawn by careful blocking in, as shown in Fig. 2. The blocking in being complete, the details should be carefully examined as to their curvature, because every detail is slightly different, and every variation in curve has its meaning.

Plate 142—In Fig. 2 the rosettes are shown blocked in by straight lines, the containing curves of the large leaves are also shown; but, in addition to this, the student should carefully block in the sub-lobes of these leaves. The proportions of ornament of this kind should be carefully noticed, as they are less common than upright drawings.

Plate 143—This is a fairly good example of continuous growth, the details tending to take the attention of the student away from that continuity.

Plate 144—The foundation curves in this are simple, but the details require careful blocking in, and the stems, where they are banded together on the centre line, must be carefully managed.

Plate 145—The foundation of this drawing is a semi-circle. After drawing it, great care should be taken to get the principal curves flowing gradually into one another, as in Fig. 1. A curve is tangential to another when it will not cut, even if produced. In the finished drawing great care must be taken to get the interlacing of the tendrils correct.

Plate 146—This depends on careful drawing of the ellipses, see Chapter II. Principle 6.

Plate 147—After drawing the midribs of the leaves, as in Fig. 1, the masses of the leaves should be carefully mapped out, as shown in Fig. 2, overlapping one another; then the varied details put in, touching these curves.

Plate 148—Great care must be taken in this to get the flow of line continuous, especially where the joints occur. The student must not allow himself to lose sight of the continuity of growth by these details. The directions of the straight lines, crossing the curves, are very important, see Fig. 2.

Plate 149—In this example the five-sided rosettes are best drawn in circles, and then the loops marked, as shown in Fig. 2. The principal curve must be drawn continuous at first, as it is broken up by sheath leaves in parts.

Plate 150—This is an example of inlaid work, which accounts for the overlappings of the scrolls being treated differently from those at the top of the next drawing, Plate 151.

All the scrolls should be drawn as single curves first, then doubled throughout, and lastly the details added.

Plate 151—The principal curves in this are broken up or hidden by sheath leaves, and therefore great care must be taken that the part of the stem seen must suggest the hidden remainder.

Plate 152—The acanthus leaves must have their sub-lobes blocked in, by first marking the loops. For the centre ornament additional cross lines may be used.

Plate 153—This drawing is based on a square; the leaves must be divided up by single lines at first as shown in Fig. 2. The clusters of berries should be blocked in by drawing triangles round them.

Plate 154—After drawing the principal curves, block in the sublobes of the leaves, before adding the details.

Plate 155—Notice that the rosettes in this are based on squares, which should be drawn as suggested in Fig. 2. The dolphin heads require great care.

Plate 156—This drawing is the angle of a border, and to test the containing lines, the student should produce the upper ones to meet the lower ones, when a square should be formed. This square will show that the directions of the lines are correct. The stems should be drawn as single lines first, then doubled throughout before the details are added.

Plate 157—Be careful to get the tendrils suggesting that they grow out of the sheath leaves. The flower cups should be blocked in as shown in Fig. 2, and the feathers drawn at first by continuous curves.

Plate 158—The details in this drawing are rather difficult and require careful blocking in to get their comparative size in relation to the drawing and their distances from other parts.

Plate 159—This is a good example of dolphin ornament, the lower part of the ornament suggests the tail of the fish and the branching foliage the fins. Notice the blocking in suggested in Fig. 3, and the method of getting a good scroll in Fig. 4.

Plate 160—The rosettes in this are difficult, owing to their irregularity, they are best commenced by circles, otherwise it is difficult to get them the right size. Notice that there is balance in some parts between the details, and not symmetry throughout.

Plate 161—This example depends on careful blocking in; to attempt it without method would end in hopeless failure; therefore, keep to the steps as suggested in Figs. 1 and 2. Fig. 3 shows how the details are added to the blocking in lines.

Plate 162—This example looks rather intricate in the finished drawing, but if it be commenced as suggested in Figs. 1 and 2, and the loops marked before the lobes of the leaves are blocked in, it will be managed all right. All the curves should be drawn continuous at first, and, after the drawing is complete, the interlacing shown, by rubbing out the parts not wanted.

Plate 163—The thick stem in this should be drawn continuous, as in Fig. 1, the outer curve first, afterwards the branching details as shown in Fig. 2. A vertical and a horizontal line are helpful in this to get the attitude of the scroll.

Plate 164—The foundation of this drawing is simple, but the details should be carefully planned out by equal divisions, as shown in Fig. 2; the principal lines of the shield are also shown in Fig. 2.

Plate 165—This drawing depends on careful mapping out of the masses of foliage. The details should be commenced by marking the loops.

Plate 166—This plate contains rosettes based on squares which should be divided up as shown in Fig. 2, care being taken to get the right inclination of these squares.

Plate 167—The upper rosettes in this are twelve-leaved, and are best started as shown in Fig. 2. Notice that the spirals are diminishing in thickness as they twine round the rosettes; also that the centre stem has three stages of thickness.

Plate 168—After drawing the principal curves, as shown in Fig. 1, great care must be taken with the blocking in of the flowers and leaves, the details being useless if they are in the wrong places.

Plate 169—In the five-sided rosettes, the small detached curves are intended to suggest undulation or bending in the flower cup, and must be very carefully drawn; they are better left out if the student cannot give the necessary care to them. Notice the method of drawing the centre leaves in Fig. 2, namely by marking the loops first; and notice also the blocking in of the flowers at the upper part by triangles.

Plate 170—The foundation curve of this is a circle, which should be got by drawing centre line, cross line, and one or two others, as shown in Chapter III., "How to draw a circle," next the principal curves, shown in Fig. 2, should be added, and lastly the sub-lobes of the leaves blocked in. The scrolls, in the fan-like central part, should have an additional curve to keep them in position.

Plate 171—After drawing the principal lines in Fig. 1, great care must be taken with the blocking in of the flowers, to get their right attitude and size.

Plate 172—This drawing is made up largely of single lines, and depends on the flow of those lines for its effect. The drops at the sides must be vertical, so as to suggest that they are hanging. Notice the elements of which this drawing is composed, namely, crown, shield, rose, shamrock, thistle, oak leaves and acorns. This was given at a "College of Preceptors" Examination, Jubilee year.

Plate 173—After drawing the principal lines, great care must be taken with the blocking in of the sublobes of the acanthus leaves, otherwise the drawing will be difficult.

Plate 174—After drawing the principal curves in single lines, double them throughout, as shown in Fig. 2, then mark the position of the sheath leaves. Notice the different treatment of the upper and lower rosettes; continuity of growth must be carefully observed in this as there is so much ornament on the stems to break it up.

Plate 175—This is rather a difficult example owing to the straggling nature of it. The blocking in of the flowers should be carefully noticed in Fig. 2, and the distances of the buds from the other parts should be noticed.

Plate 176—This is an exercise on acanthus leaves, and the loops and folds should be very carefully drawn in the direction of growth. The flower cups and the tendrils should be blocked in by lines at right angles to the direction of the tendrils.

Plate 177—Notice carefully the way the foliage is blocked out in Fig. 2, and be careful to get the continuity of curve where the joint occurs in the upper part.

Plate 178—This plate is an exercise on continuity; the stems are frequently broken up by sheath leaves and other details in order to test the student's ability to keep the drawing together in a continuous flow of line. Notice the methods of dealing with the details shown in Figs. 3 and 4.

Plate 179—This plate is rather full of trifling details, therefore it is necessary to realise the principal curves, as in Fig. 1, and then to mass the other details together as in Fig. 2.

Plate 180– The two four-sided rosettes or flowerettes at the upper part should be carefully blocked in by lines joining the four points ; this will form a good foundation on which to work these parts.

Plate 181—The flow of line in the dolphins should be very carefully drawn before attempting any details, then the sublobes of the leaves both in the dolphins, and in the lower part of the capital, should be blocked in by starting from the loops as suggested in Fig. 2.

Plate 182—After the principal lines have been drawn as in Fig. 1, this exer e affords good practice in blocking in, the wings and heads of the birds, as well as the foliage requiring to be massed together before attempting their details.

Plate 183—The four diagrams here divide the work up into such easy stages, and such definite method, that the careful student cannot very well go wrong; care should be taken, however, to get the overlapping of the tendrils correct. The rosettes, as shown in Fig. 2, should be started from the loops.

Plate 184—After marking the principal curves of the lockplate, and the key-hole, as in Fig. 1, the shapes of the leaves should be blocked in, as shown in Fig. 2.

Plate 185—This appears rather complicated in the finished drawing, but if all curves and leaves be drawn continuous at first the difficulty will be considerably diminished. The stems are of equal thickness throughout.

Plate 186—This Plate is fairly easy, owing to the fact that after getting the principal lines drawn, the remainder of the work is mere filling in. Notice that the ornament on the lower part of the bowl, is not symmetrical.

Plate 187—This is an example of a hinge for a door, after getting the first flowing lines, however, the details are easy.

Plate 188—This example, after getting the large curves, depends on careful blocking in before attempting any details.

Plate 189—This, and the two or three following are fairly difficult examples, but if the method suggested in Figs. 1 and 2 be carefully followed, the difficulty will be easily overcome. All the foliage requires blocking in and working from the loops ; Figs. 3, 4, and 5, show methods of blocking in the other details.

Plate 190—Notice in this drawing the various elements of which it is composed, and refer to Chapter I. on Elements. In this case the student is left to pick out the principal lines for himself, to block in the various parts, and test his ability in the method of procedure, suggested throughout the course.

Plate 191—This is simple in its principal lines, but rather intricate in its details, so requires great care and delicate work generally.

Plate 192—This plate will be found difficult, unless the principal lines, as suggested in Fig. 2, are carefully placed first ; beyond that stage the filling in of the details is easy.

CHAPTER V.

SUGGESTED SHORT COURSES.

Short Course for Students :—

For students who have already had a good amount of practice at drawing, or who, after doing a little, find themselves blessed with more than ordinary natural ability, the following selection of the Plates is made. To students who wish to acquire the ability without trouble, or without a considerable sacrifice of time, perhaps the best suggestion that could be given is that there is no royal road to success.

Plates 3, 6, 8, 11, 15, 19, 21, 27, 32, 33, 34, 36, 38, 40, 42, 43, 46, 50, 55, 56, 64, 70, 71, 73, 74, 77, 80, 87, 95, 96, 98, 99, 100, 101, 105, 110, 111, 113, 115 and 117, that is one a week for 40 weeks. The book contains nearly 5 drawings per week, if worked at steadily through the year.

No drawing in the above course should be made the same size as the copy, nor yet twice the size, but all should be a little larger.

In schools or colleges where the students are young, they may first make the drawing the same size, measuring with their pencil only, and never using another pencil, paper, compass, &c., to help. This should be at the discretion of, and under the direction and supervision of the teacher, the object being to get the largest possible amount of usefulness out of the one pencil used, and to train the student's eye to what is right.

The same copy may be afterwards drawn a little larger without measuring. This has been found *to produce good results in practice.*

The book has not been designed for the Standards, but teachers may get a large amount of teaching matter from it for their classes.

COURSES FOR THE STANDARDS.

Standards I. and II. (Straight lines)—

Plate	1	Figs. 1 and 2		Plate	19	Fig. 1
,,	2	,, 1 and 2		,,	49	,, 1
,,	7	Fig. 1		,,	50	,, 1
,,	10	,, 1		,,	66	,, 1
,,	12	,, 1				
,,	13	,, 1				

Also Figs. 1 of several other plates by omitting the curves.

The number of examples for these Standards is inadequate, but teachers may get help by referring to Chapter 3 on Methods.

Standard III.—

Plate	1	Figs. 4 and 6		Plate	26	Fig. 1
,,	2	,, 4 and 6		,,	27	,, 1
,,	3			,,	29	,, 1
,,	4			,,	30	,, 1
,,	9	Figs. 1 and 2		,,	31	
,,	10	Fig. 2		,,	32	Fig. 1
,,	11	,, 1		,,	34	Figs. 1 and 2
,,	13	,, 2		,,	36	Fig. 1
,,	14	Figs. 1 and 2		,,	38	Figs. 1 and 2
,,	15	,, 1 and 2		,,	39	Fig. 1
,,	16	,, 1 and 2		,,	40	,, 1
,,	17			,,	43	,, 1
,,	18			,,	44	,, 1
,,	19	Fig. 2		,,	45	,, 1
,,	20			,,	46	,, 1
,,	21			,,	47	,, 1
,,	23			,,	52	,, 1
,,	24	Figs. 1 and 2		,,	53	Figs. 1 and 2
,,	25			,,	56	,, 1 and 2

Standard III.—*continued.*—

Plate	57	Figs. 1 and 2	Plate	76	Fig. 1
,,	59	Fig. 1	,,	77	,, 2
,,	66	,, 2	,,	86	,, 2
,,	71	,, 1	,,	87	Figs. 1 and 2

&c., &c. Fig. 1 of almost every succeeding Plate being suitable. These simple exercises, which form the bases of more elaborate drawings, are on that account, well worth practising.

Standard IV.—

Plate	4		Plate	45	Fig. 1
,,	5		,,	46	,, 1
,,	6		,,	47	,, 2
,,	7		,,	52	,, 2
,,	14		,,	53	,, 2
,,	24		,,	55	,, 1
,,	26		,,	56	,, 2
,,	27		,,	57	,, 2
,,	37	Fig. 2	,,	59	,, 2
,,	38	,, 2	,,	61	,, 2
,,	39	,, 2	,,	64	,, 2
,,	40		,,	66	,, 2
,,	42	Figs. 1 and 2	,,	68	,, 2
,,	43				

And so on, either Fig. 1 or Fig. 2 of the following plates being suitable.

Standard V.—

Plate	13	Plate	53
,,	20	,,	54
,,	23	,,	62
,,	25	,,	72
,,	28	,,	75
,,	31	,,	79
,,	34	,,	80
,,	43	and Fig. 2 of any succeeding Plates.	

Standard VI.—

Plate 14	Plate 57
,, 16	,, 58
,, 32	,, 59
,, 33	,, 60
,, 38	,, 71
,, 42	,, 77
,, 45	,, 80
,, 51	,, 91
,, 52	,, 115
,, 55	,, 123
,, 56	

and other plates or figures at the discretion of the teacher.

Standard VII.—

All Plates up to Plate 130.

PLATES.

PLATE 1.

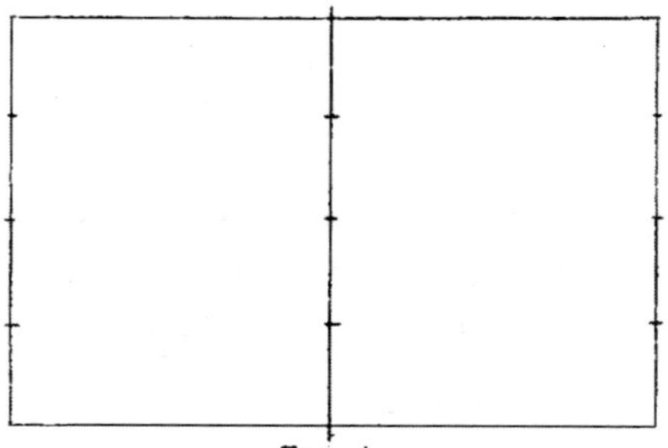

Fig. 1.

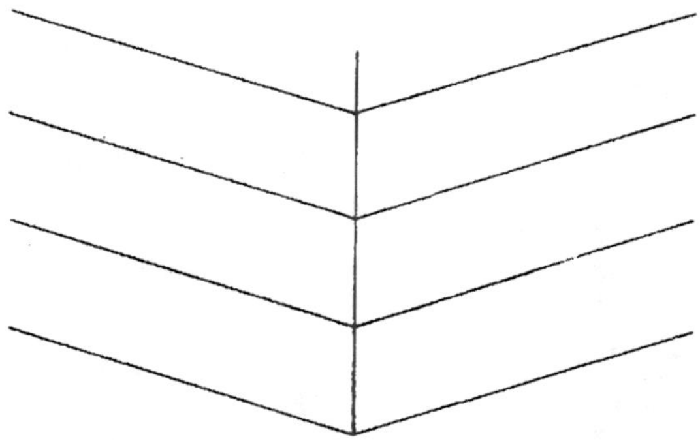

Fig. 2.

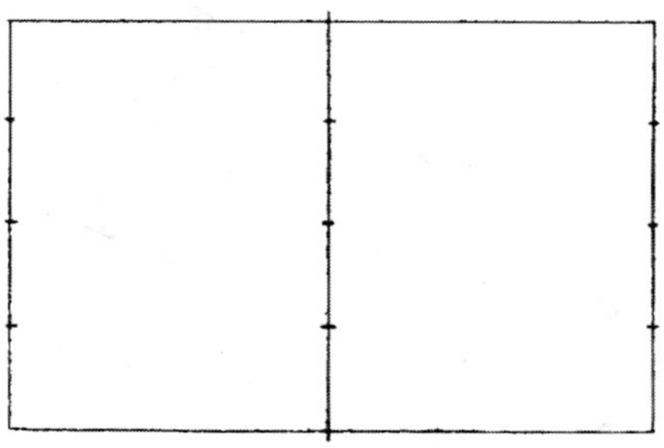

Fig. 3.

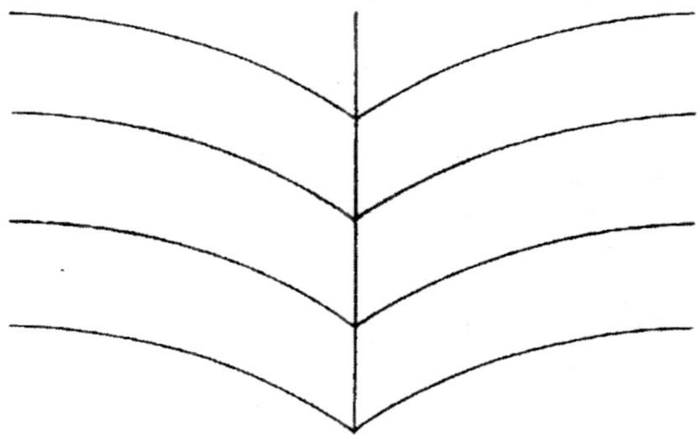

Fig. 4.

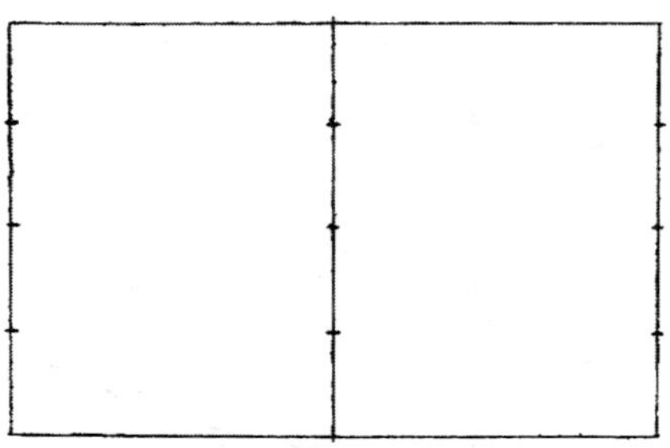

Fig. 5.

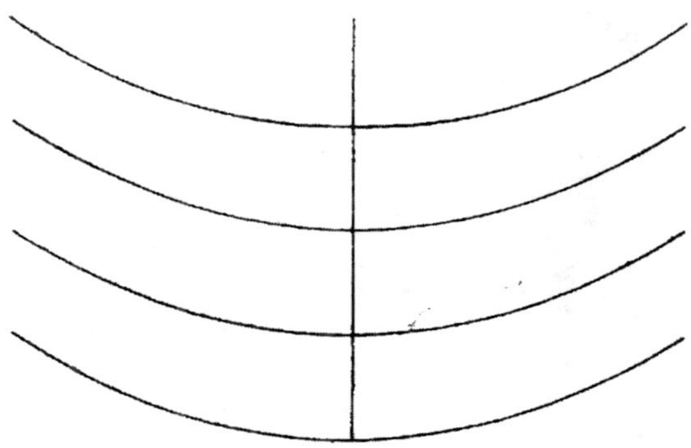

Fig. 6.

Parallel radiation from points on an axis.

PLATE 2.

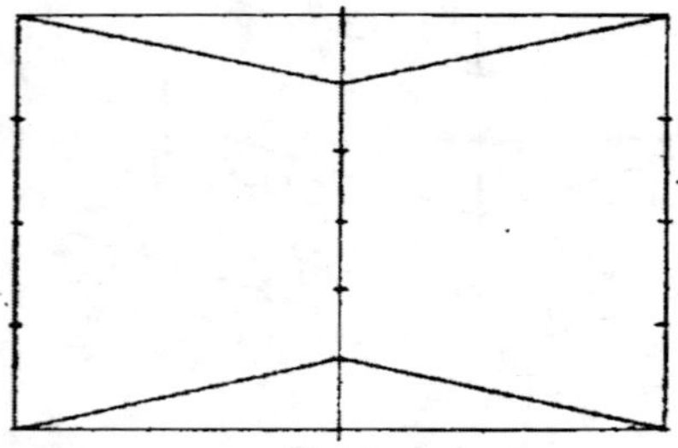

Fig. 1.

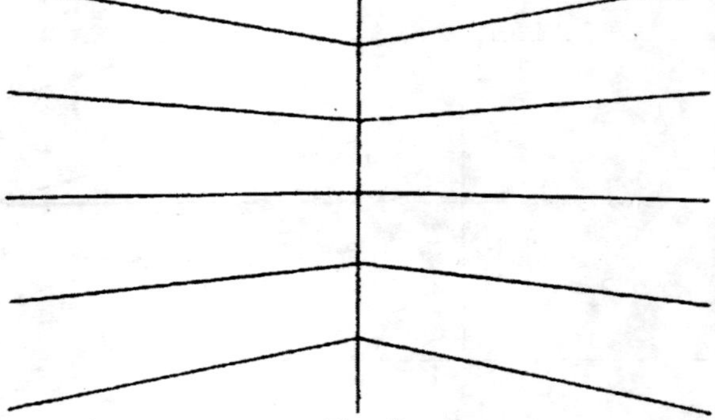

Fig. 2.

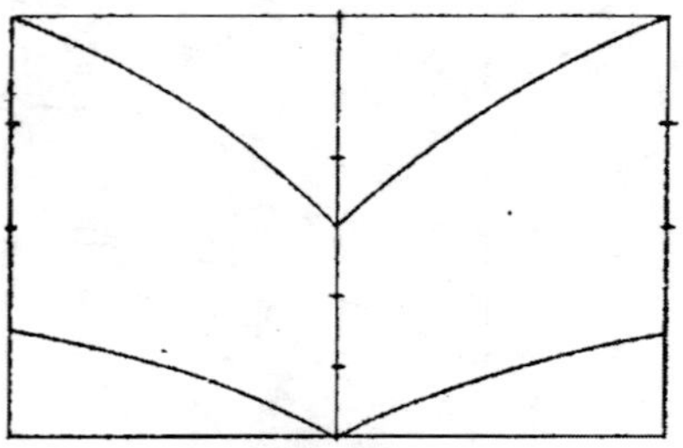

Fig. 3.

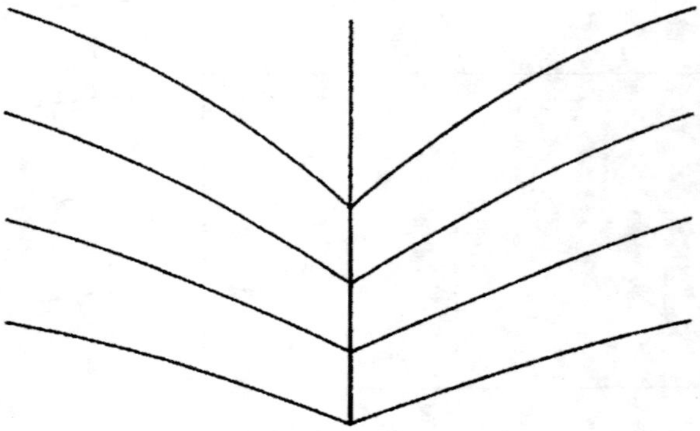

Fig. 4.

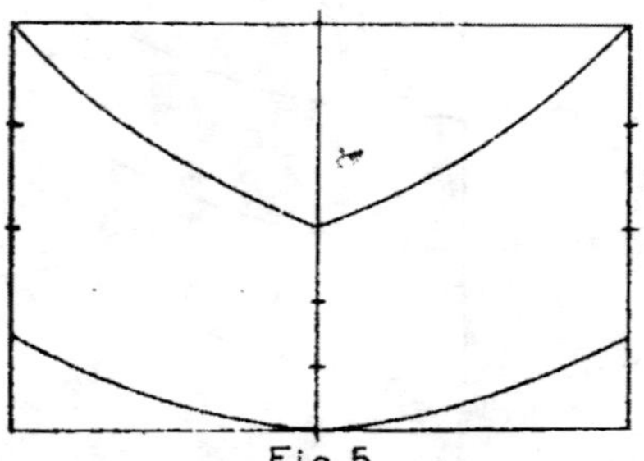

Fig. 5.

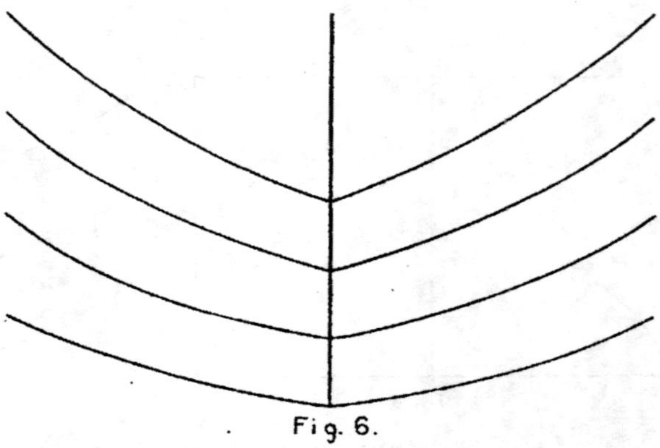

Fig. 6.

Diverging radiation from points on an axis.

PLATE 3.

Radiation from a point.

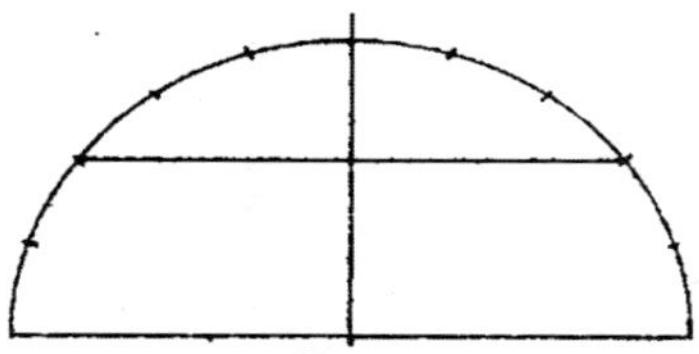

Fig. 1.

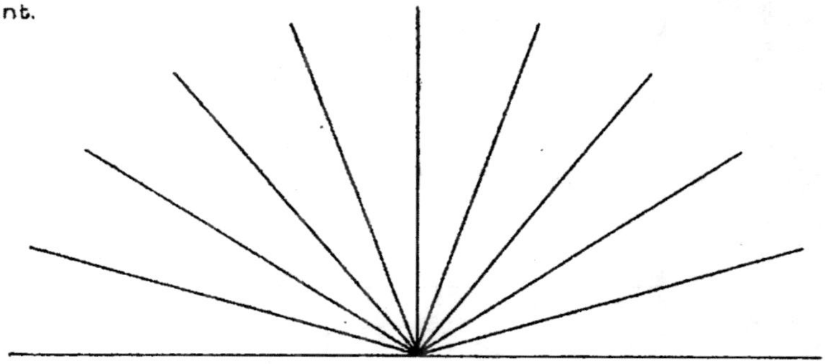

Fig. 2

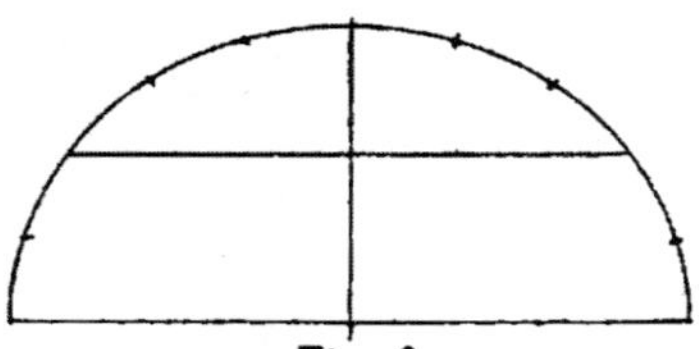

Fig. 3.

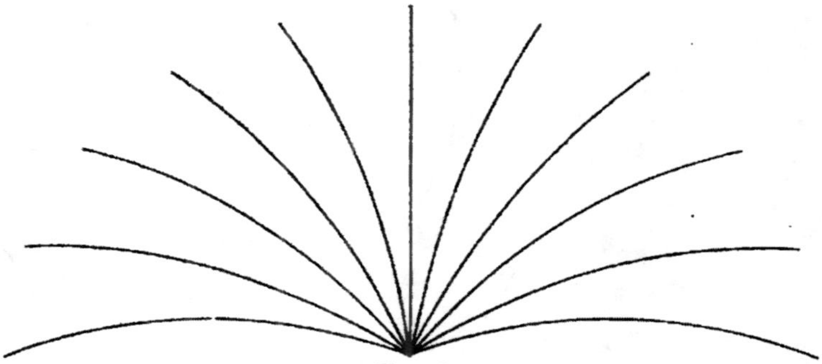

Fig. 4.

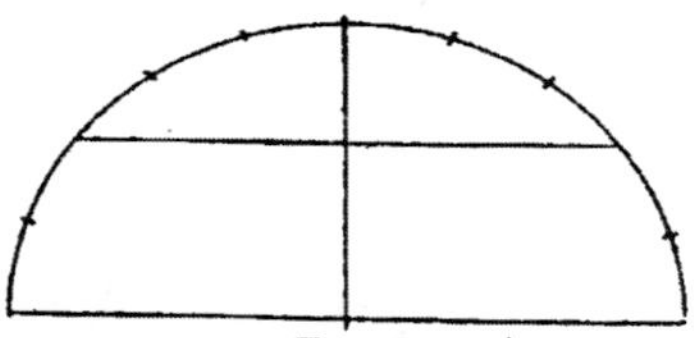

Fig. 5.

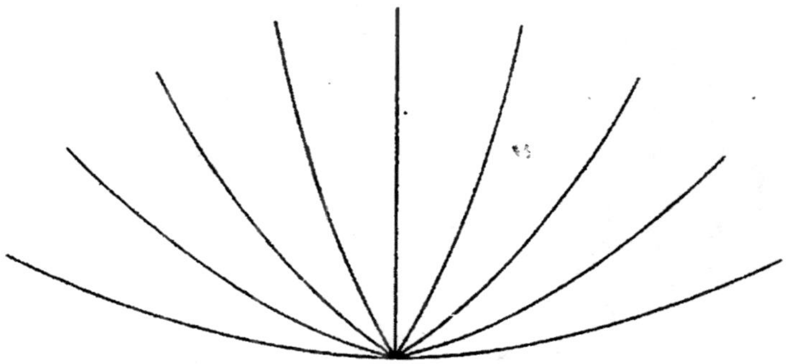

Fig. 6.

PLATE 4.

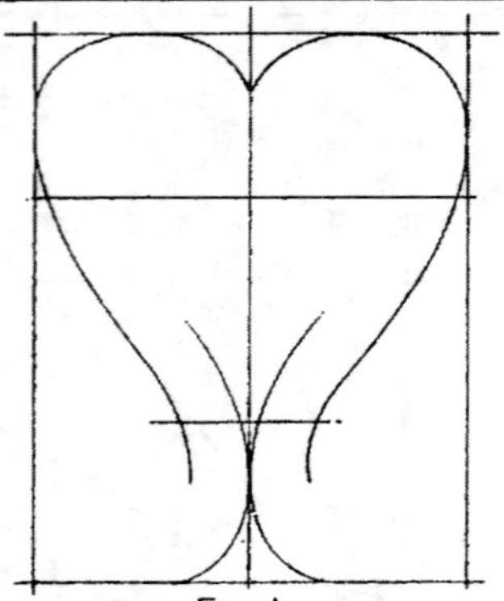

Fig. 1.

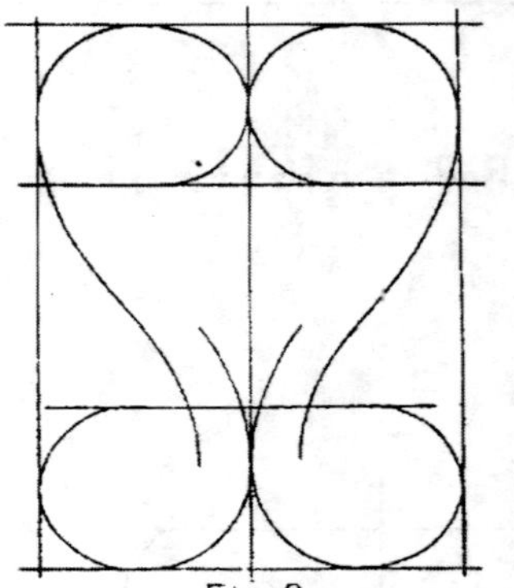

Fig. 2.

By CHARLES ARMSTRONG.

PLATE 5.

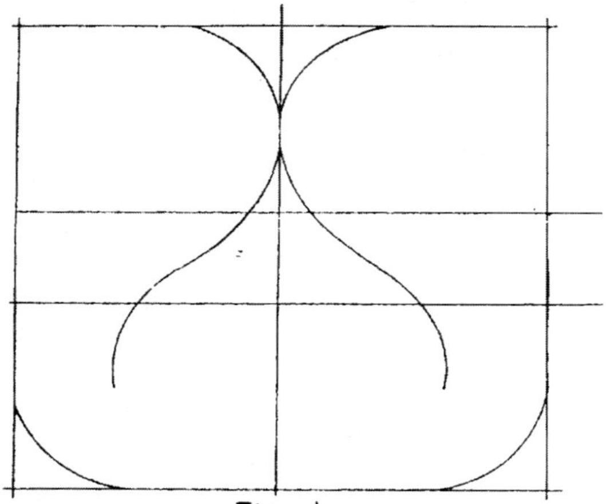

Fig. 1.

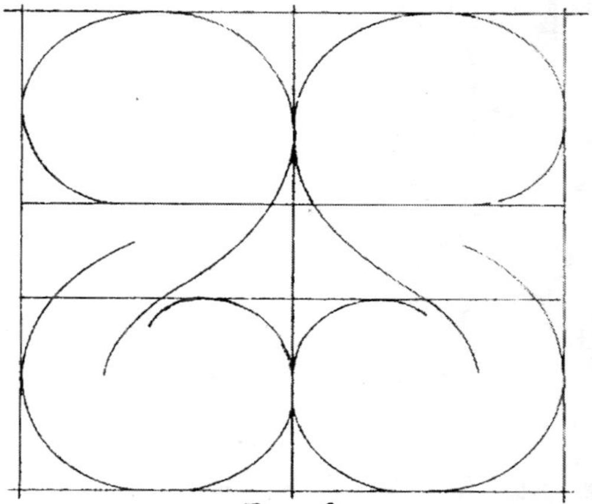

Fig. 2.

PLATE 6.

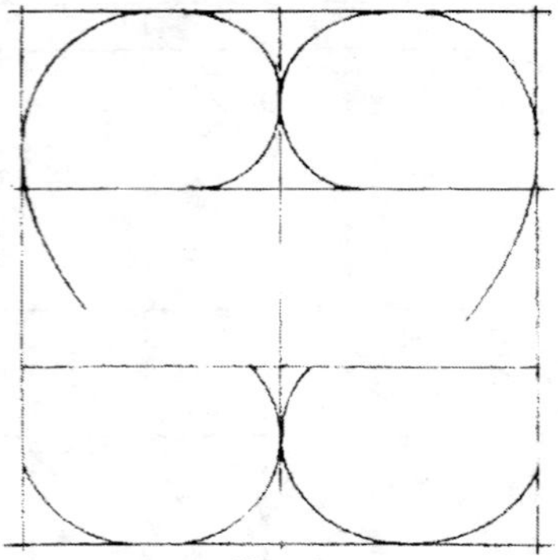

Fig. 1.

Fig. 2.

PLATE 7.

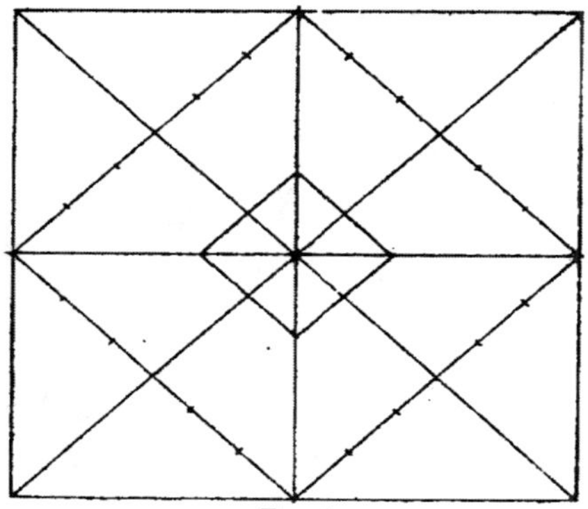

Fig. 1.

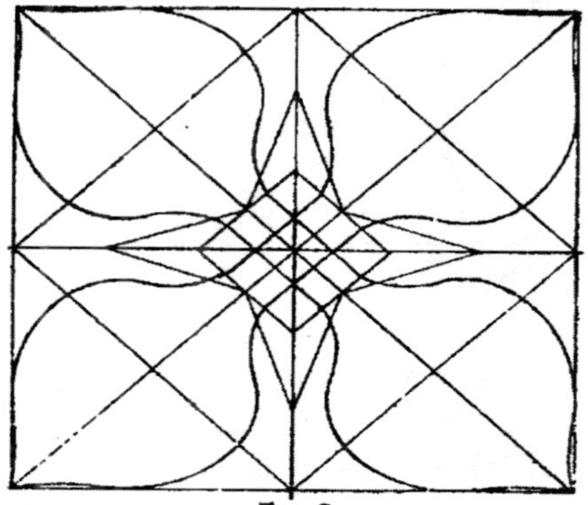

Fig. 2.

CUSACK'S "FREEHAND ORNAMENT." By CHARLES ARMSTRONG.

PLATE 8.

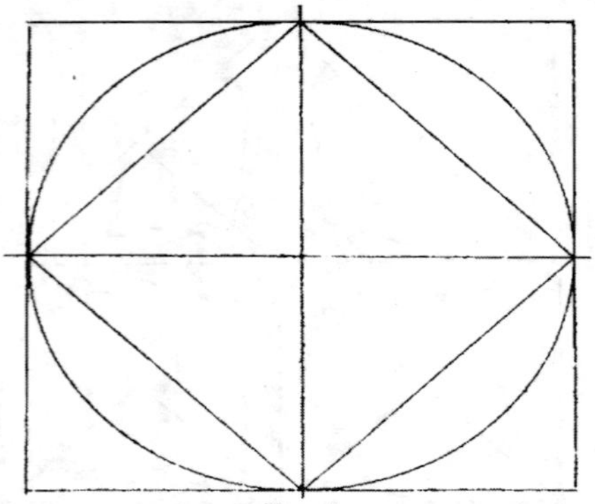

Fig. 1.

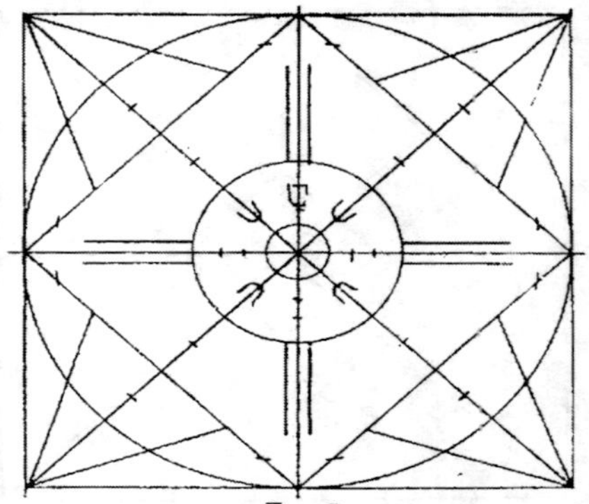

Fig. 2.

PLATE 9.

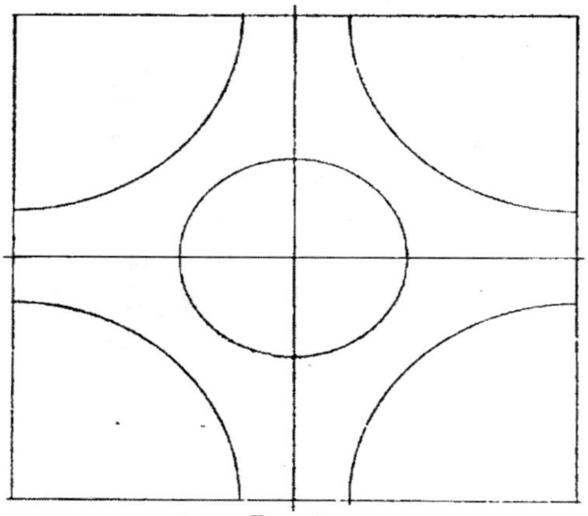

Fig. 1.

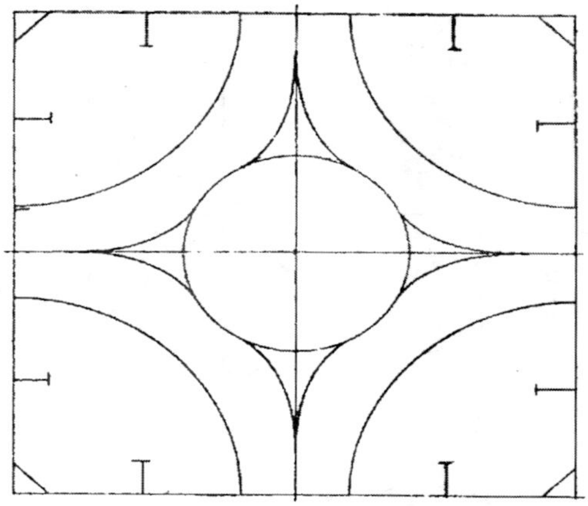

Fig. 2.

PLATE 10.

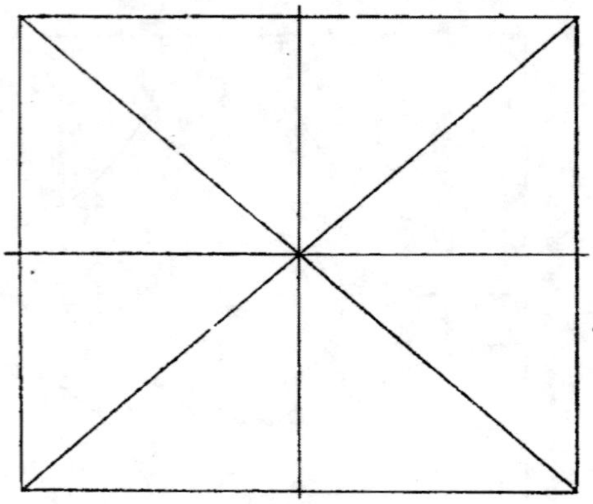

Fig. 1.

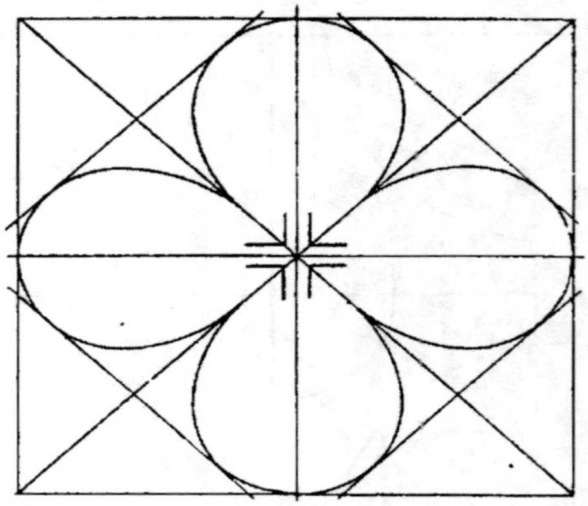

Fig. 2.

PLATE 11.

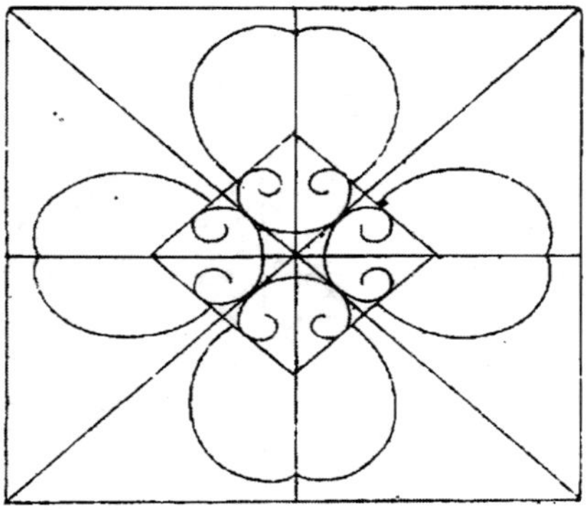

Fig. 1.

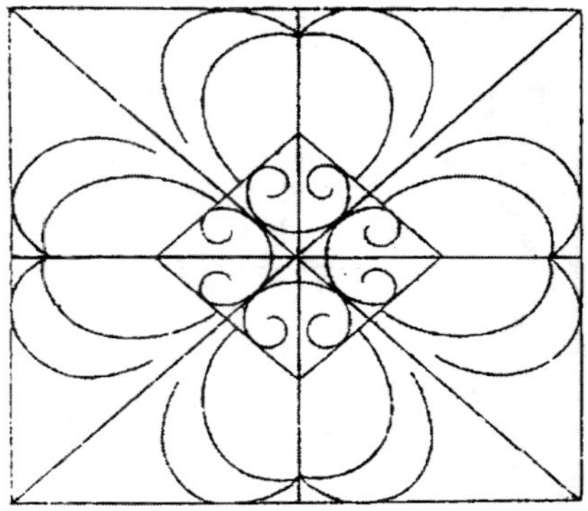

Fig 2

PLATE 12.

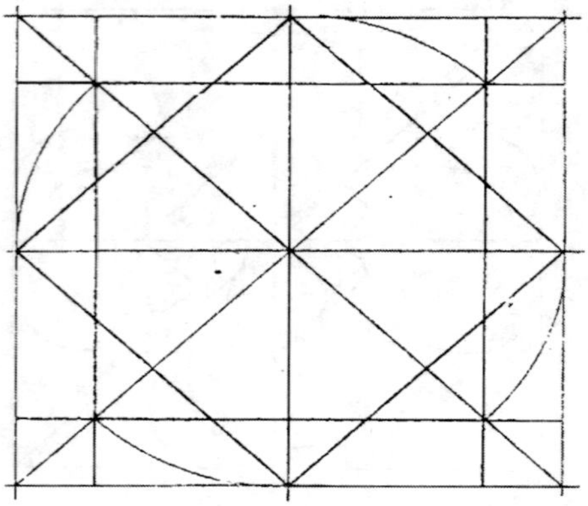

Fig. 1.

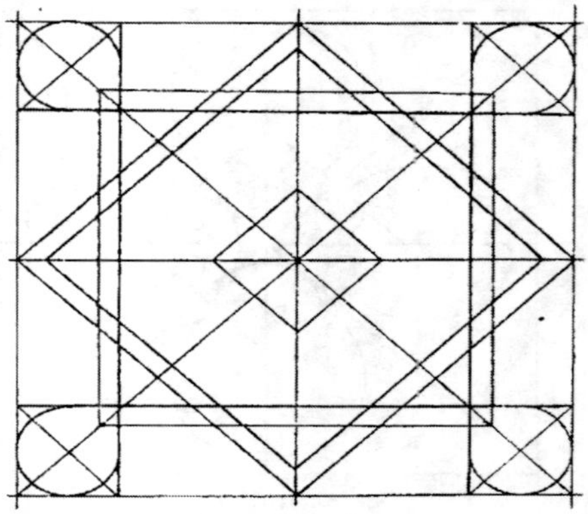

Fig. 2.

PLATE 13.

PLATE 14.

Persian Design from below the Frieze of Arches in the Throne Room of Darius I sketched from a fac-simile in the Louvre Paris.

PLATE 15.

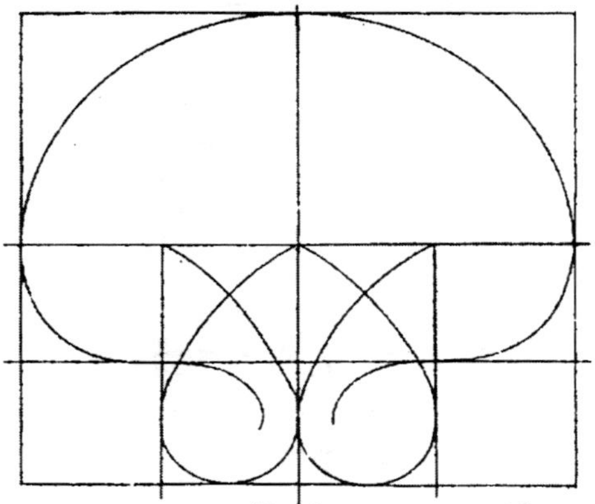

Fig. 1.

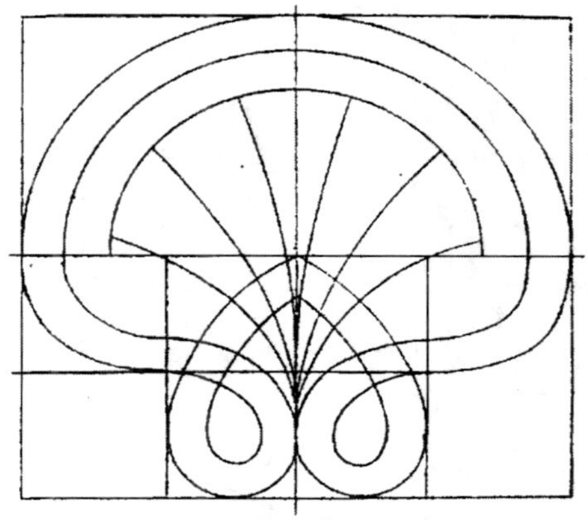

Fig. 2.

PLATE 16.

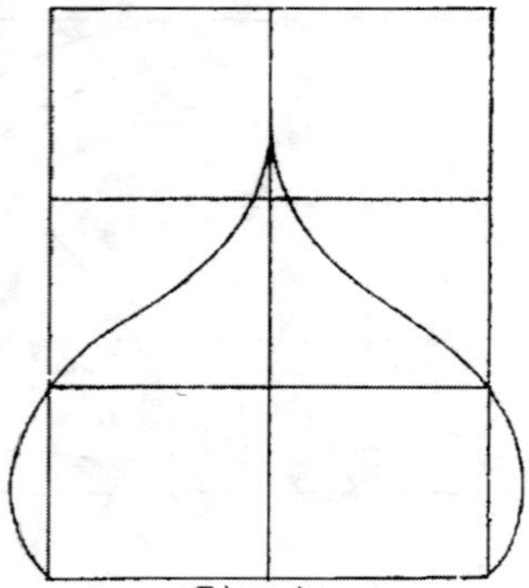

Fig. 1.

Fig. 2.

By CHARLES ARMSTRONG.

PLATE 17.

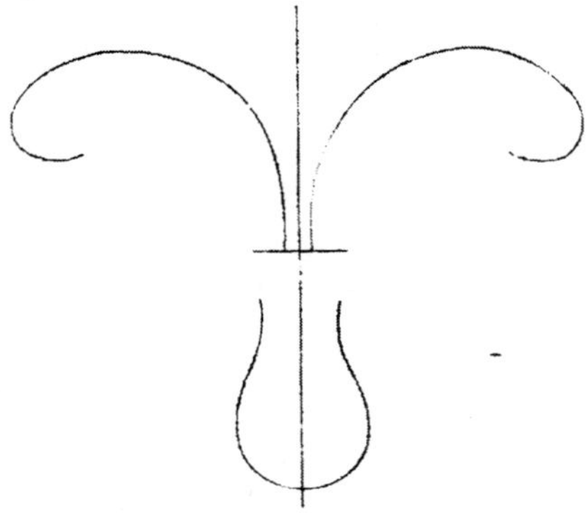
Fig 1

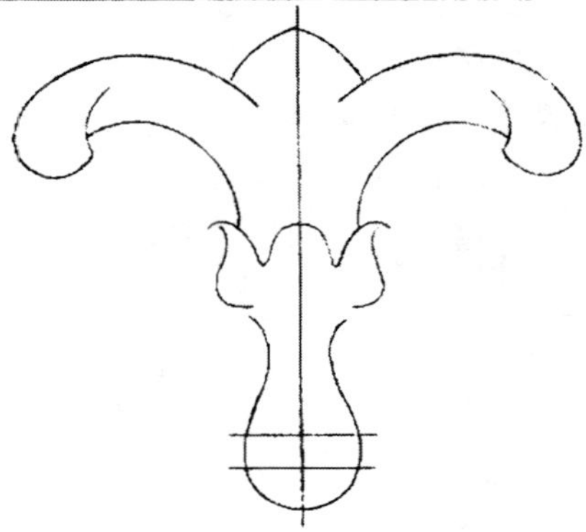
Fig 2

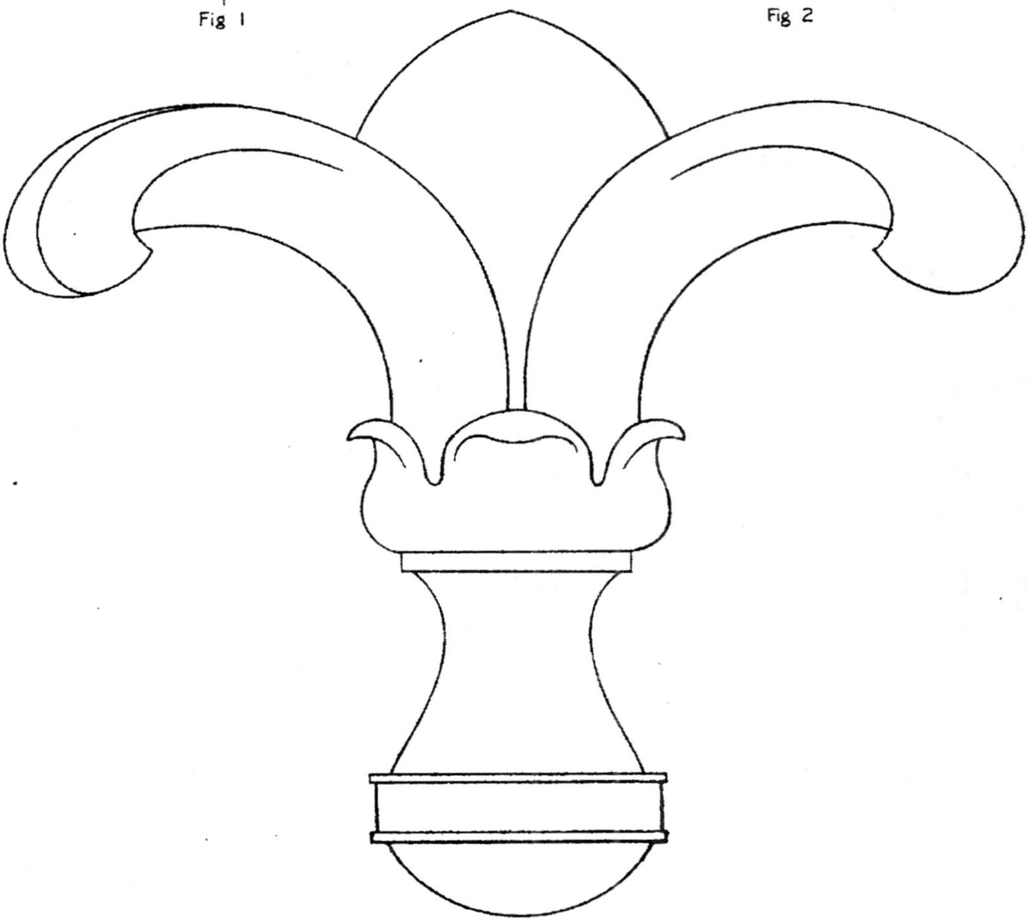

PLATE 18.

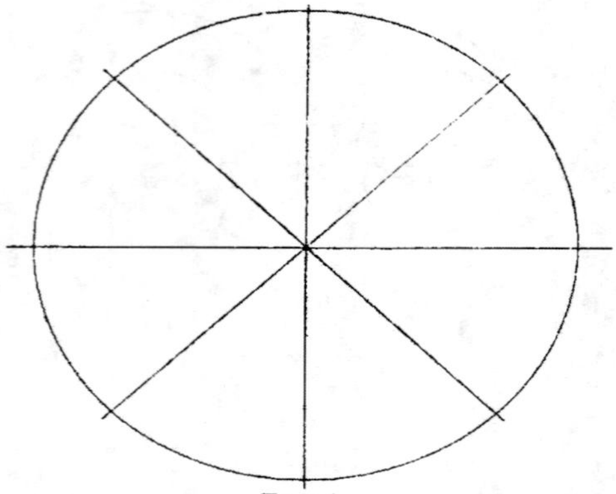

Fig. 1.

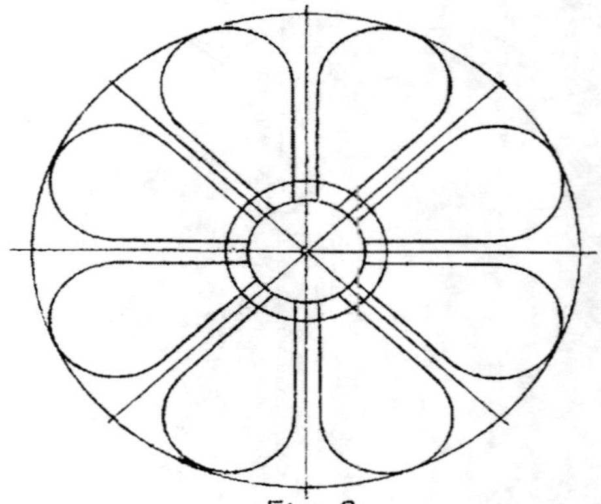

Fig. 2.

PLATE 19.

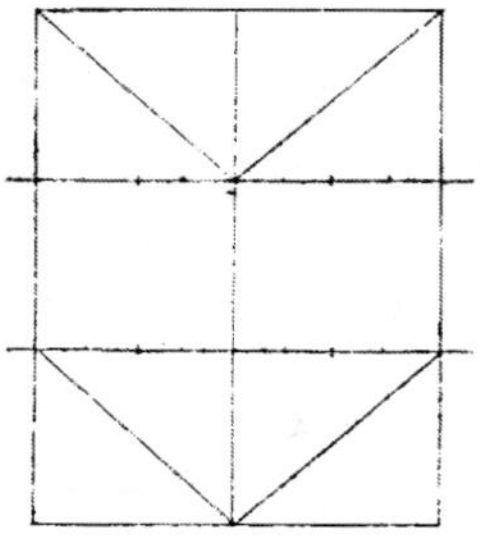

Fig. 1.

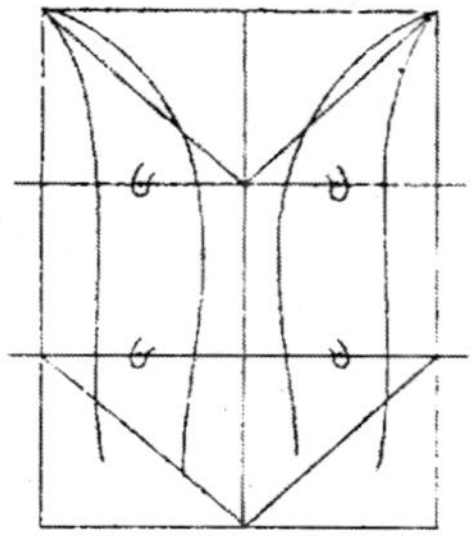

Fig. 2.

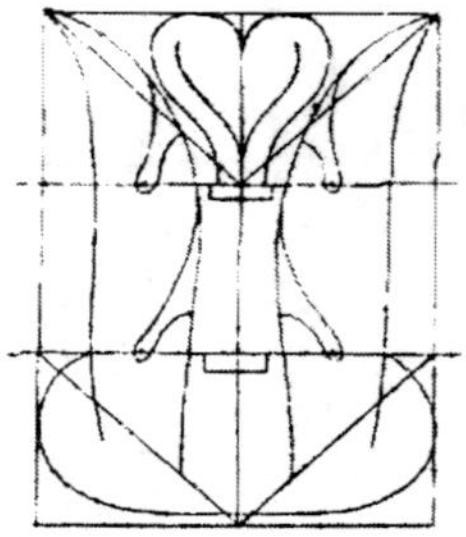

Fig. 3.

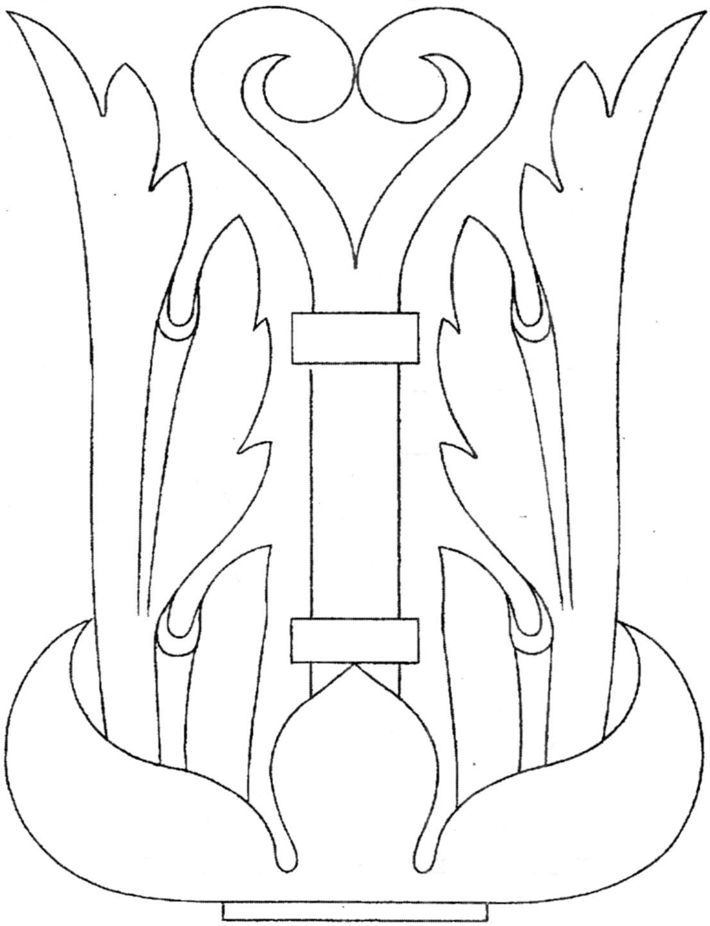

CUSACK'S 'FREEHAND ORNAMENT' By CHARLES ARMSTRONG.

PLATE 20.

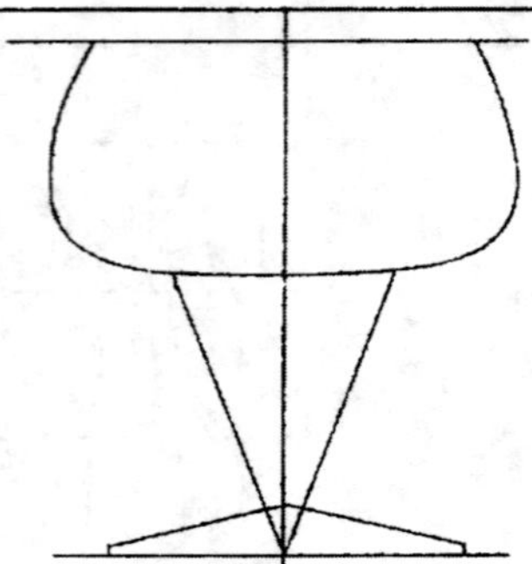

Fig 1.

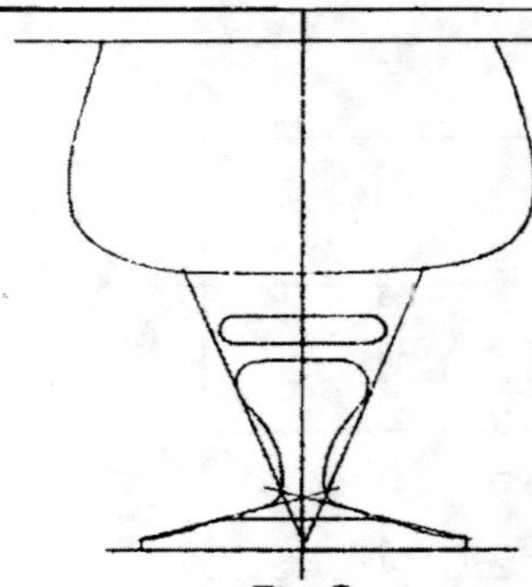

Fig 2.

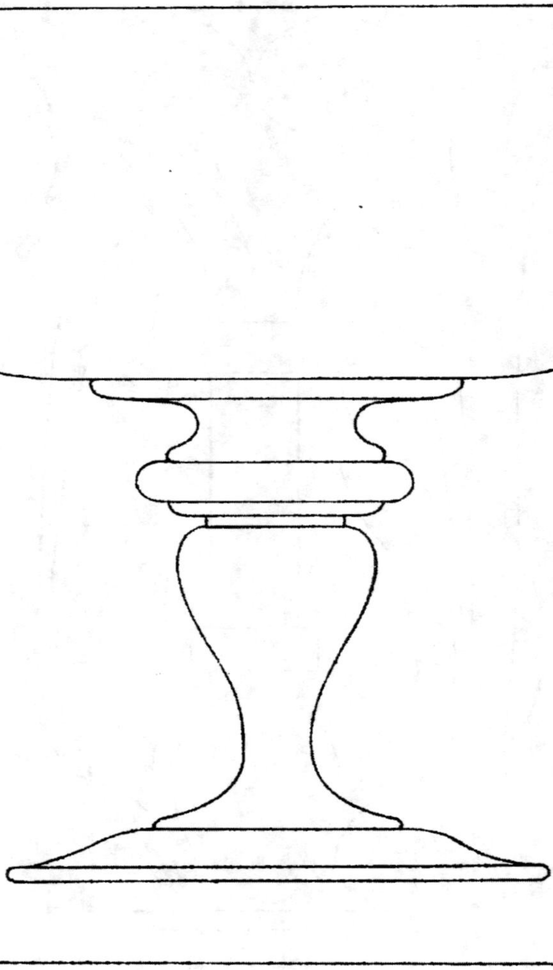

PLATE 21.

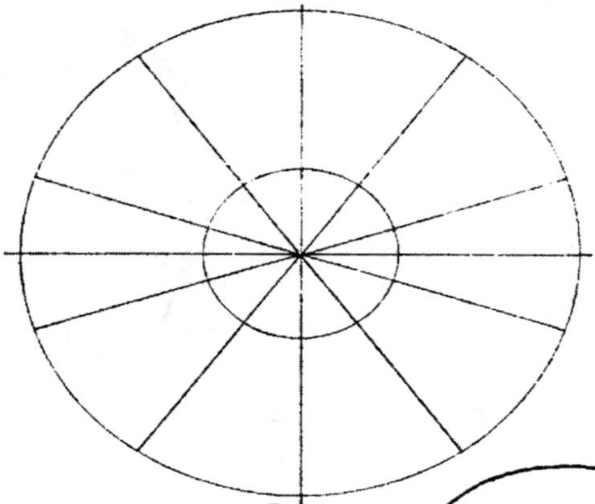

Fig. 1.

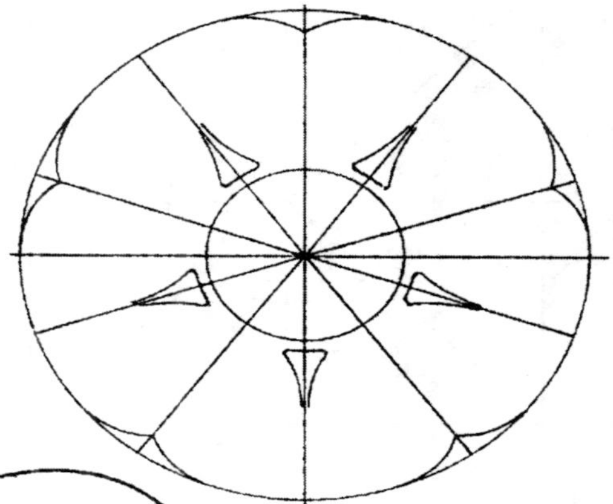

Fig. 2.

PLATE 22.

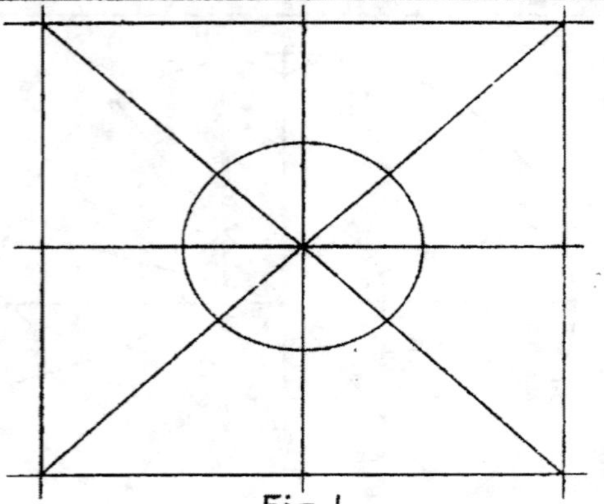

Fig.1.

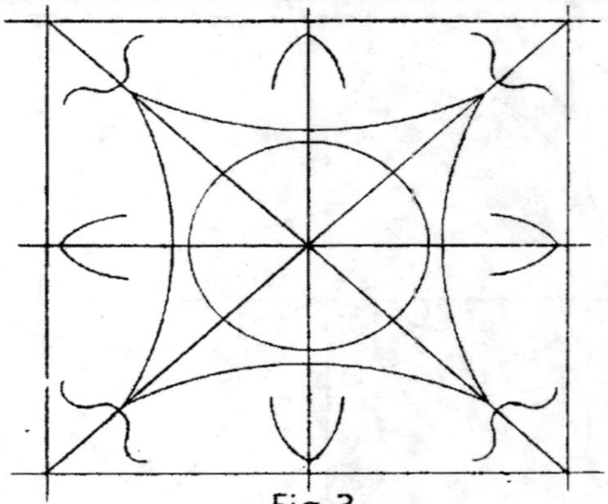

Fig.2.

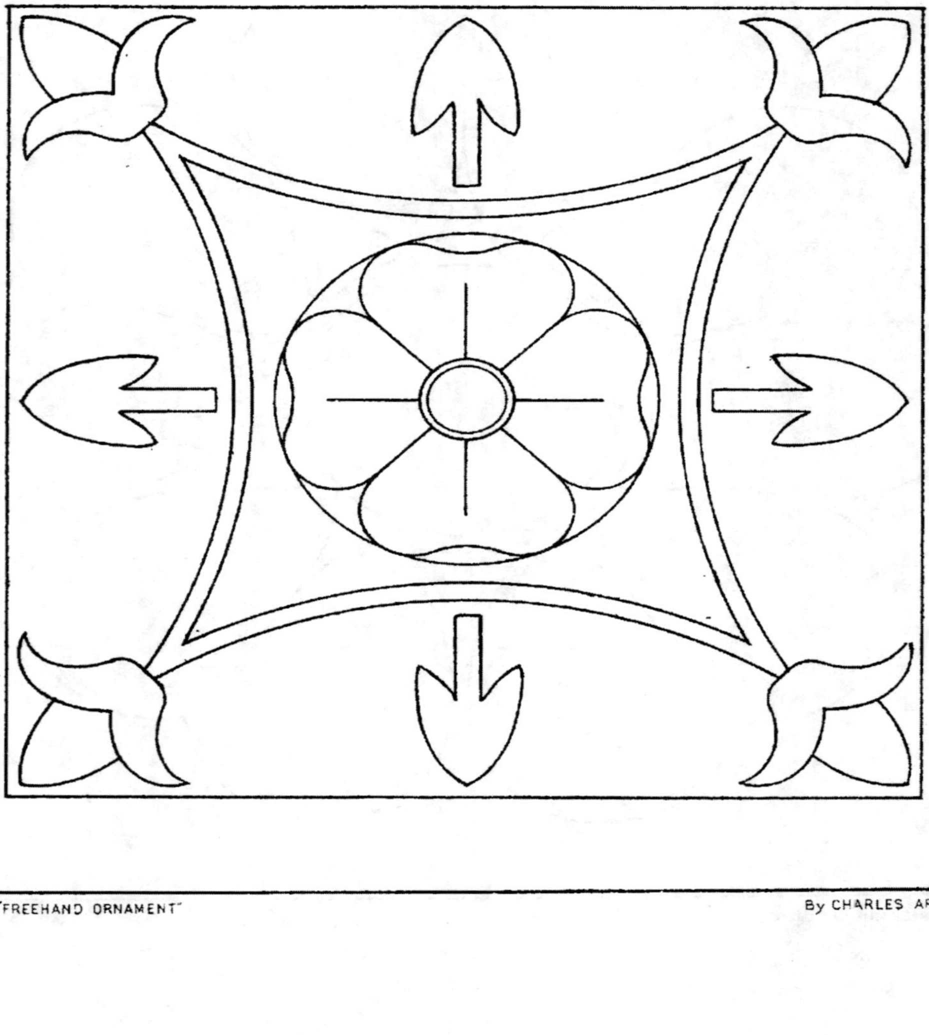

PLATE 28.

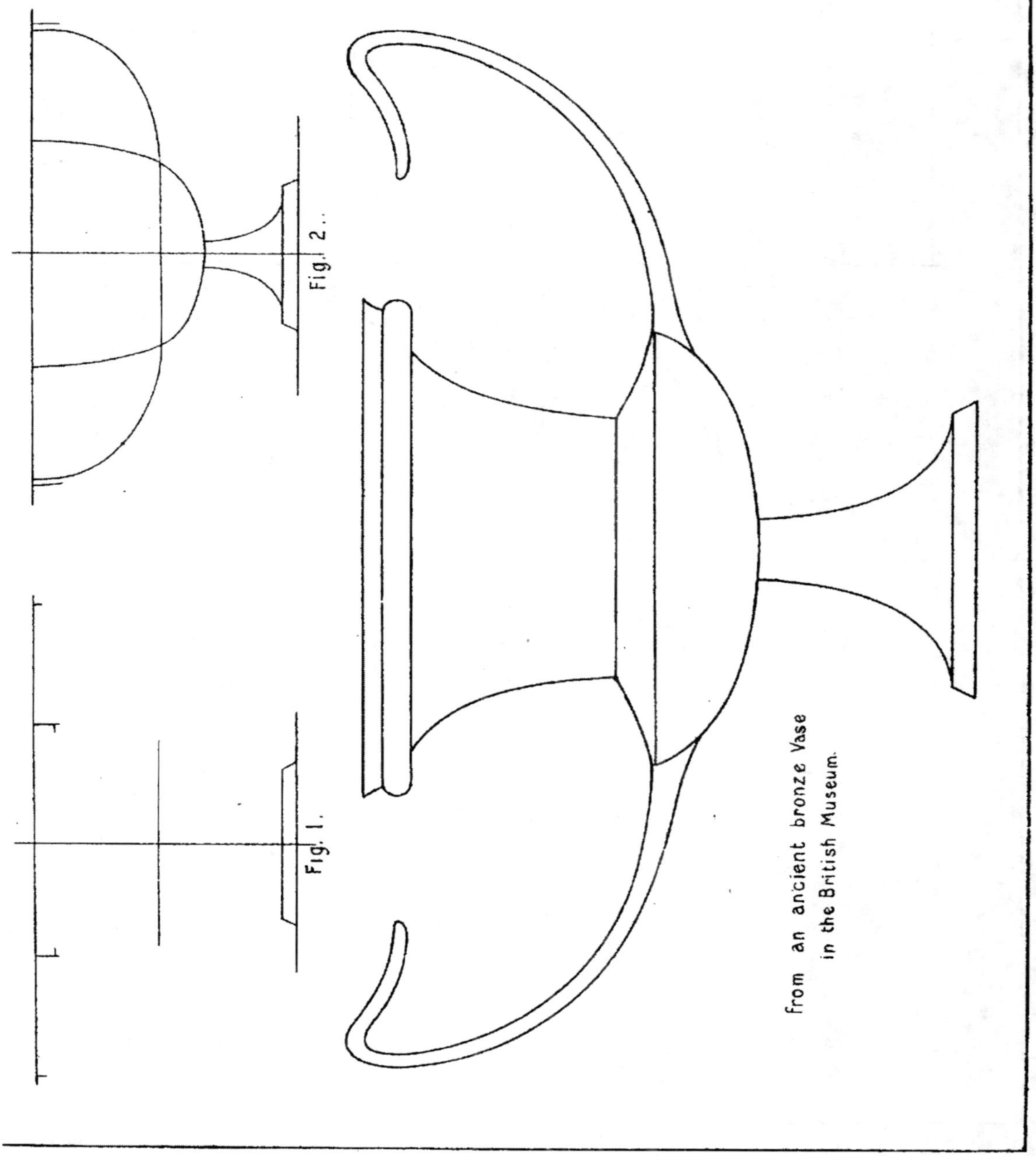

From an ancient bronze Vase in the British Museum.

PLATE 24.

Fig. 1. Fig 2.

Ornament from a Terra Cotta Etruscan Sepulchral Monument in the British Museum

PLATE 25.

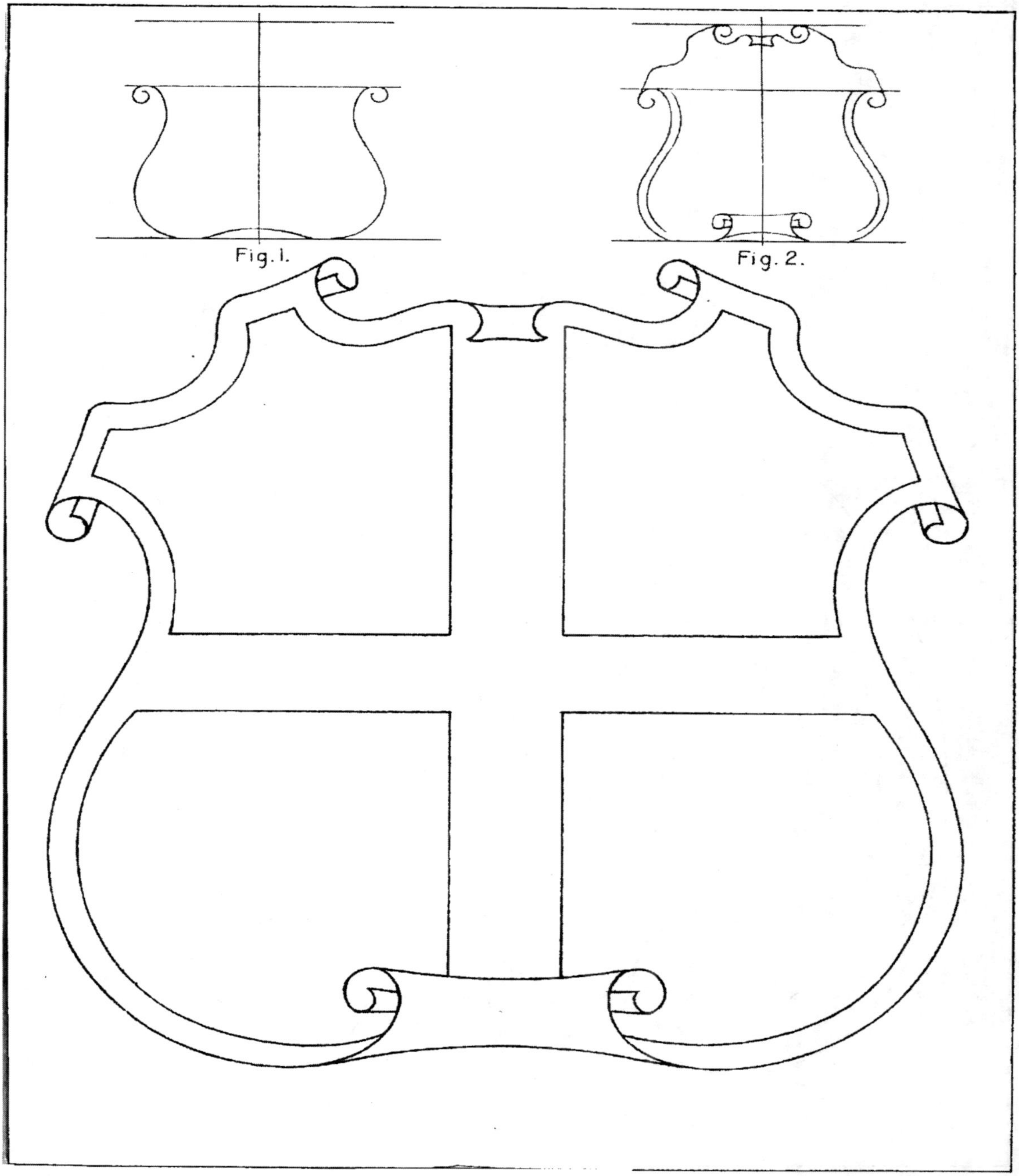

PLATE 26.

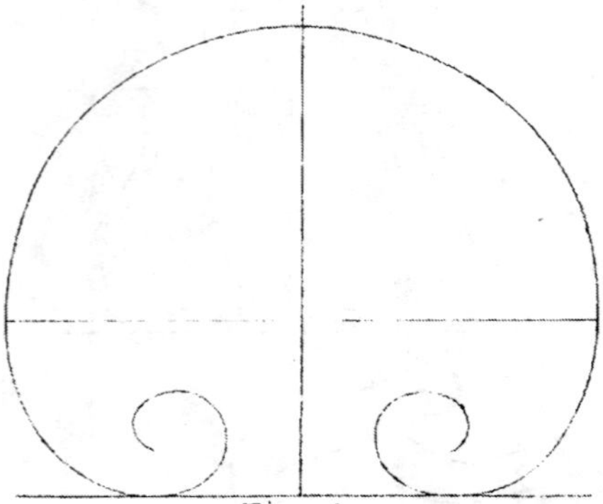

Fig. 1.

Fig. 2

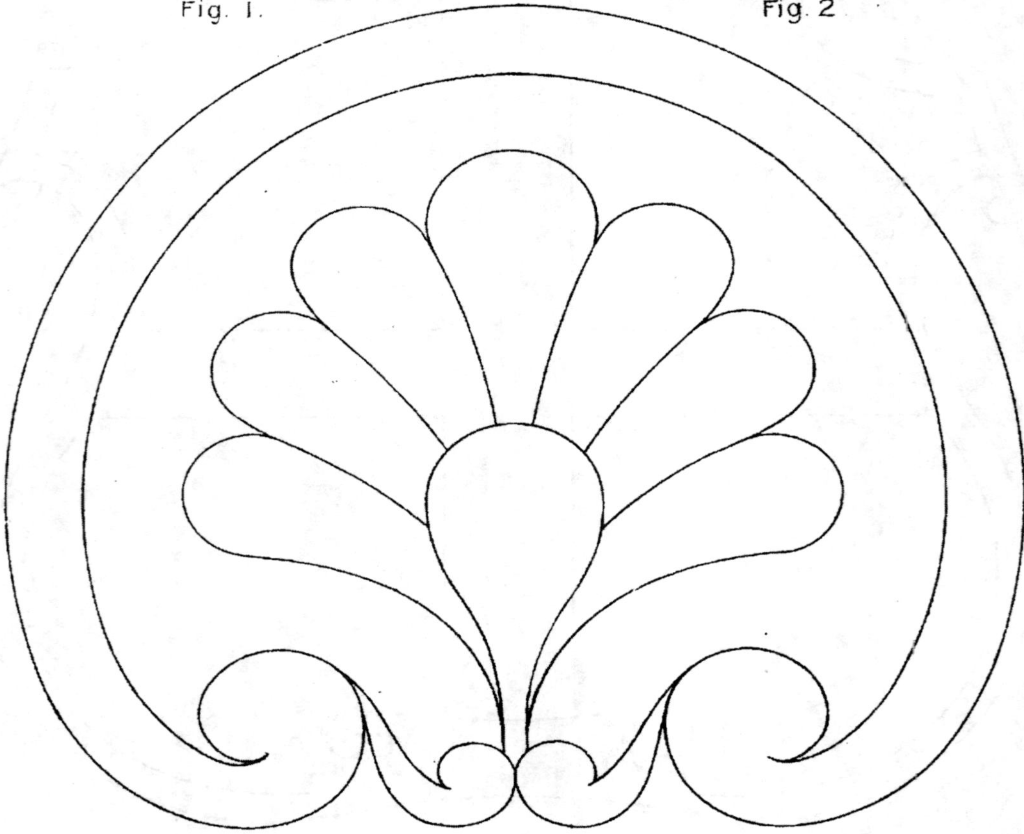

From an Asia Minor Terra cotta in the Louvre Paris

PLATE 27.

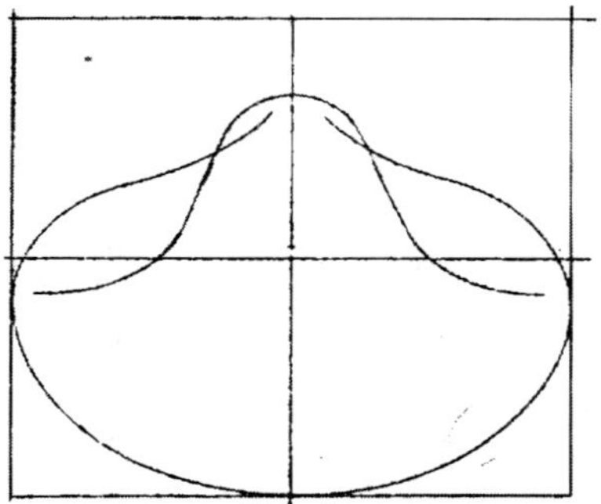

Fig. 1.

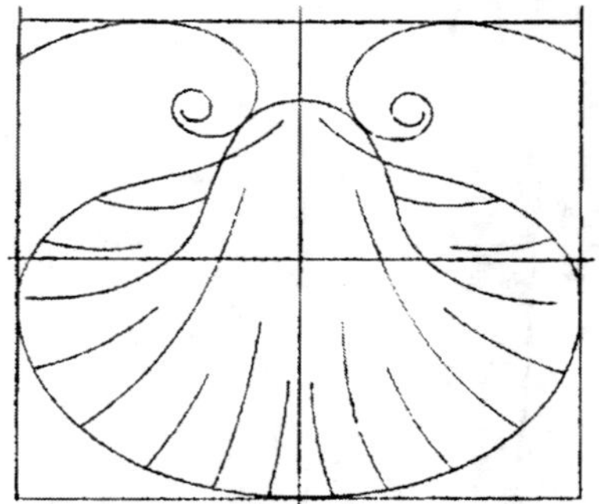

Fig. 2.

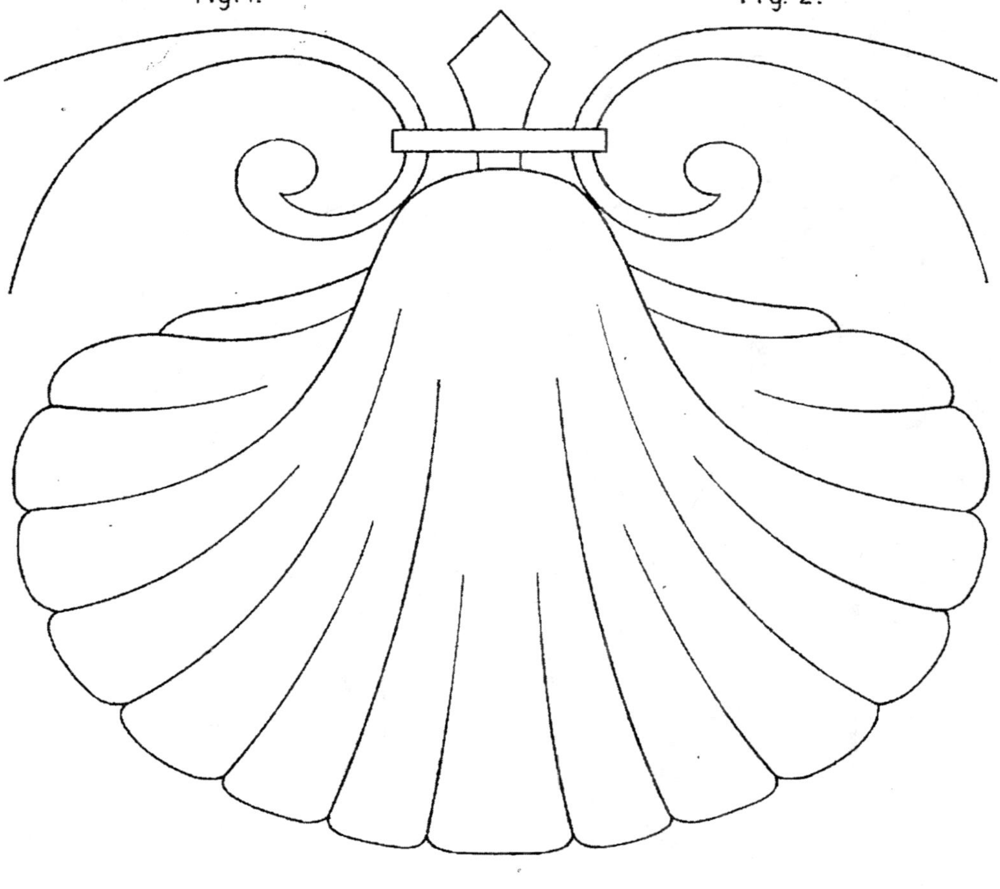

16th Century Italian,– from a painted wood moulding in the S. Kensington Museum.

PLATE 28.

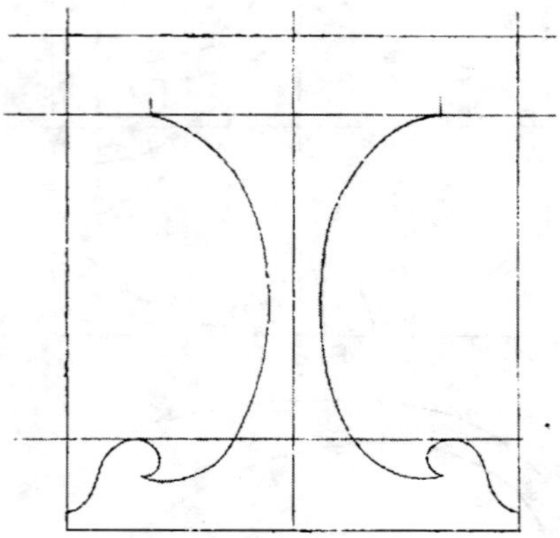

Fig. 1

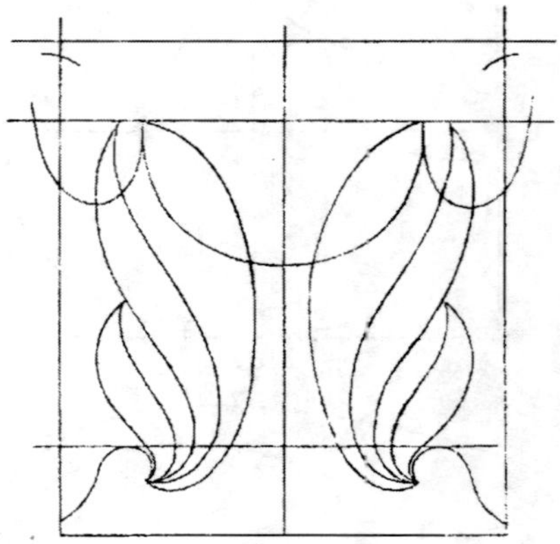

Fig 2.

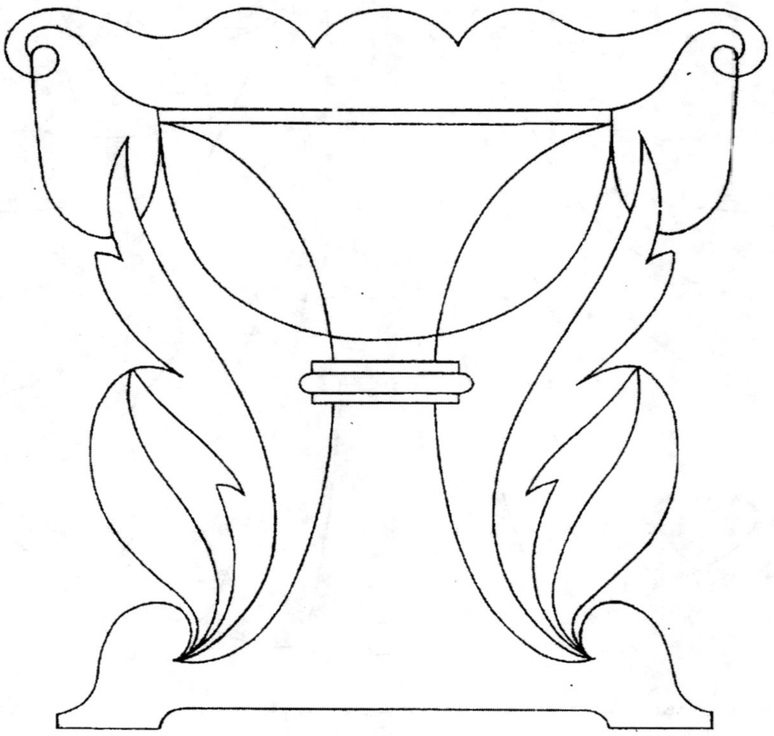

PLATE 29.

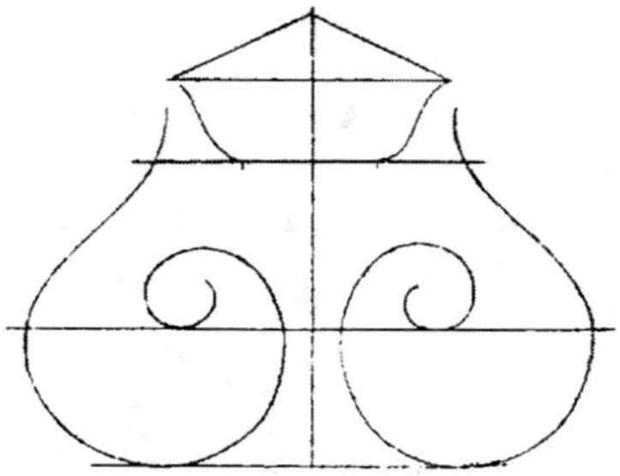

Fig. 1

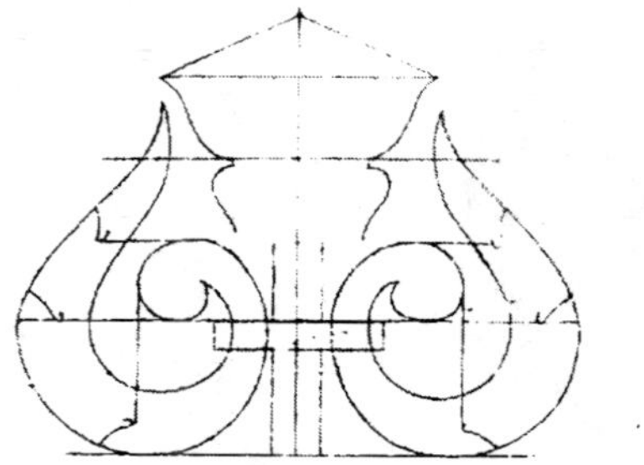

Fig. 2

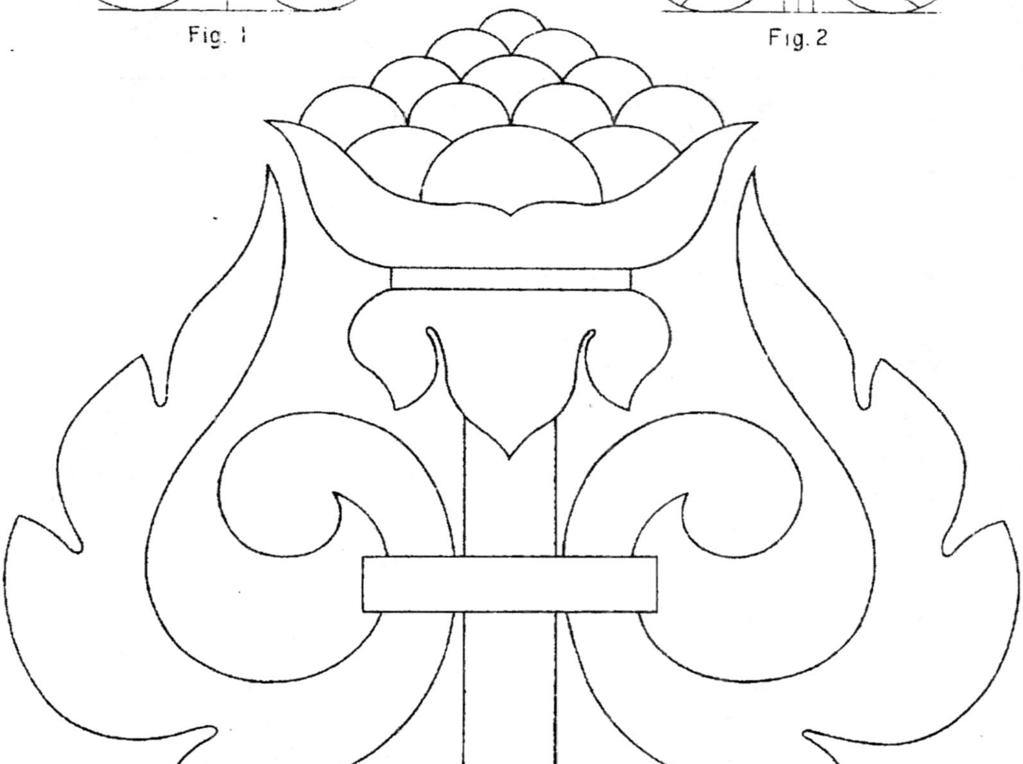

PLATE 30.

By CHARLES ARMSTRONG.

PLATE 31

From a Greek Vase in the Louvre Paris.

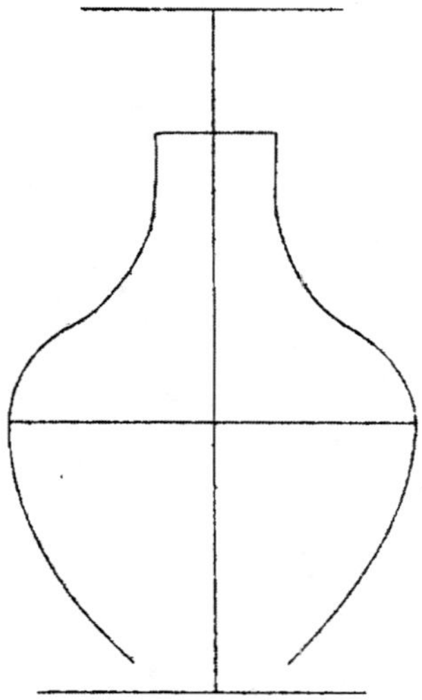

Fig. 1.

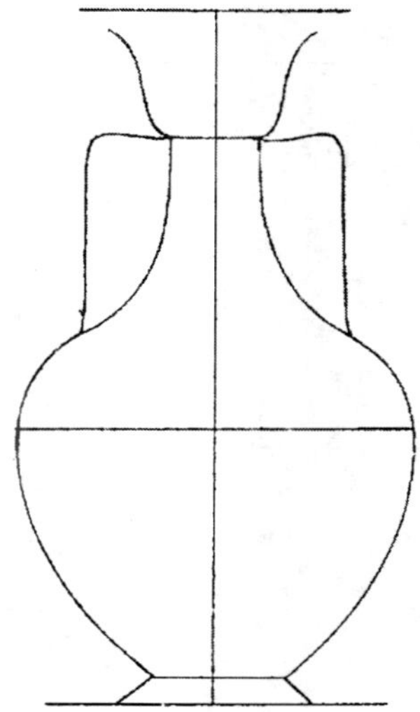

Fig. 2.

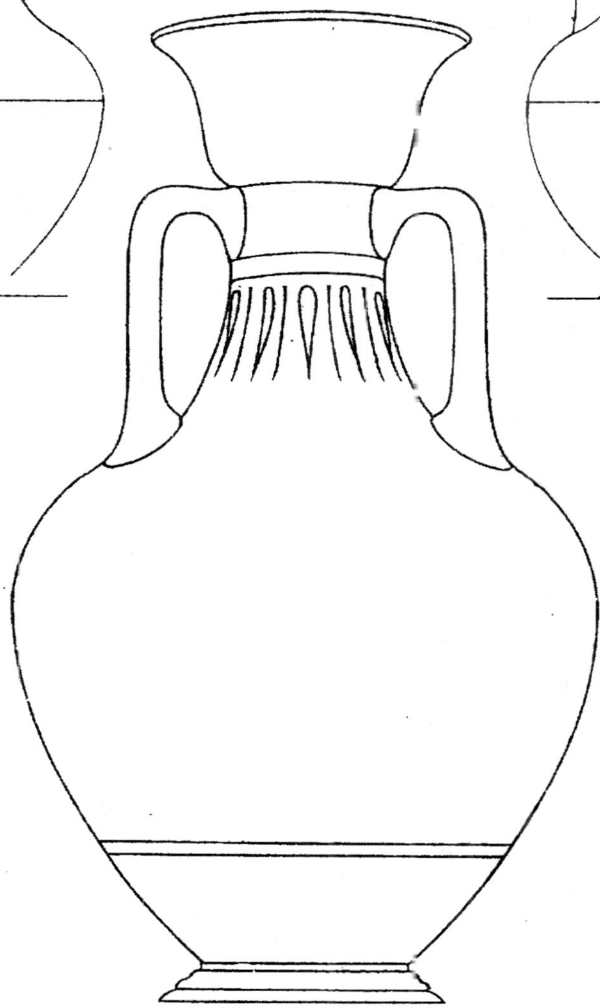

PLATE 32.

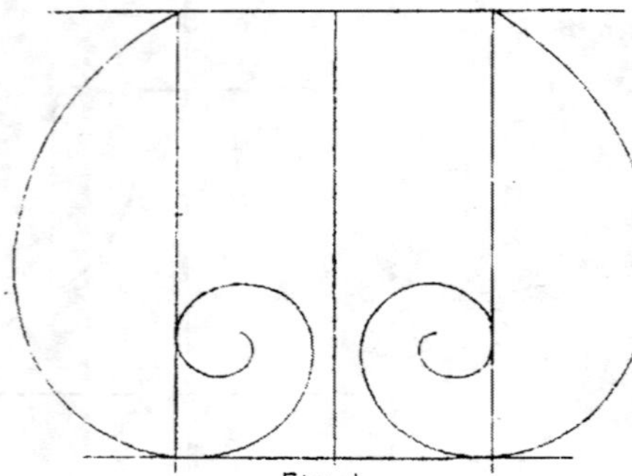

Fig. 1.

Fig. 2.

PLATE 33.

Fig. 1.

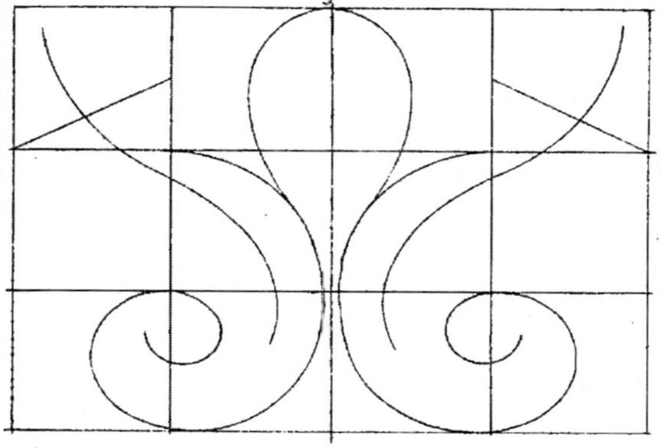

Fig. 2.

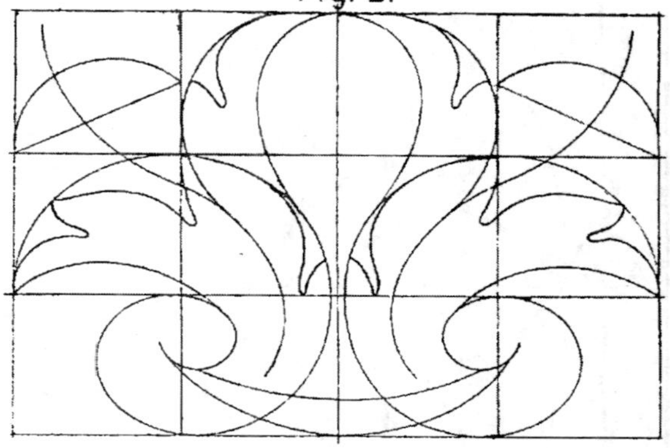

PLATE 34.

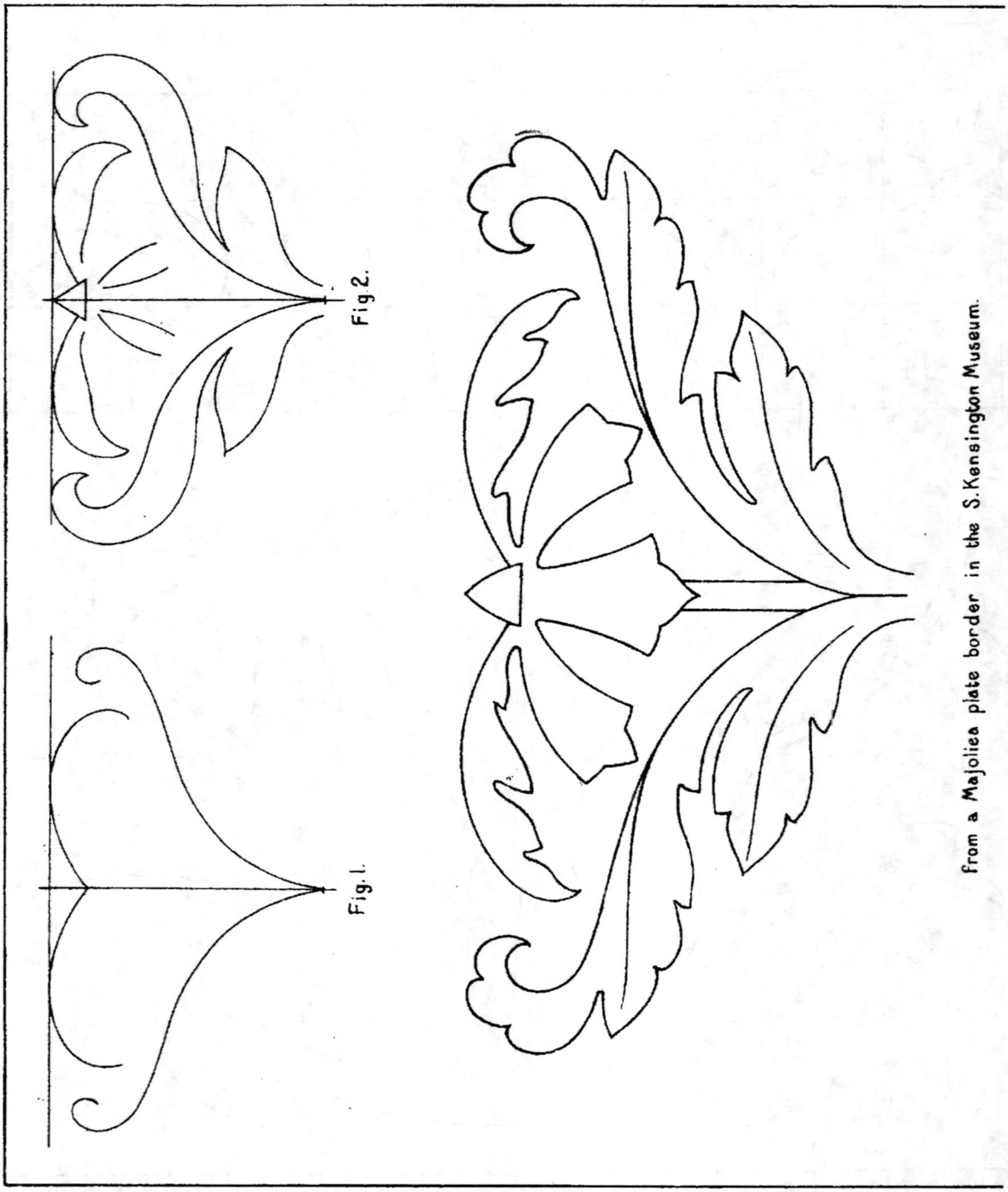

Fig. 1.

Fig. 2.

From a Majolica plate border in the S. Kensington Museum.

PLATE 35.

PLATE 36.

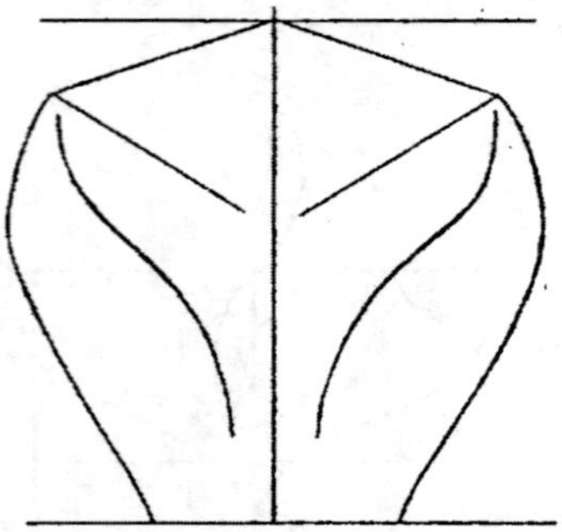

Fig. 1.

Acanthus Leaf

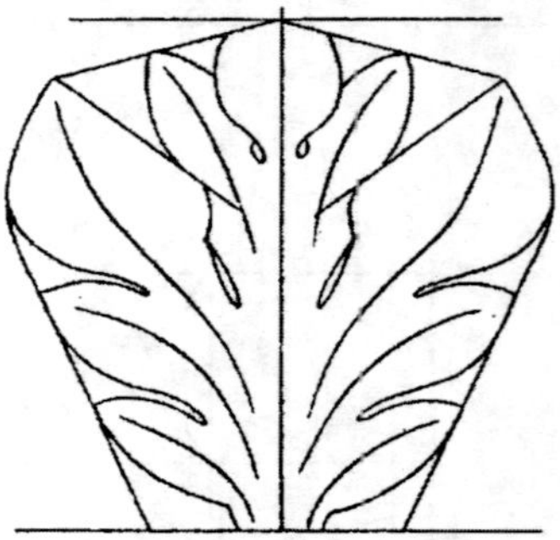

Fig. 2.

PLATE 37.

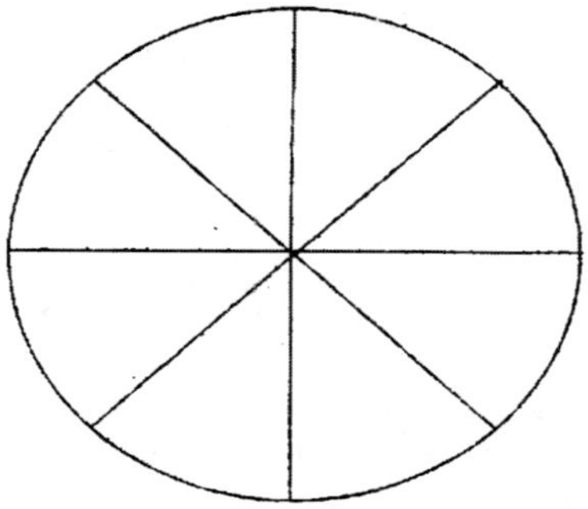

Fig. I

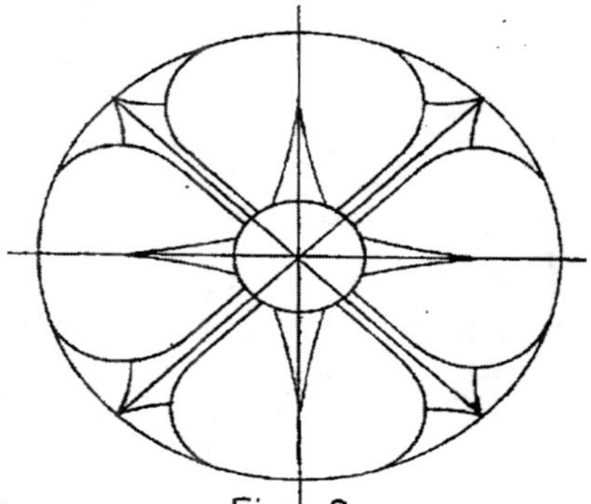

Fig. 2.

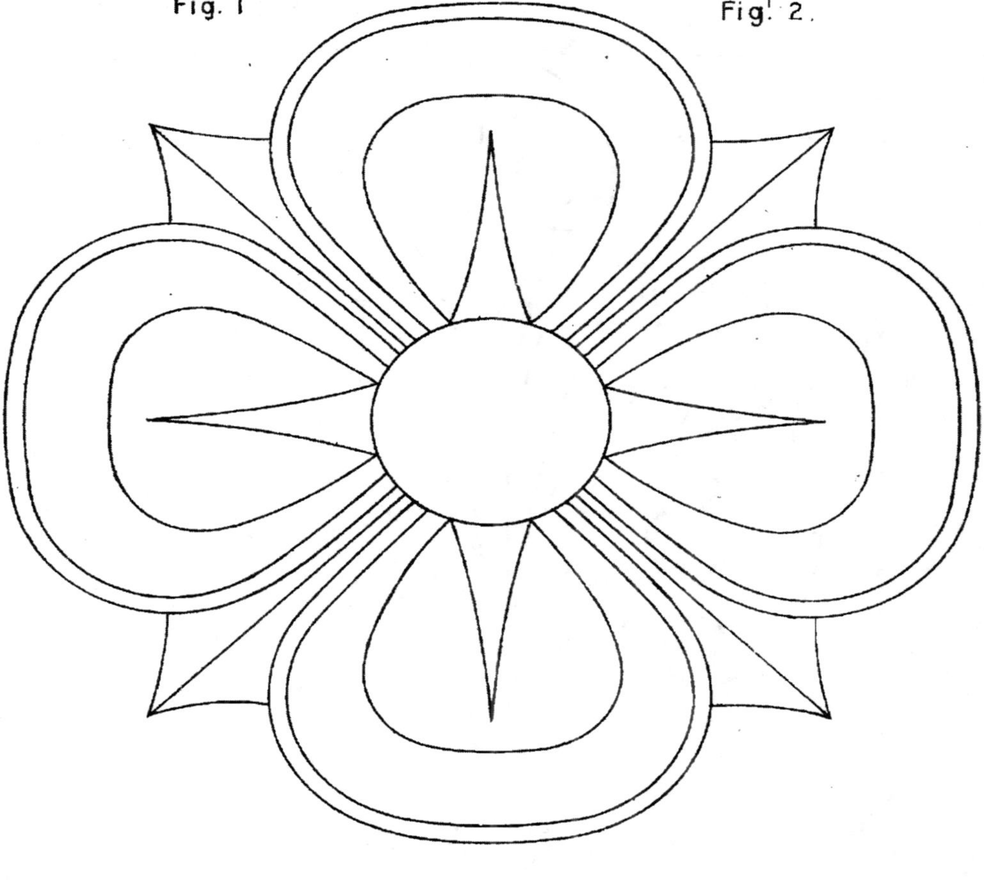

From a Sarcophagus in the British Museum 200 B.C.

PLATE 38.

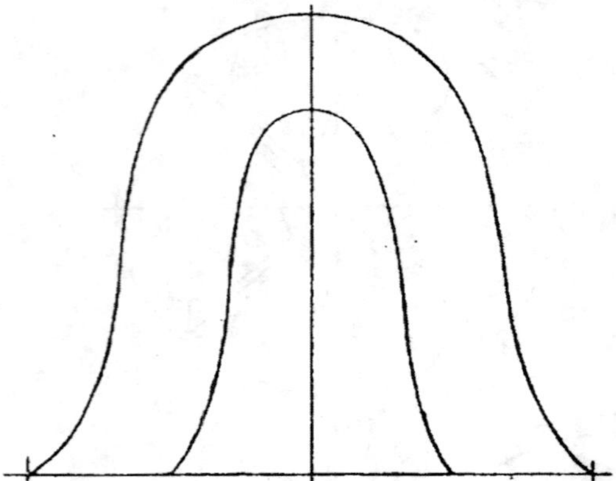

Fig. 1.

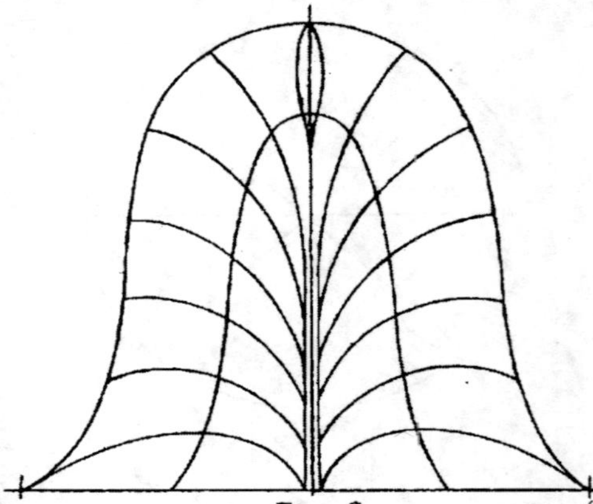

Fig. 2.

PLATE 39.

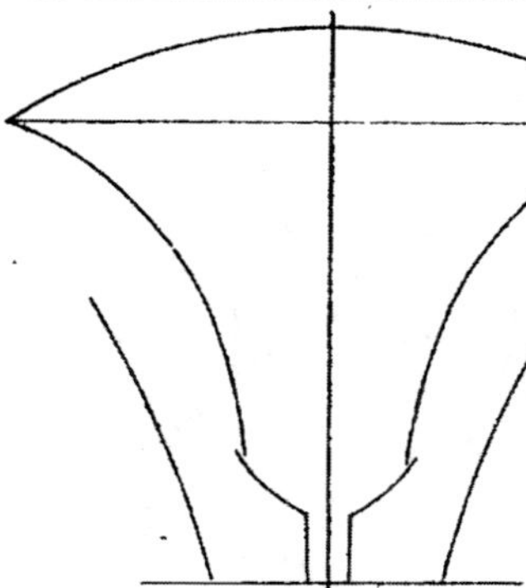

Fig. I.

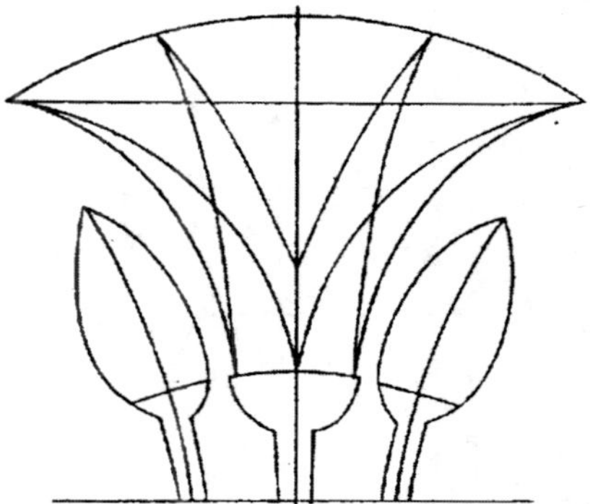

Fig. 2.

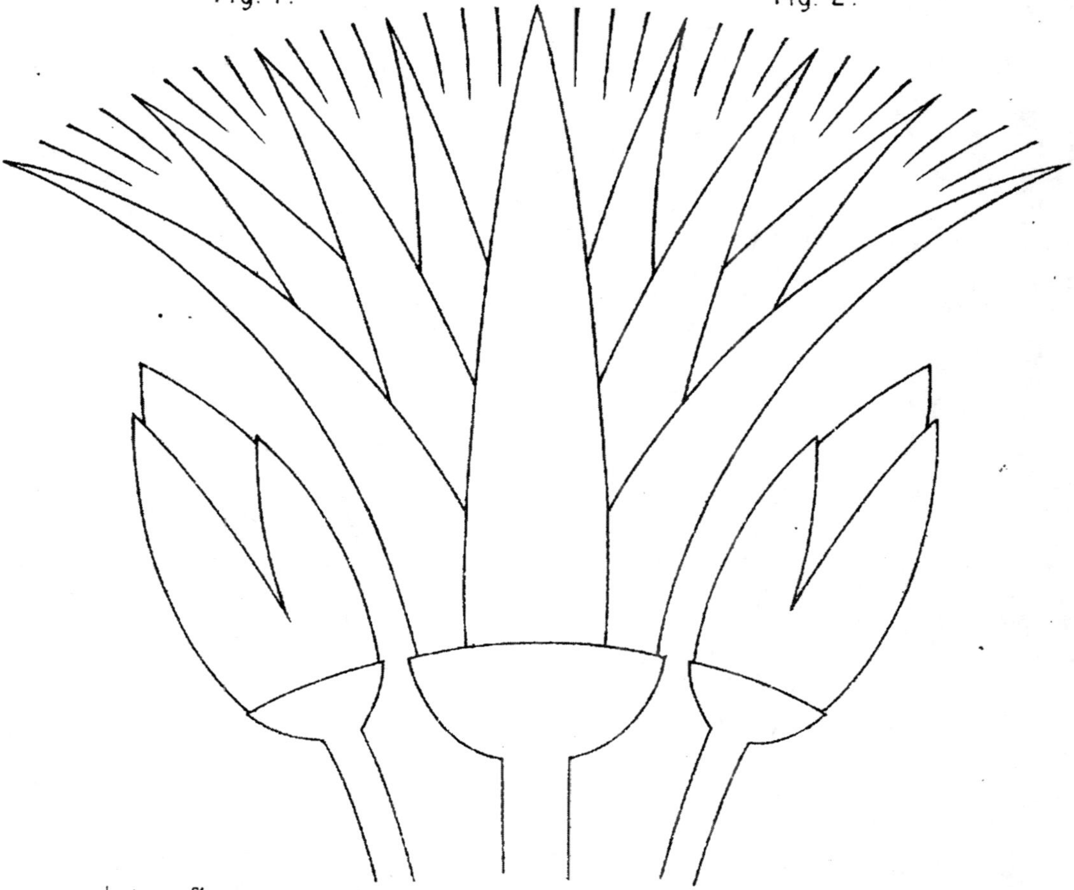

Lotus flower and buds, from an ancient Egyptian wall painting in the British Museum.

PLATE 40.

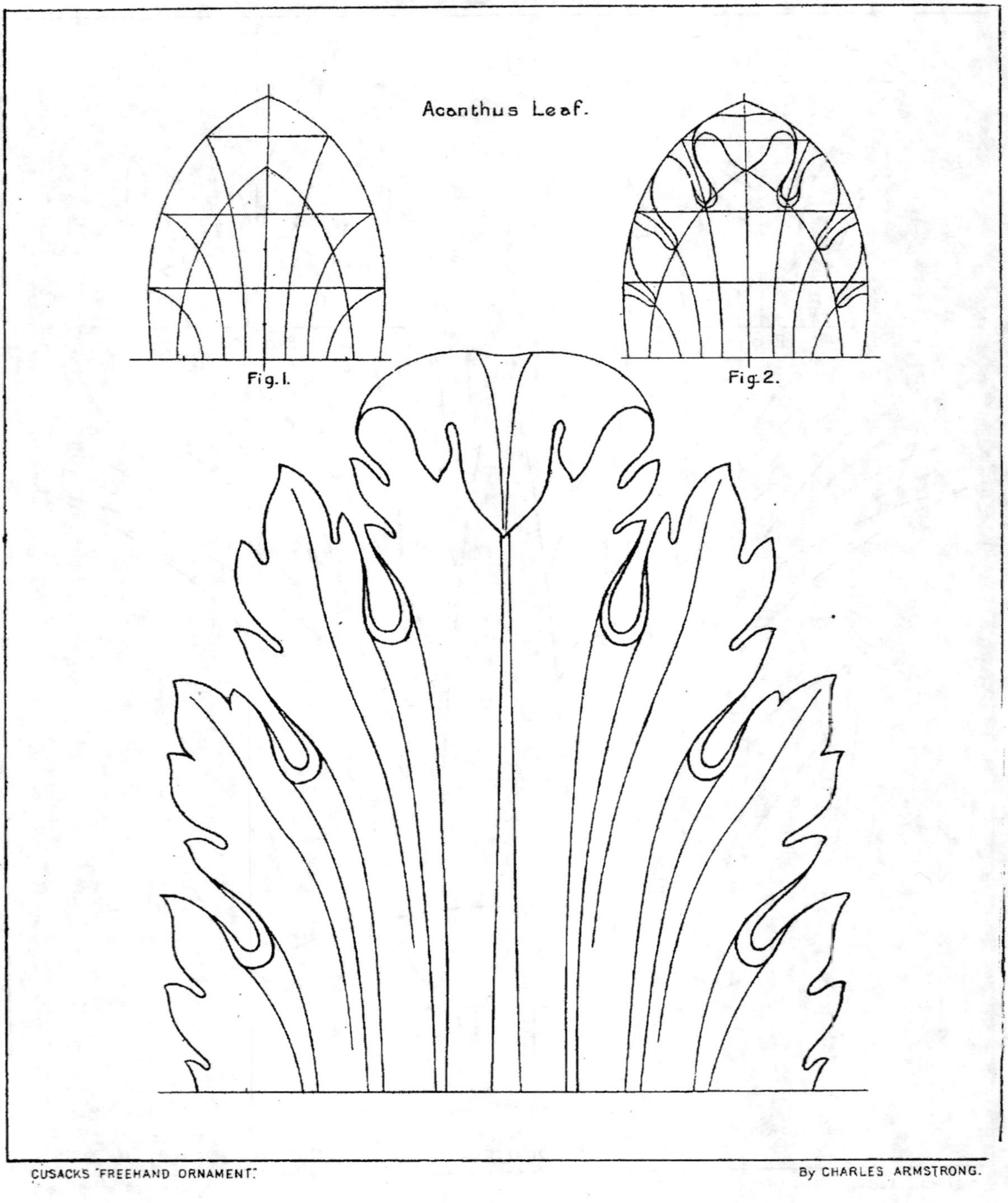

PLATE 41.

From a Moorish Vase in the S. Kensington Museum.

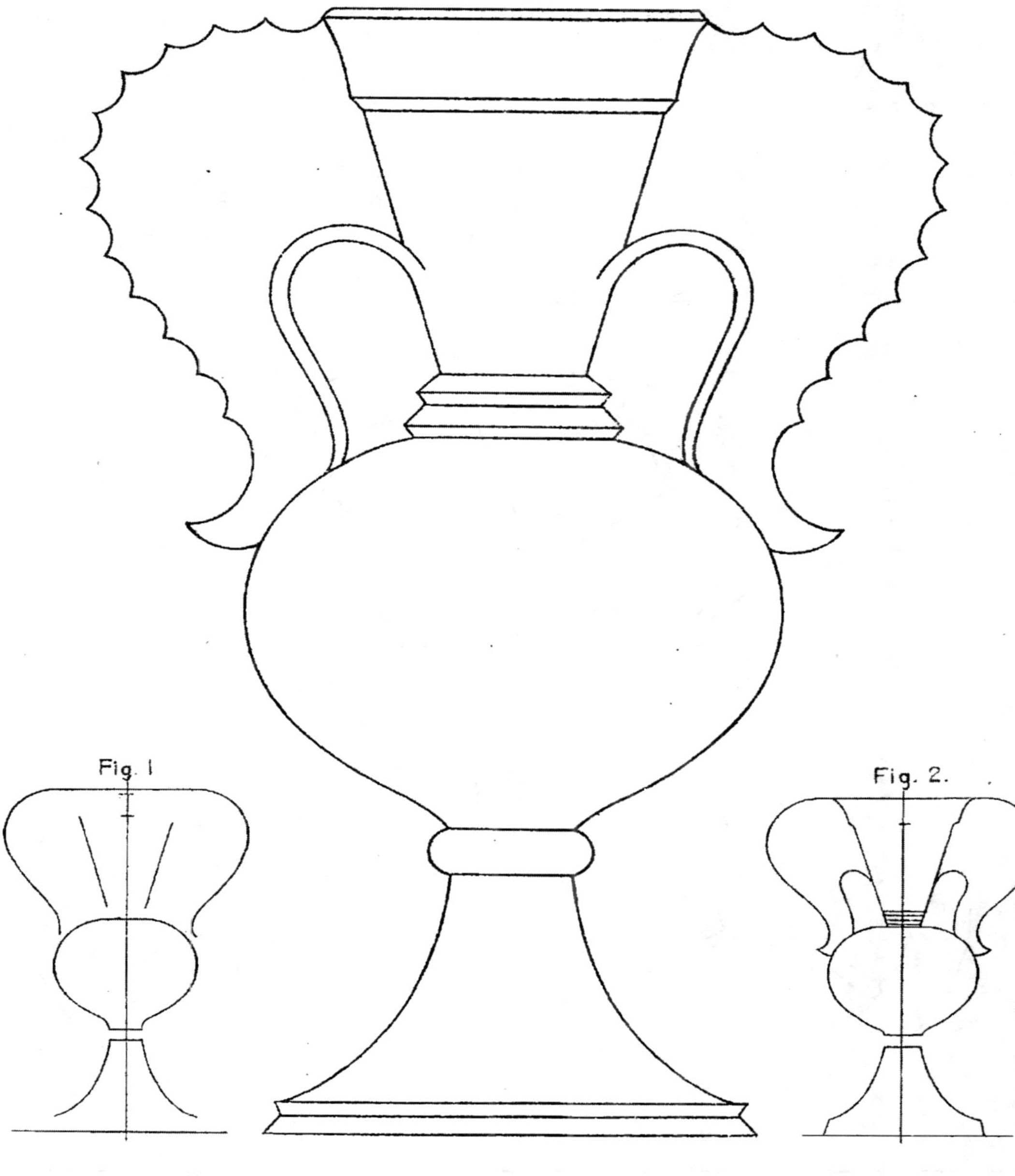

PLATE 42

PLATE 43.

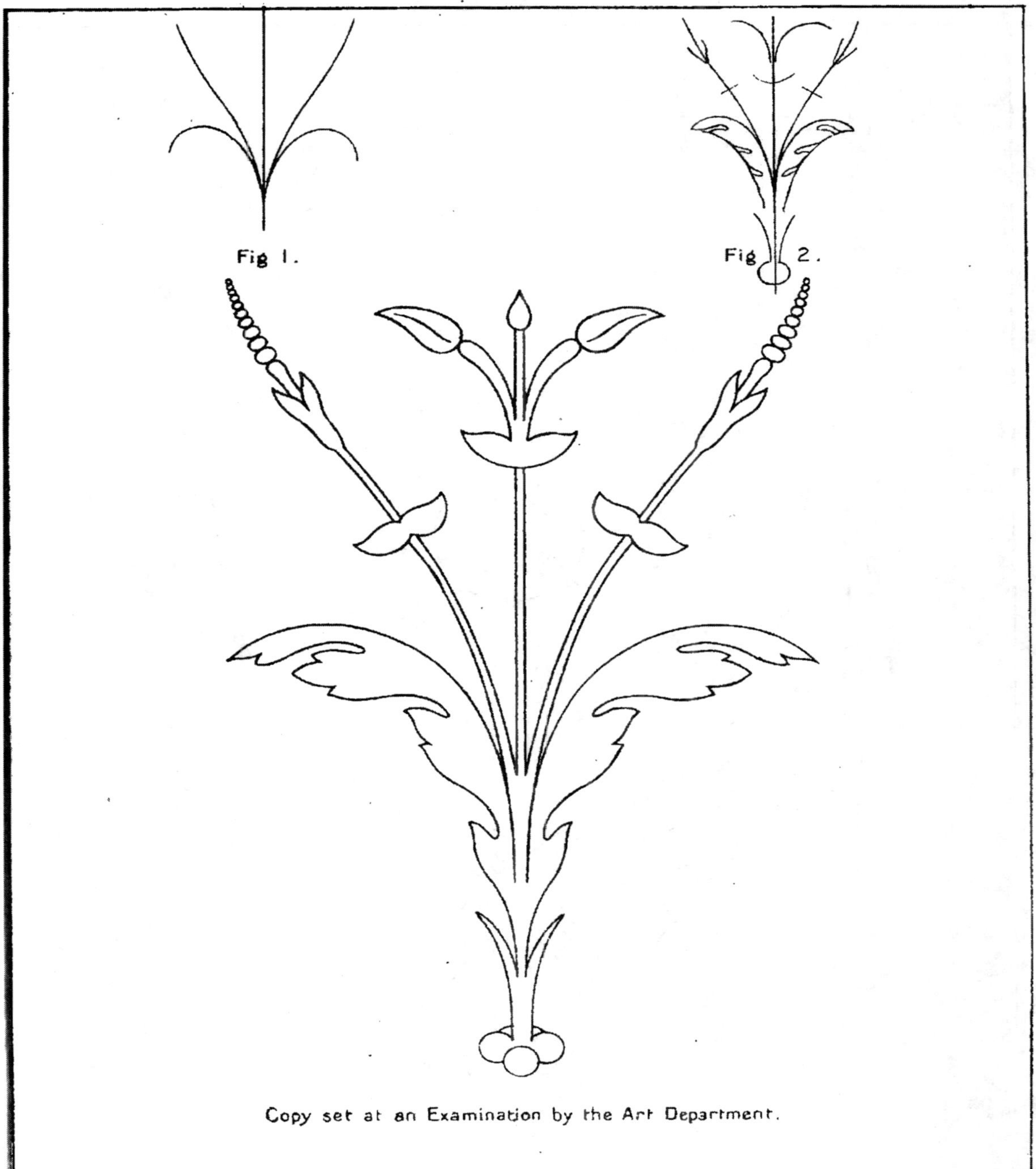

Copy set at an Examination by the Art Department.

PLATE 44.

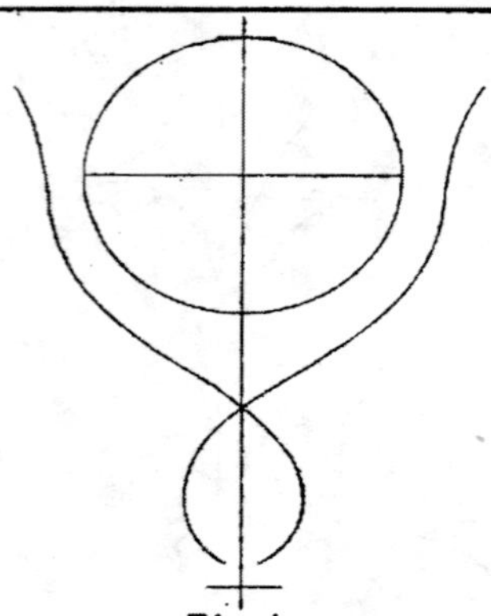

Fig.1.

Fig.2.

PLATE 45.

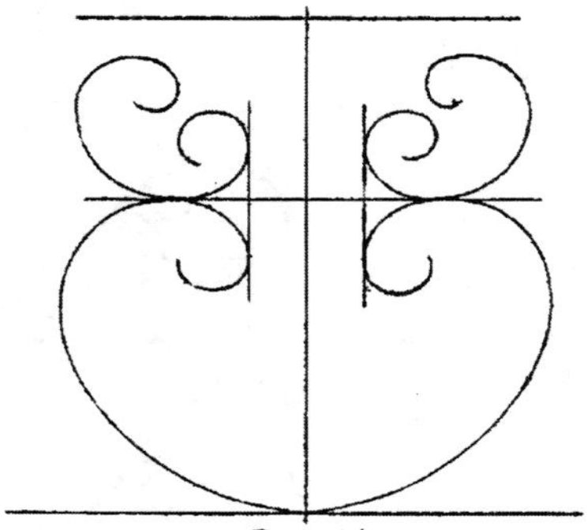

Fig. 1.

Fig. 2.

from an Italian cabinet, ivory inlaid with ebony,- in the Cluny Museum, Paris.

PLATE 46.

Fig. 1.

Fig. 2.

PLATE 47.

Fig. 1.

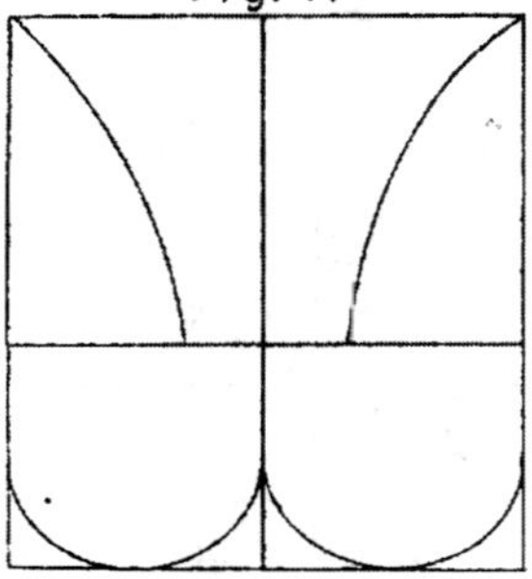

Fig. 2.

From a piece of Assyrian ornament in the Louvre Paris.

PLATE 48.

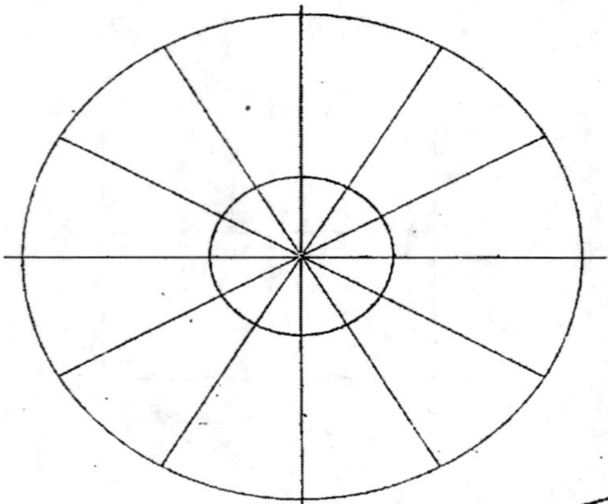

Fig. 1.

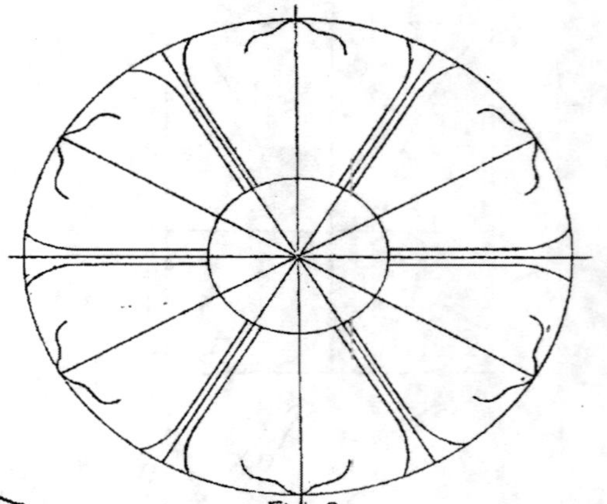

Fig. 2.

PLATE 49.

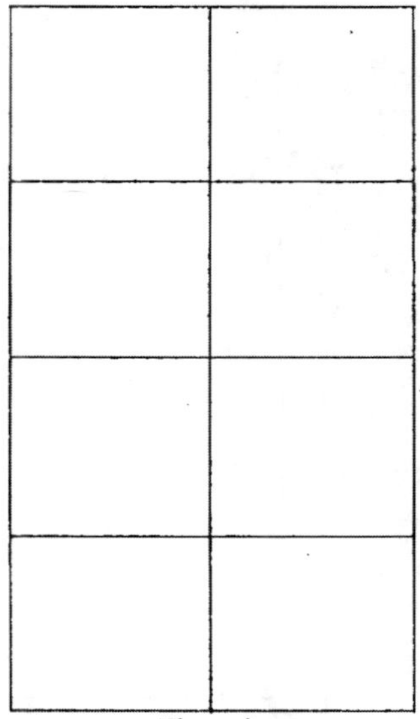

Fig. 1.

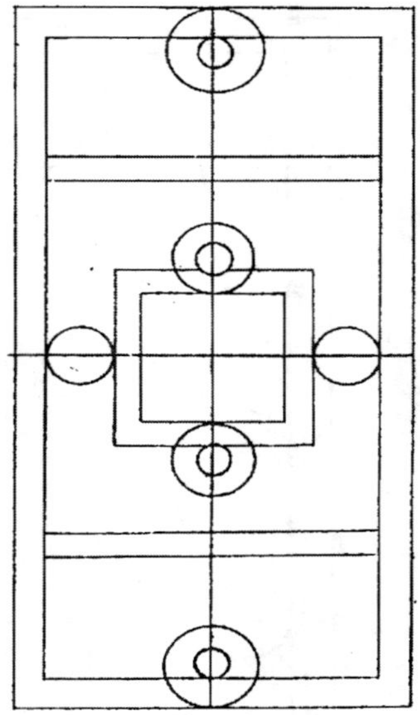

Fig. 2.

From 16th Century Strap work in the Trocadero Museum Paris

PLATE 50.

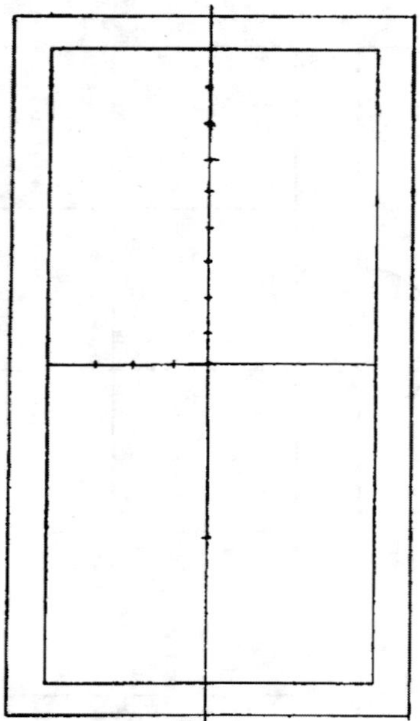

Fig. 1.

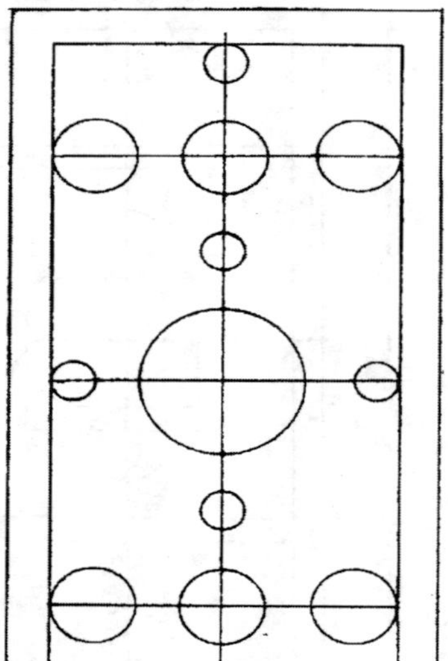

Fig. 2.

PLATE 51.

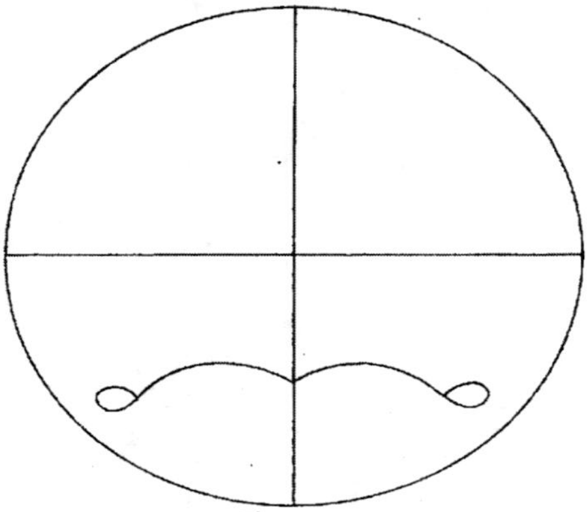

Fig. 1.

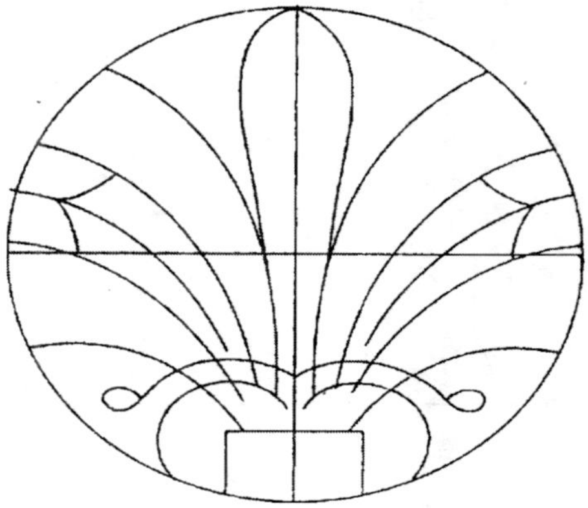

Fig. 2.

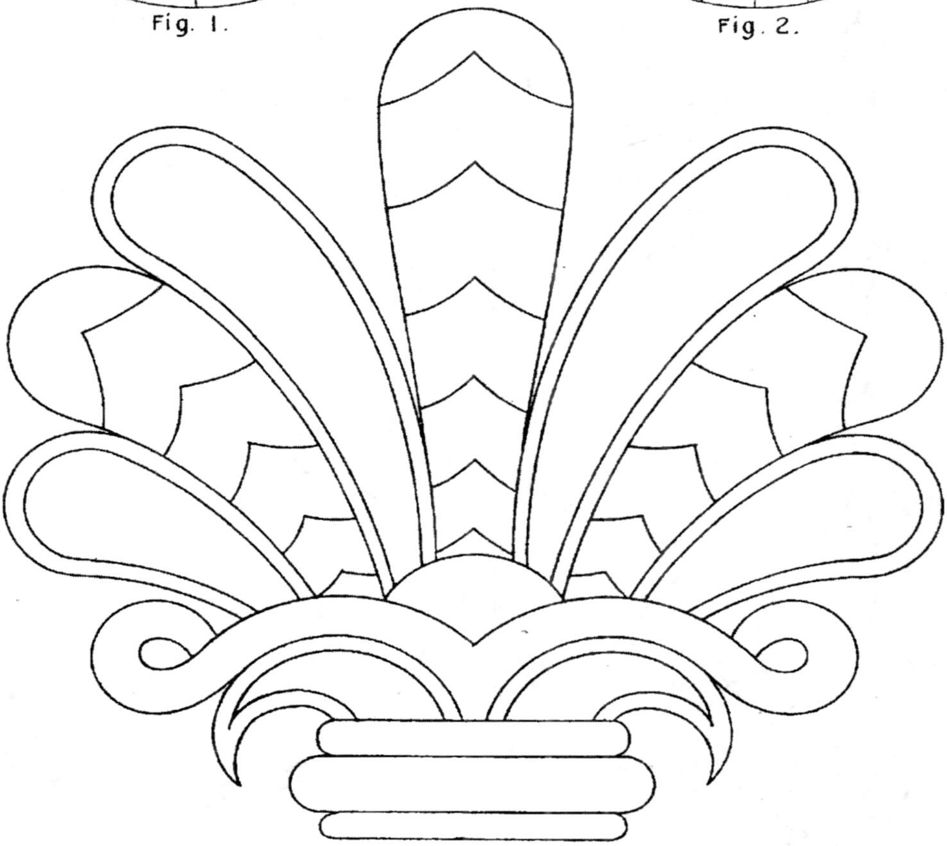

from a piece of Assyrian glazed brick in the British Museum.

PLATE 52.

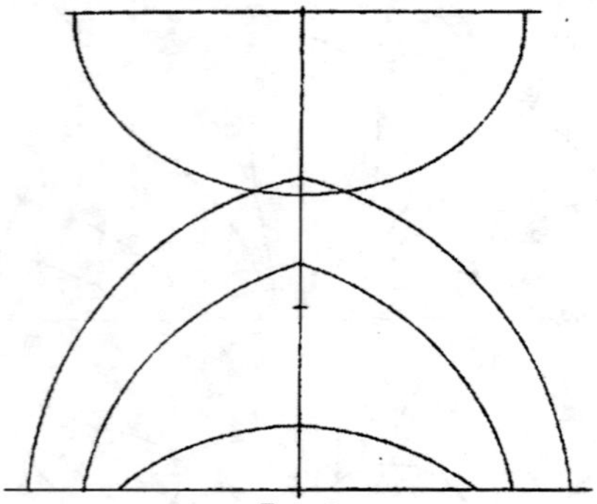

Fig. 1.

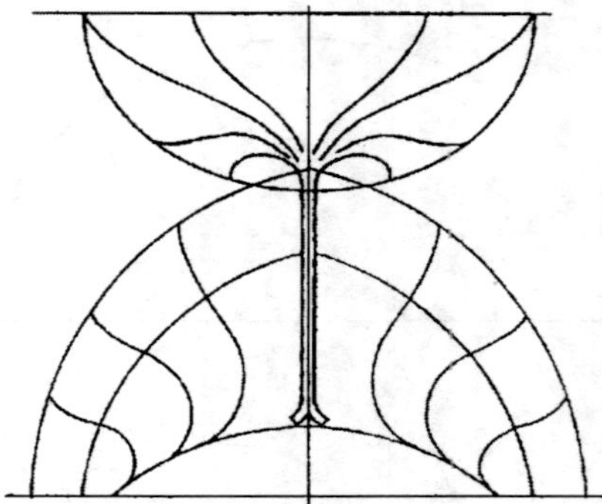

Fig. 2.

PLATE 53.

from a painted moulding– 16th Century, Italian. in the S. Kensington Museum.
Fig. 1.
Fig. 2.

PLATE 54.

Fig. 1

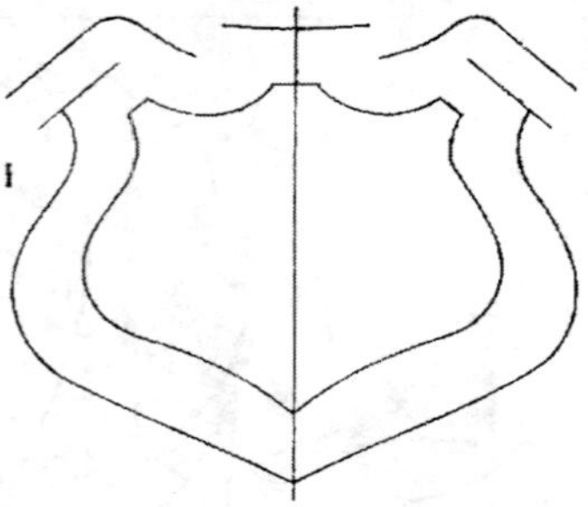

Fig. 2.

PLATE 55.

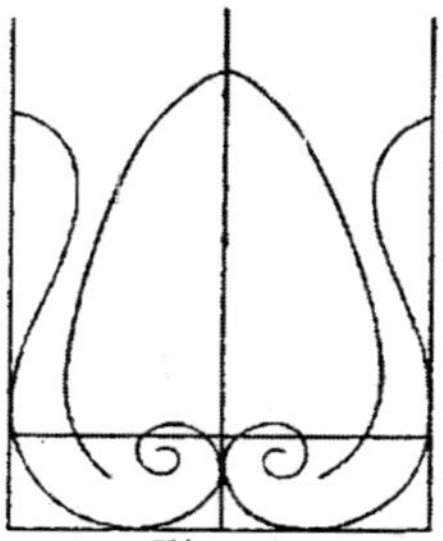

Fig. I.

Fig. 2.

From a 3rd Century B.C. Greek Vase in the S. Kensington Museum

PLATE 56.

Fig. 1.

Fig. 2.

From a 16th Century Italian Majolica Vase in the South Kensington Museum.

PLATE 57.

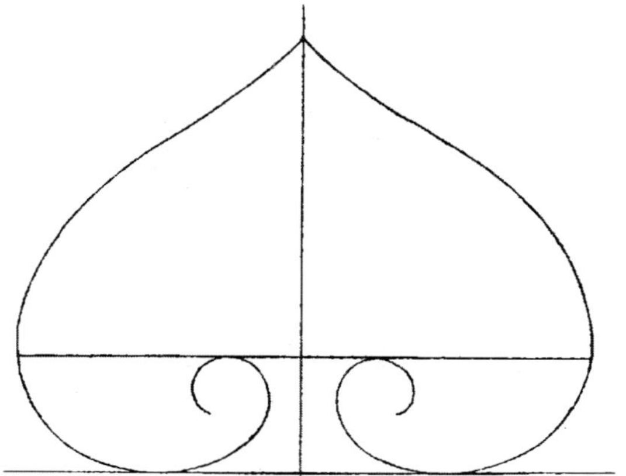

Fig. 1.

Fig. 2.

PLATE 58.

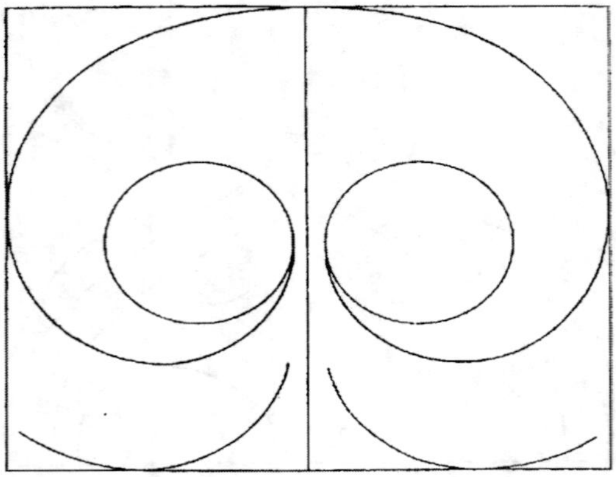

Fig. 1.

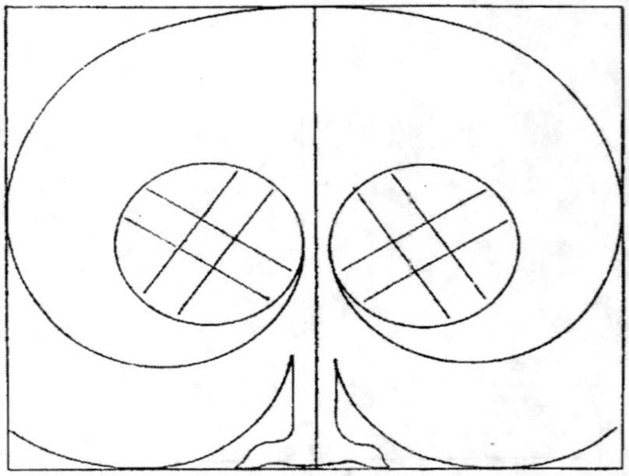

Fig. 2.

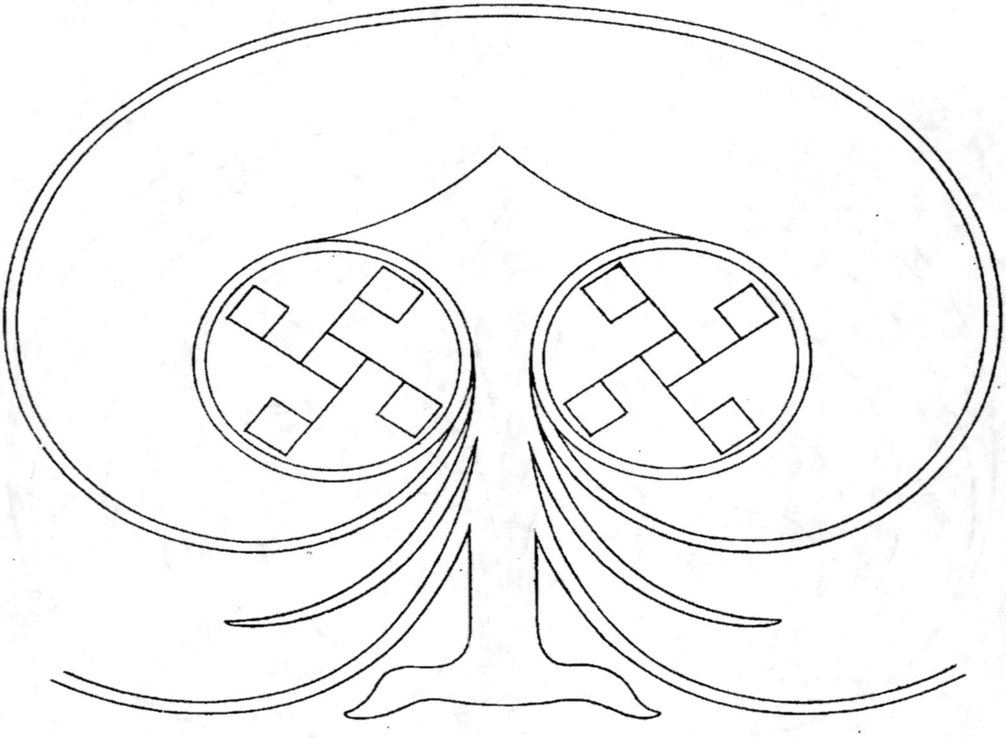

Ornament from a bronze Celtic Shield found in the Thames near Battersea, now in the British Museum.

PLATE 59.

Fig. 1.

Fig. 2.

PLATE 60.

Fig.1.

Fig.2.

from a Persian Tile in the S.Kensington Museum.

PLATE 61.

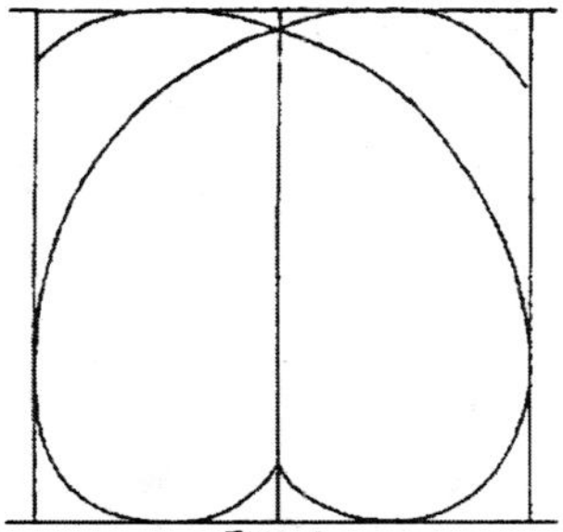

Fig. 1.

Fig. 2.

13th Century Romanesque frieze Ornament.

PLATE 62.

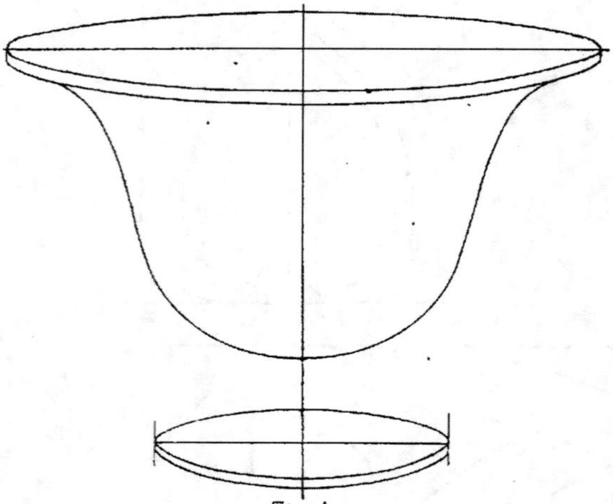

Fig. 1.

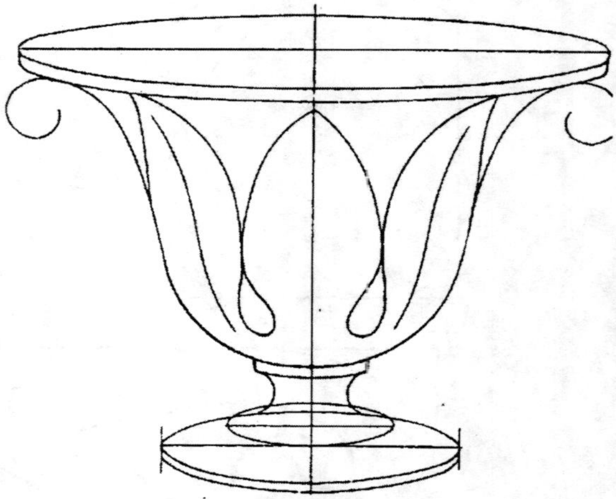

Fig. 2.

PLATE 63.

15th Century (Perpendicular Style) window head in one Stone from Hexham Priory.

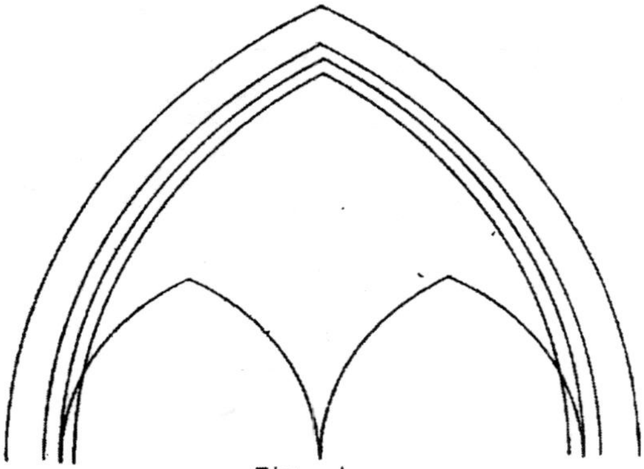

Fig. 1.

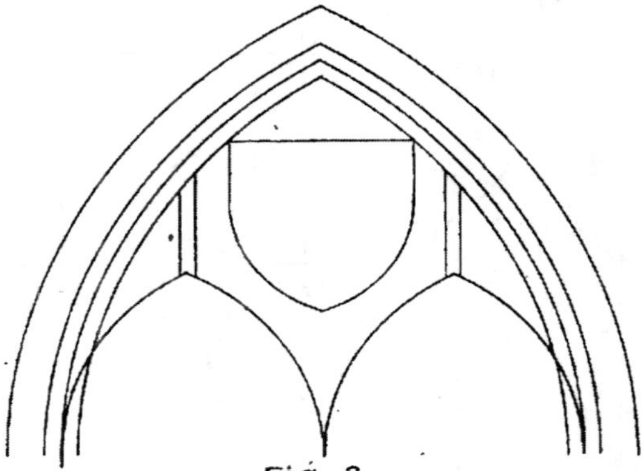

Fig. 2.

PLATE 64.

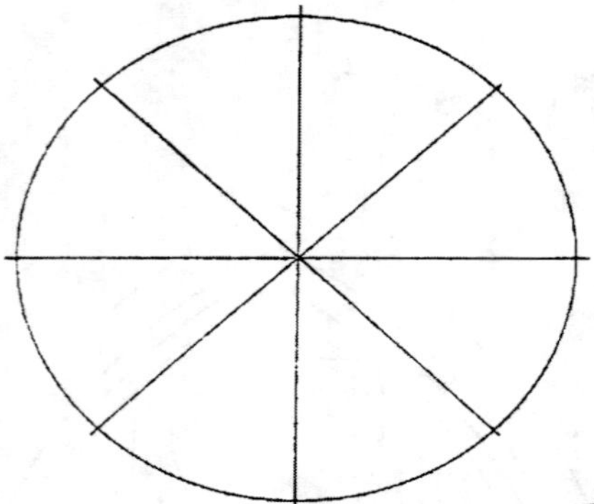

Fig. 1.

Fig. 2.

PLATE 65.

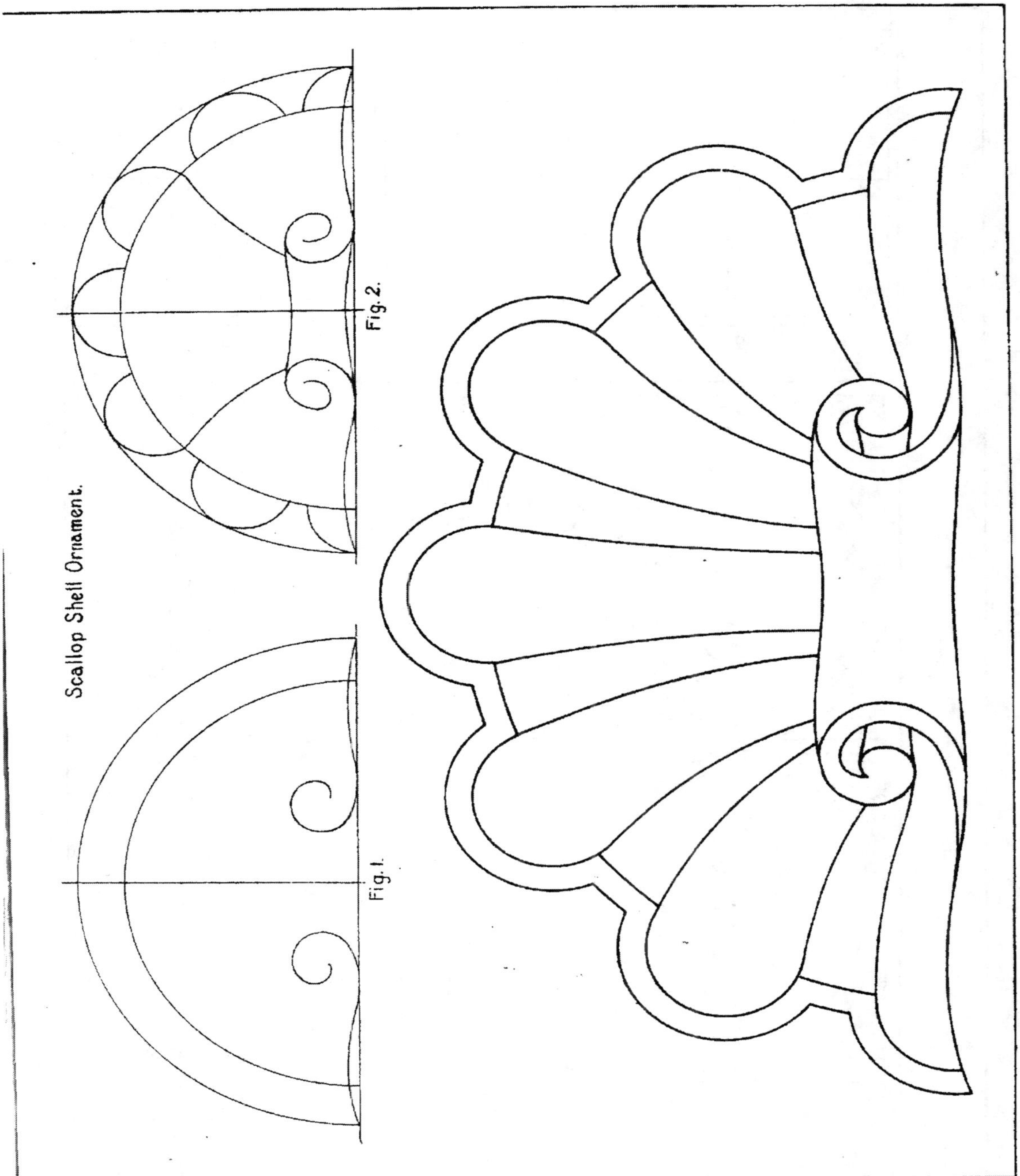

PLATE 66.

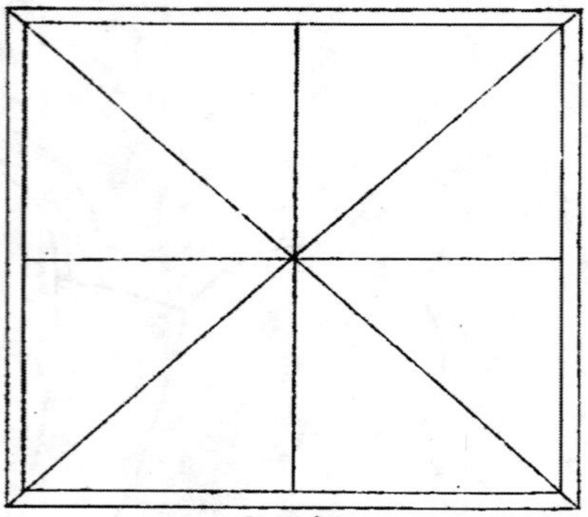

Fig. 1.

Fig. 2.

PLATE 67.

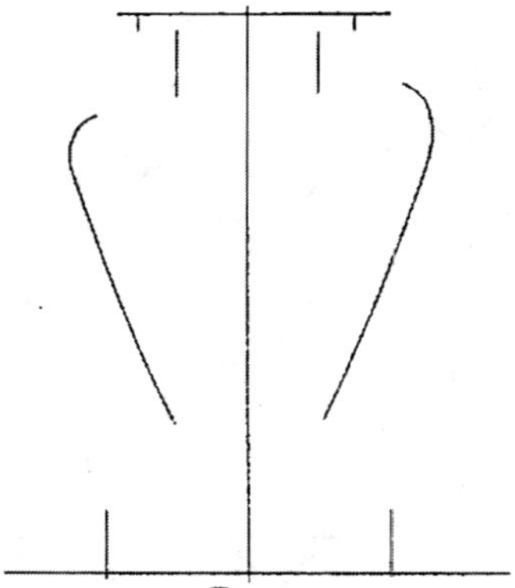

Fig. 1.

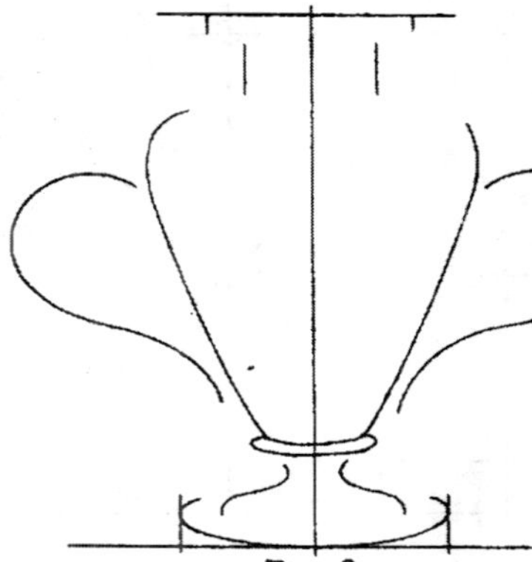

Fig. 2.

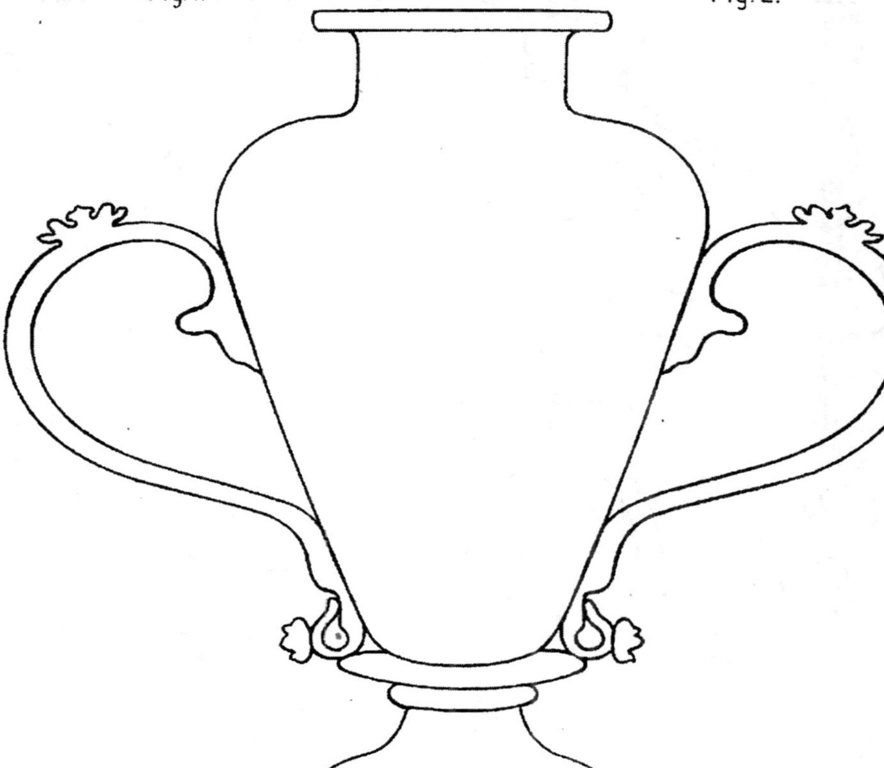

From a 17th Century Spanish Vase in the S. Kensington Museum.

PLATE 68.

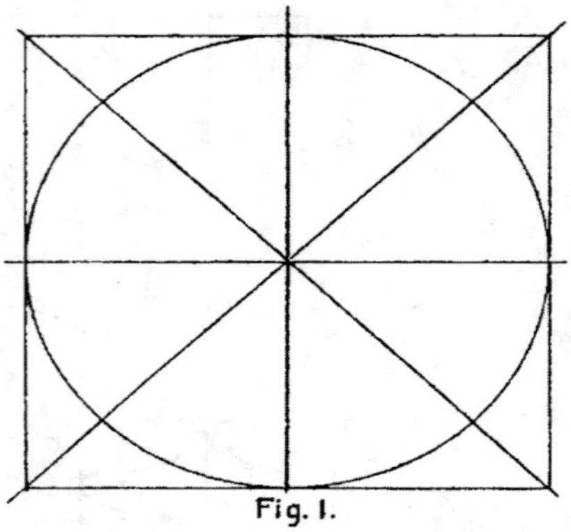

Fig. 1.

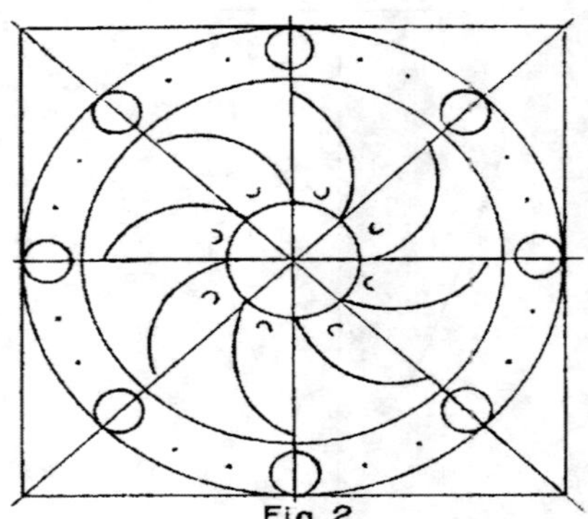

Fig. 2.

Rosette from a cast in the Trocadero, Paris.

PLATE 69.

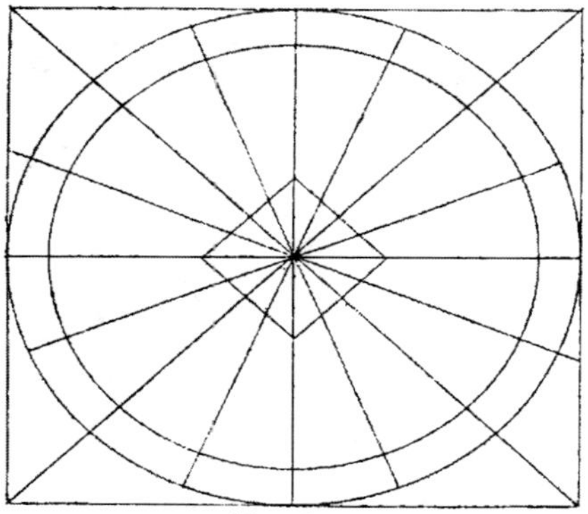

Fig. 1.

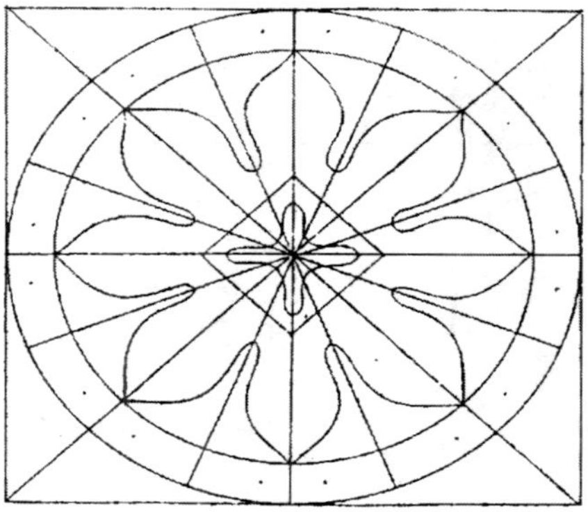

Fig. 2.

Rosette from a cast in the Trocadero, Paris.

PLATE 70.

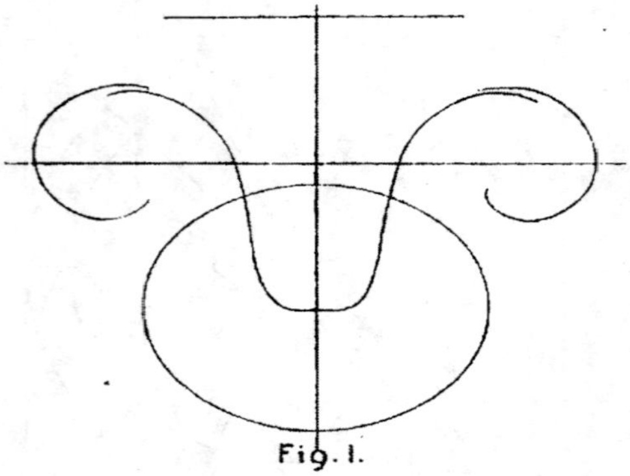

Fig. 1.

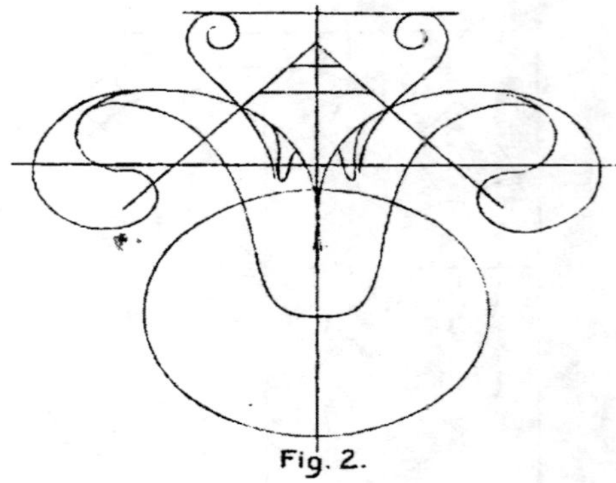

Fig. 2.

from a 16th Century Italian Majolica Vase in the S. Kensington Museum.

PLATE 71.

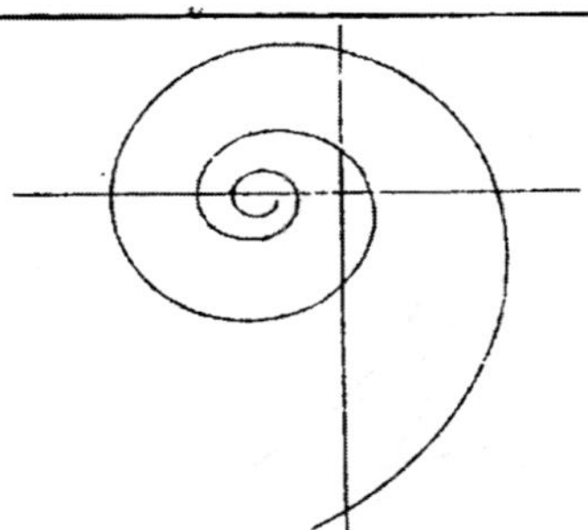

Fig. 1.

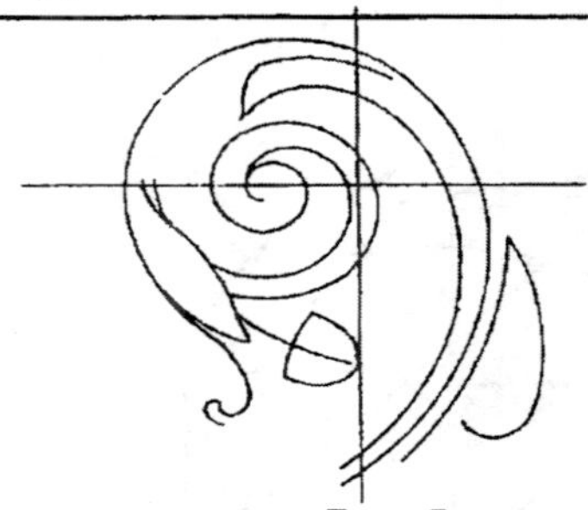

Fig. 2.

PLATE 72.

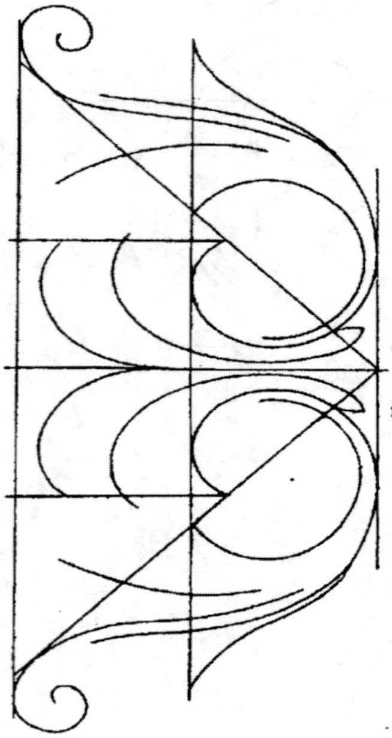

Fig. 2.

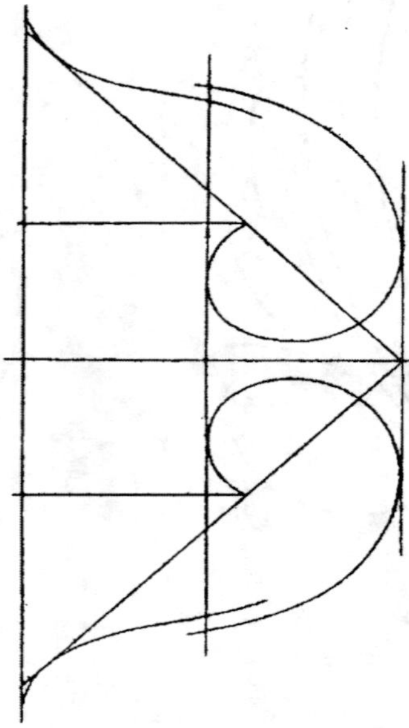

Fig. 1.

From 15th Century Italian Stone work in the S. Kensington Museum.

PLATE 73.

Fig. 1.

Fig. 2.

Copy set at an Examination by the Art Department.

PLATE 74

Fig. 1.

Fig. 2.

From a 16th Century Italian Majolica Vase in the S. Kensington Museum.

PLATE 75.

Vase from Cyprus,
in the Louvre Paris.

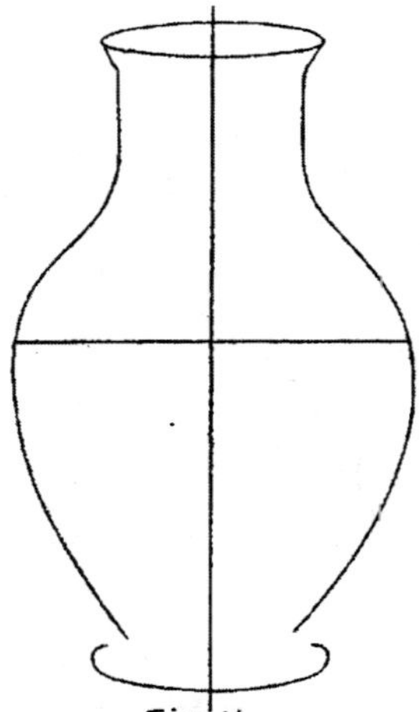

Fig. 1.

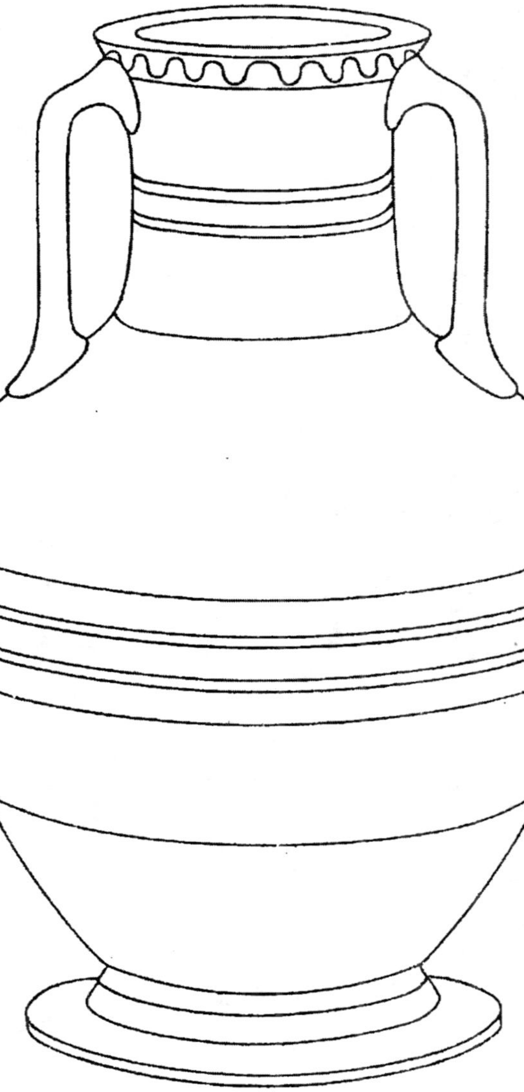

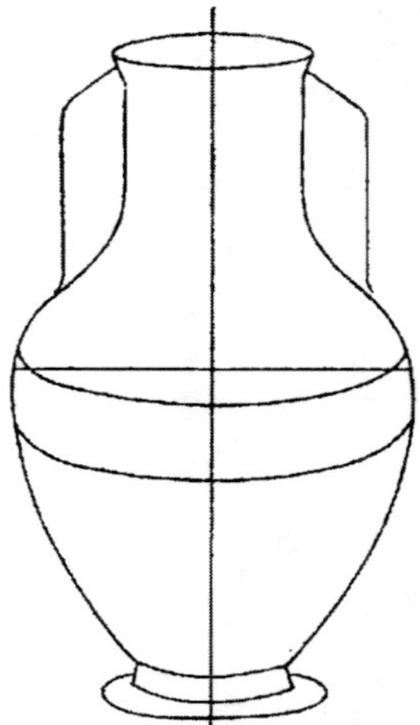

Fig. 2.

PLATE 76.

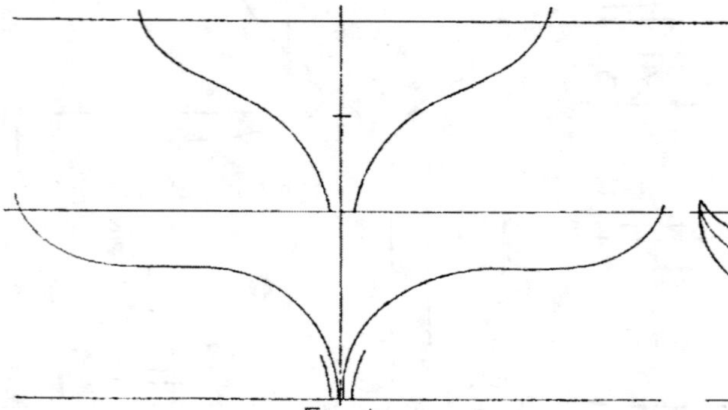

Fig. 1.

Fig. 2.

PLATE 77.

Acanthus leaf ornament.

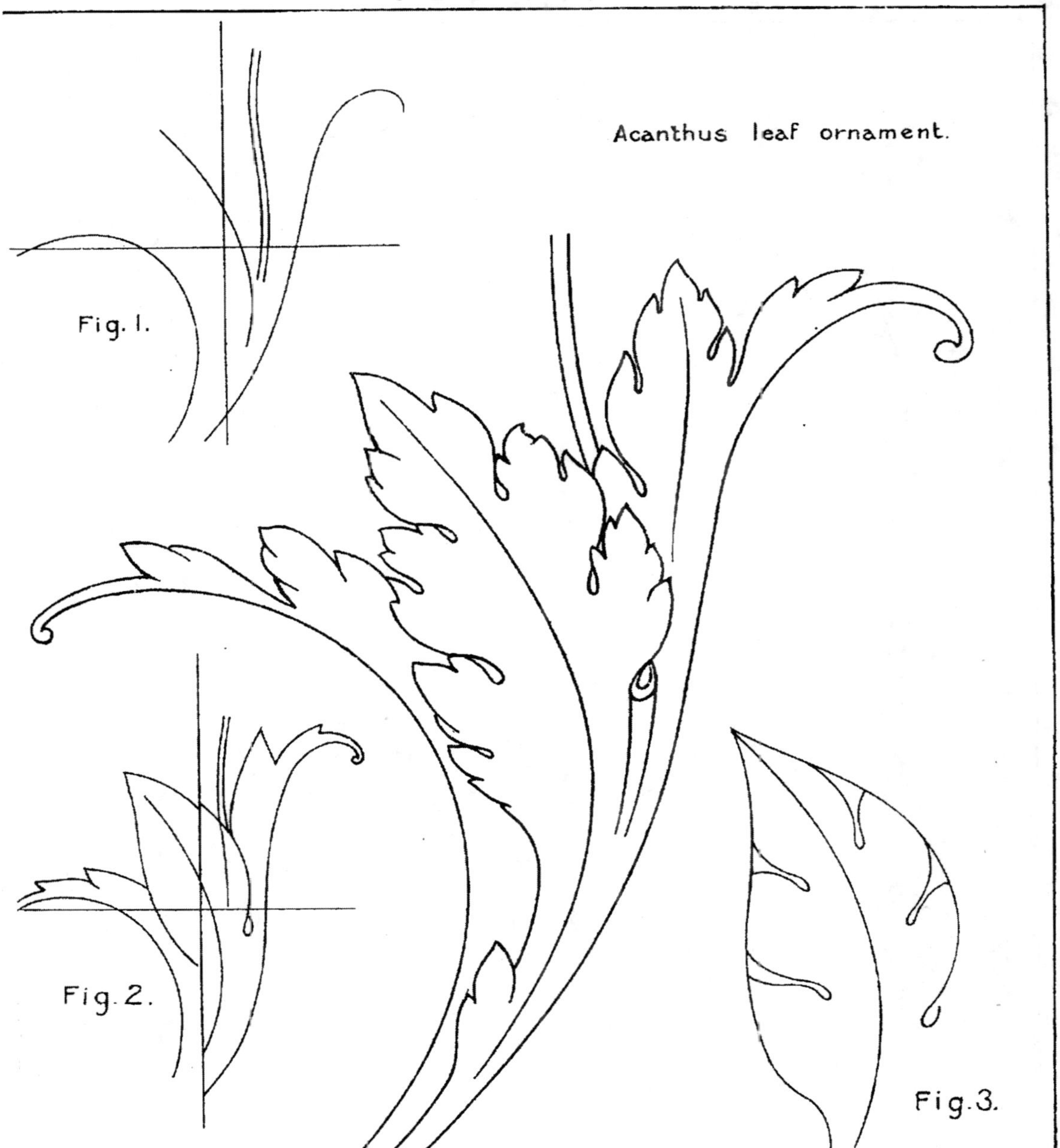

PLATE 78.

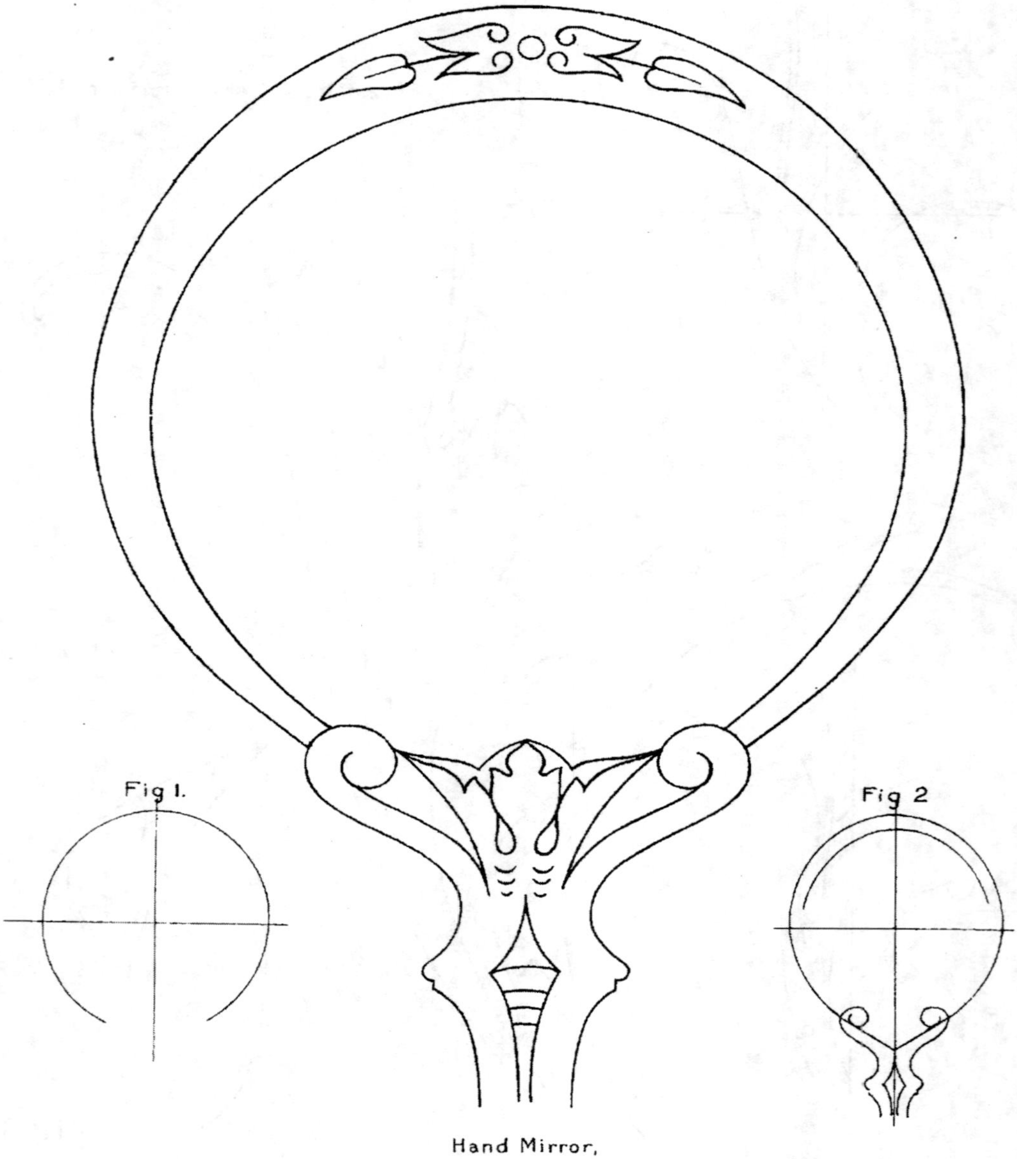

Fig I.

Fig 2

Hand Mirror,

Copy set at a College of Preceptor's Examination.

PLATE 79.

Fig. 2.

Fig. 1.

From an Indian Tile in the S. Kensington Museum

PLATE 80.

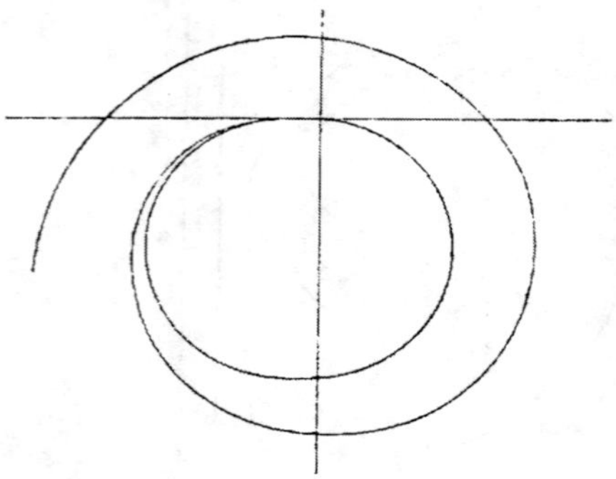

Fig. 1.

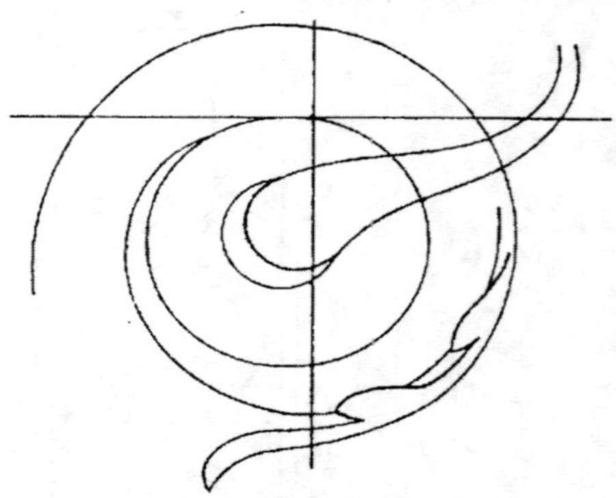

Fig. 2.

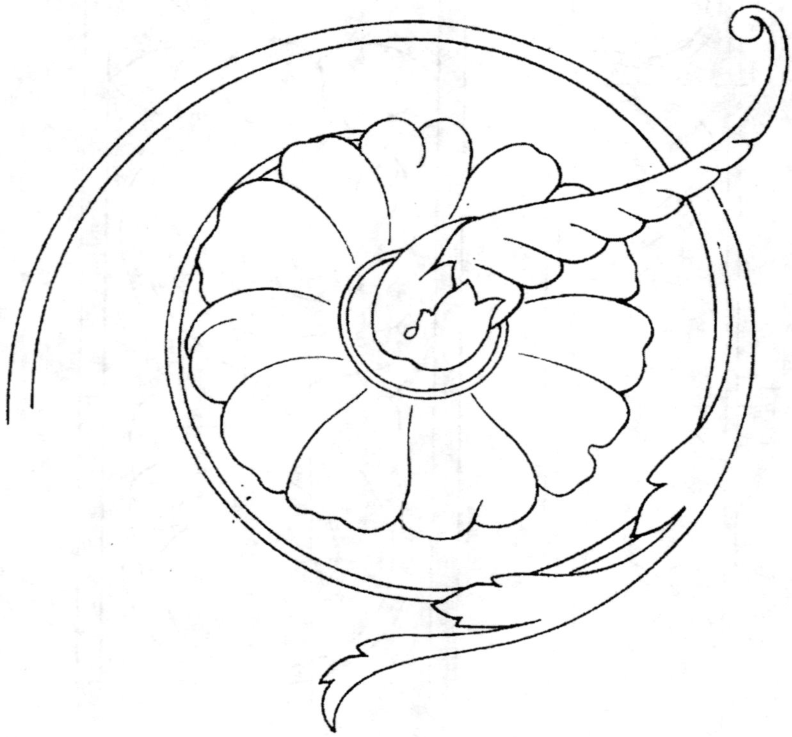

PLATE 81.

Fig. 1

Fig: 2

PLATE 82.

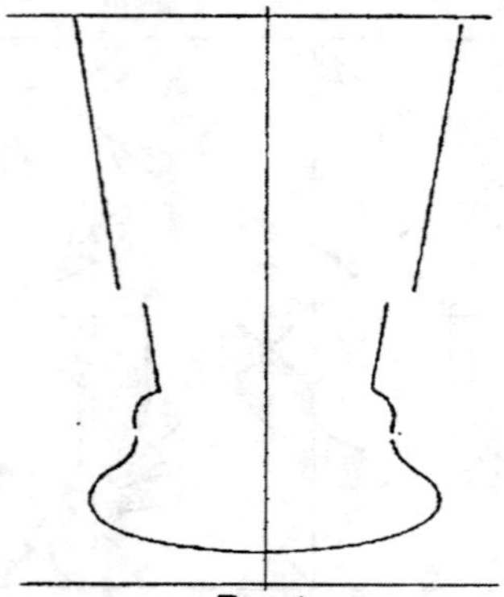

Fig. 1.

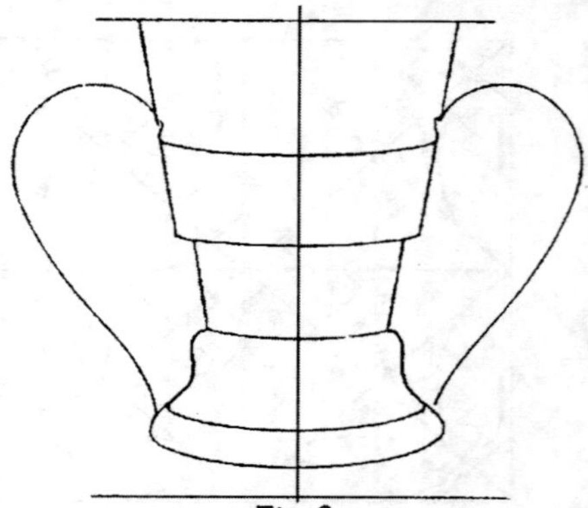

Fig. 2

from a Spanish Vase in the S. Kensington Museum.

PLATE 83.

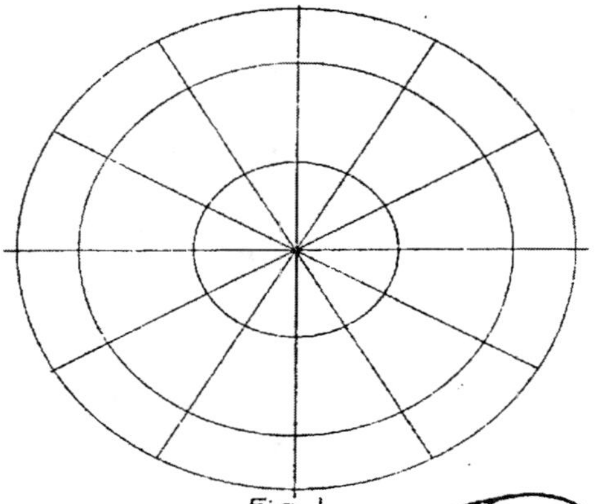

Fig. 1.

Fig. 2.

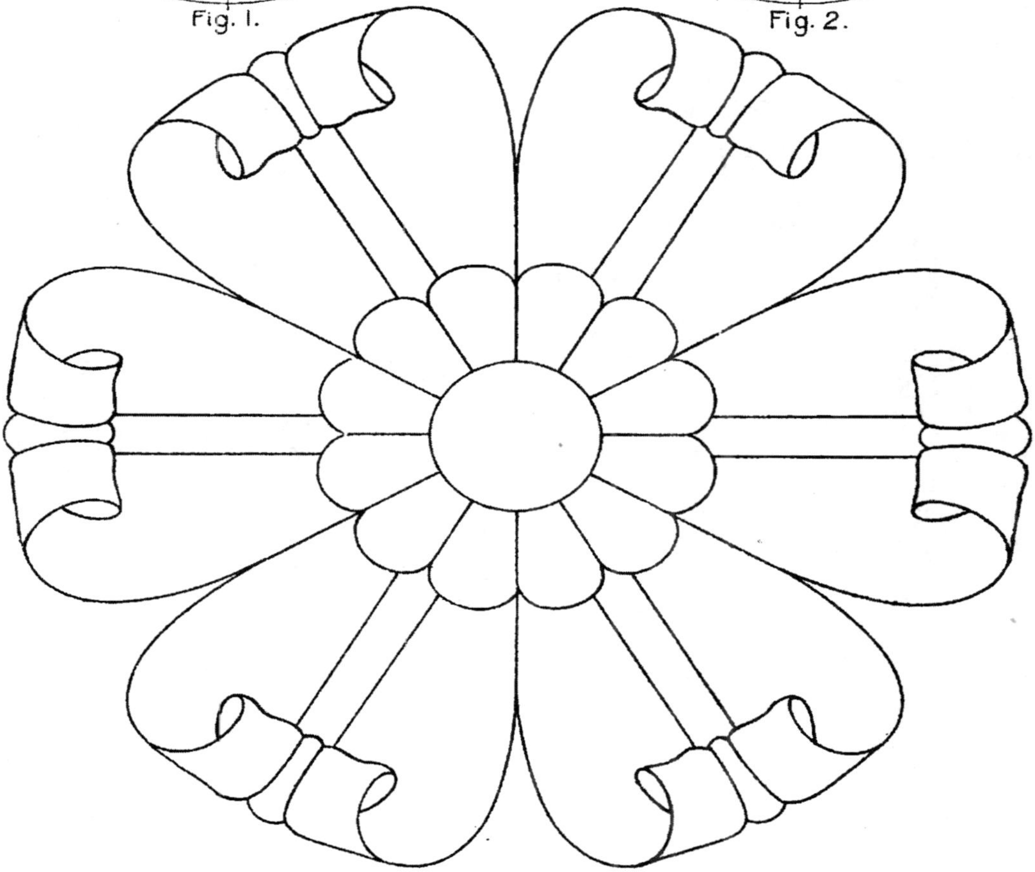

PLATE 84.

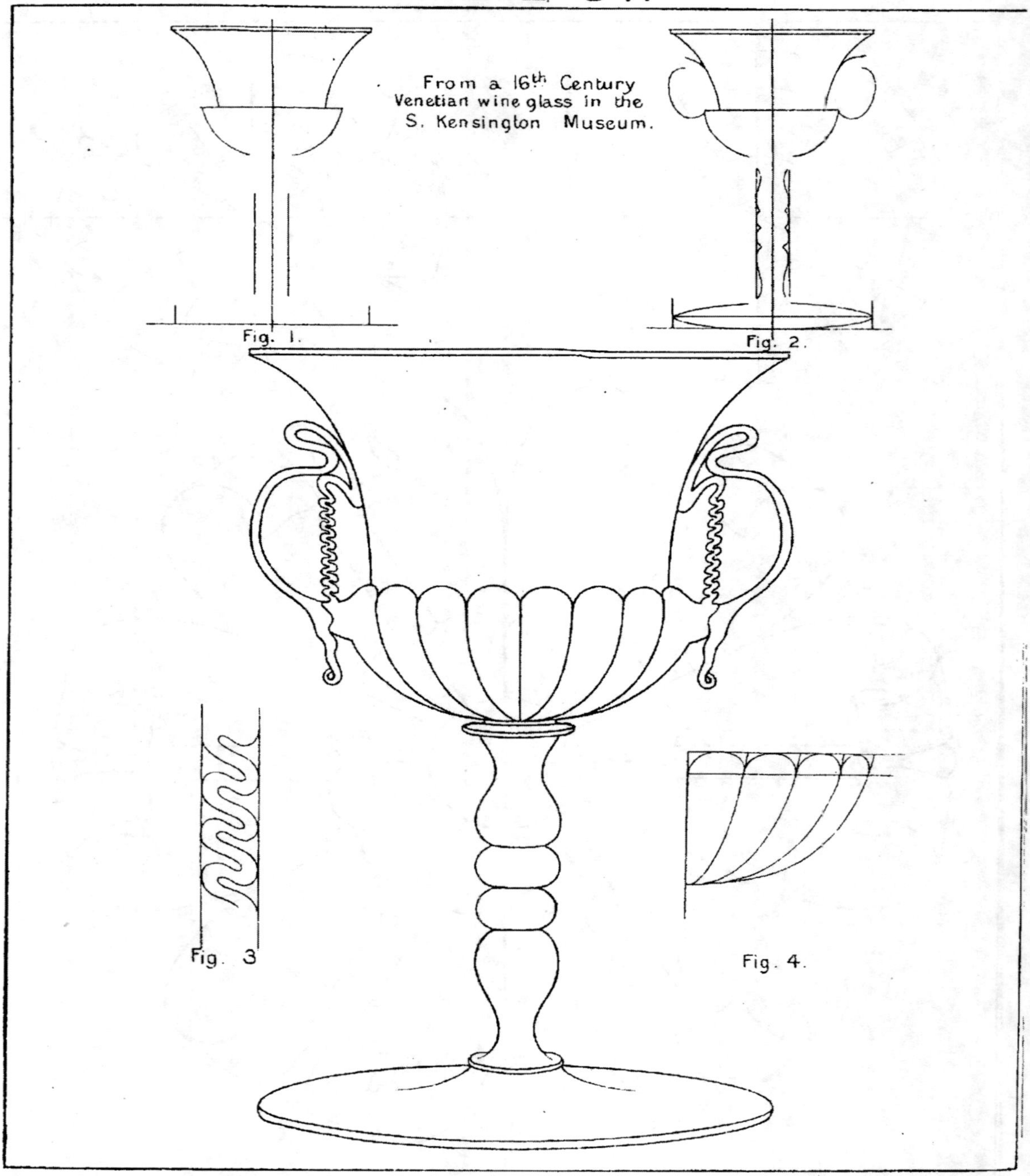
From a 16th Century
Venetian wine glass in the
S. Kensington Museum.
Fig. 1.
Fig. 2.
Fig. 3
Fig. 4.

PLATE 85.

from an Arabic Terra Cotta in the British Museum.

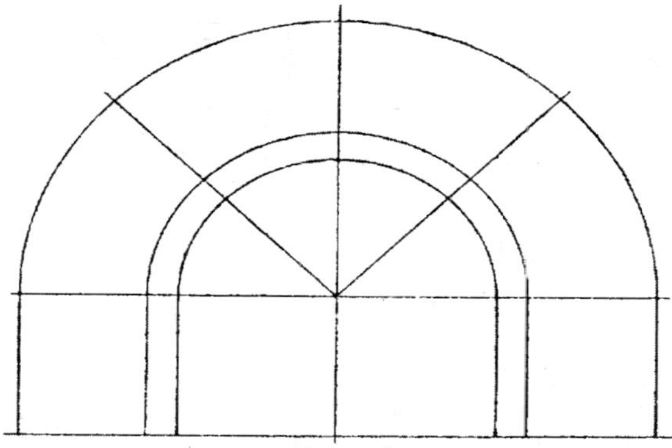

Fig. 1.

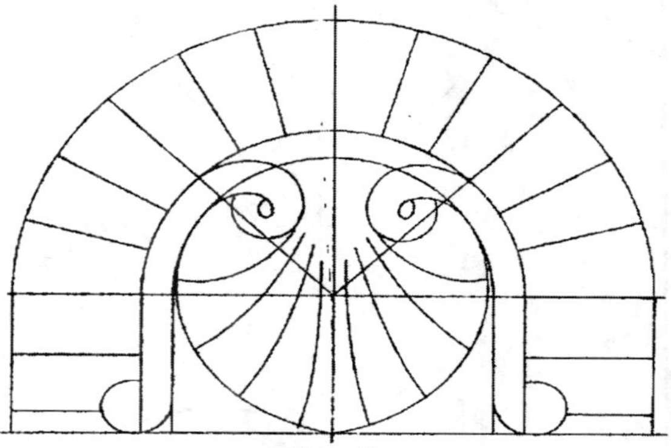

Fig. 2.

PLATE 86.

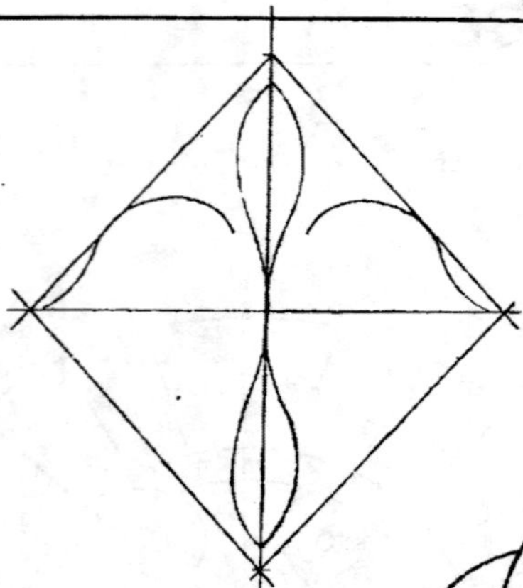

Fig 1

Fig 2

PLATE 87.

By CHARLES ARMSTRONG.

PLATE 88.

PLATE 89.

From the wrought iron Railings
round the Luxembourg Gardens, Paris.

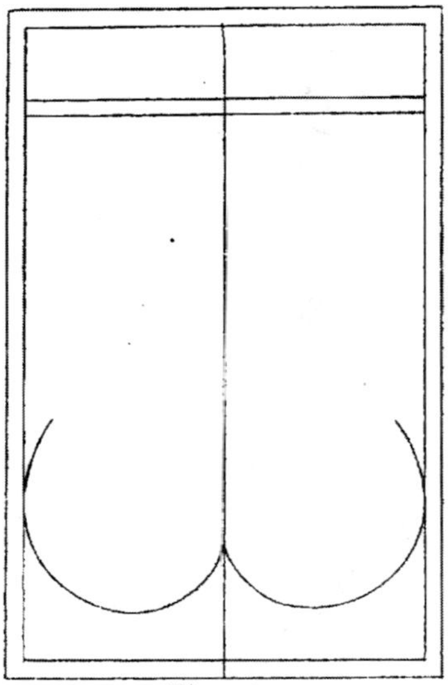

Fig. 1.

Fig. 2.

PLATE 90

Fig. 1.

Fig. 2.

Angle of a Scroll border in wrought iron 16th Century Italian
in the S. Kensington Museum.

PLATE 91.

PLATE 92.

PLATE 93.

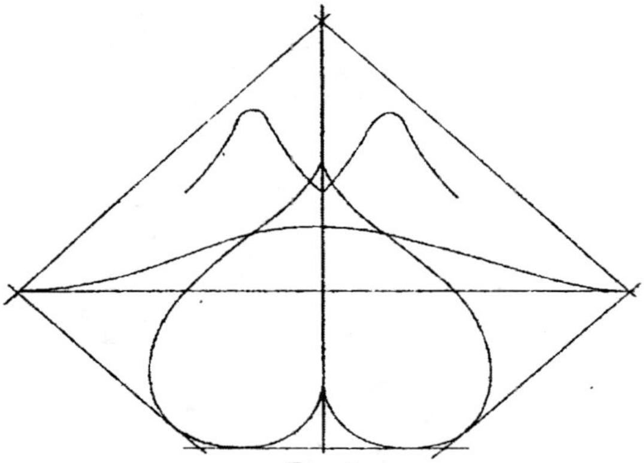

Fig. I.

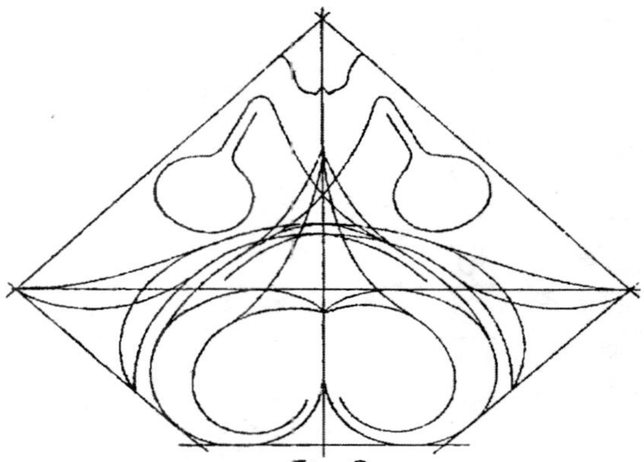

Fig. 2.

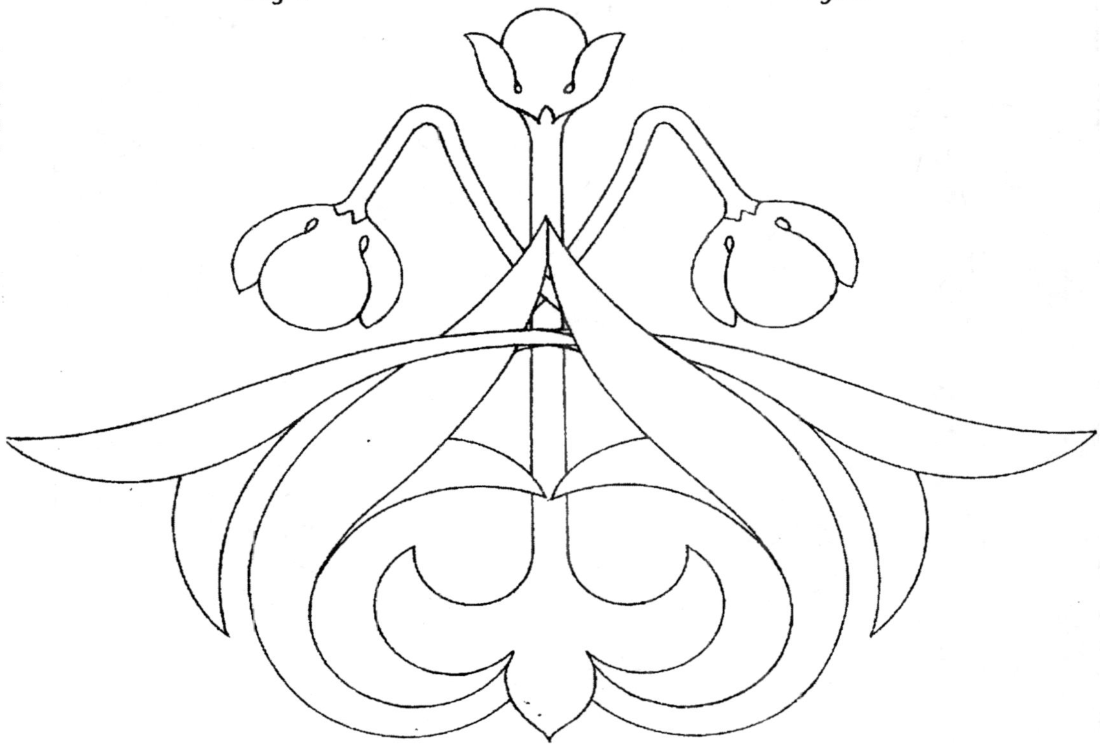

PLATE 94.

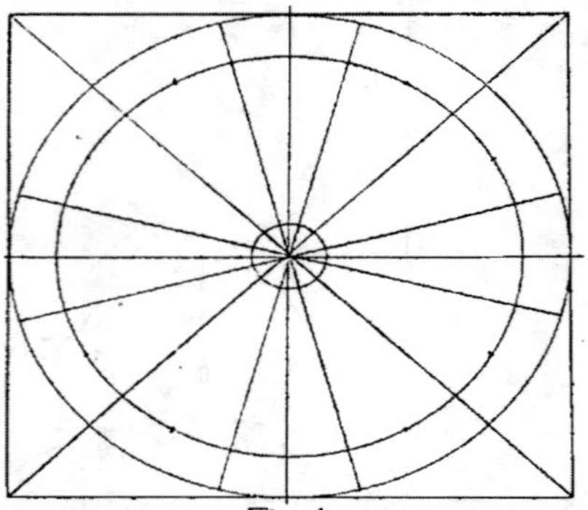

Fig. 1.

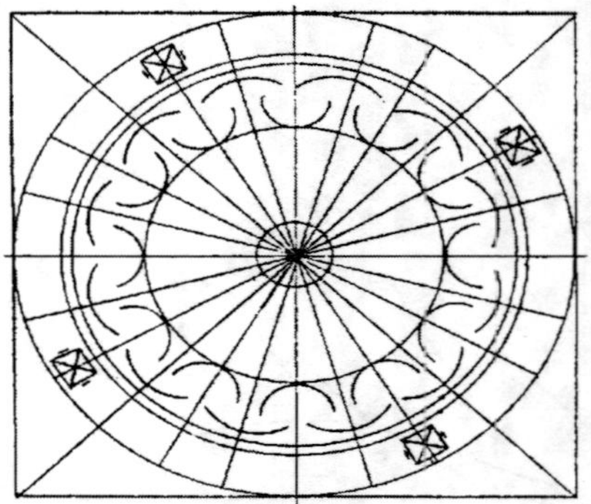

Fig. 2.

Rosette, from a cast in the Trocadero, Paris.

PLATE 95.

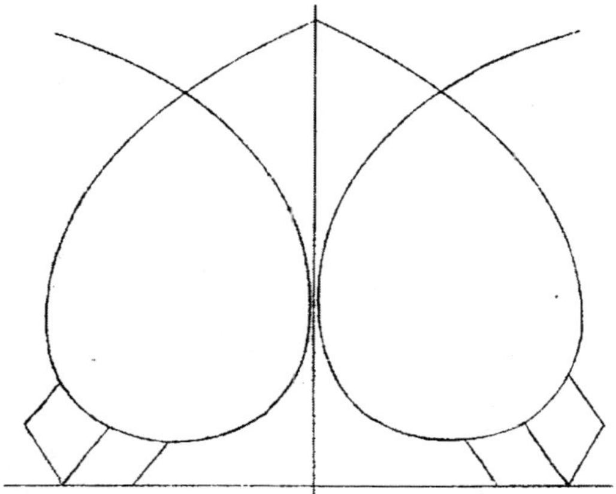

Fig. 1.

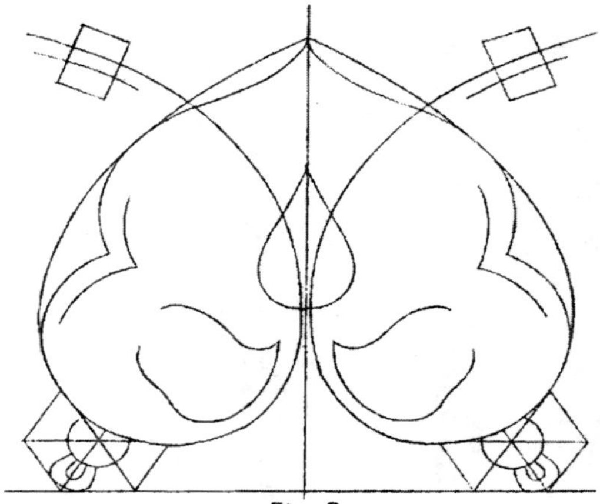

Fig. 2.

from a Persian Tile in the S. Kensington Museum.

PLATE 96.

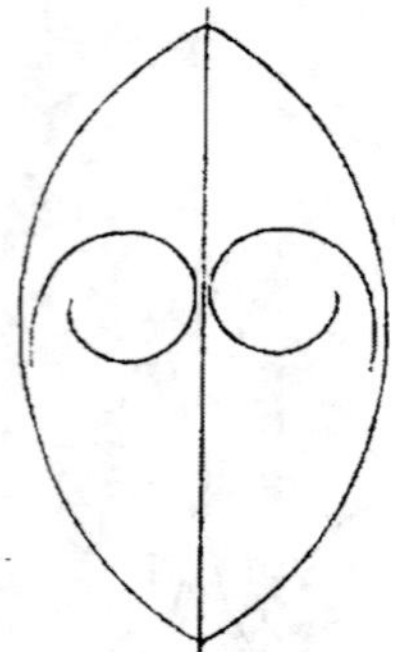

Fig. 1.

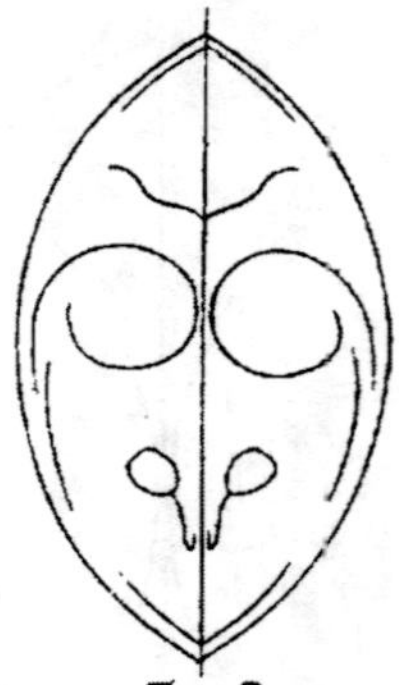

Fig. 2.

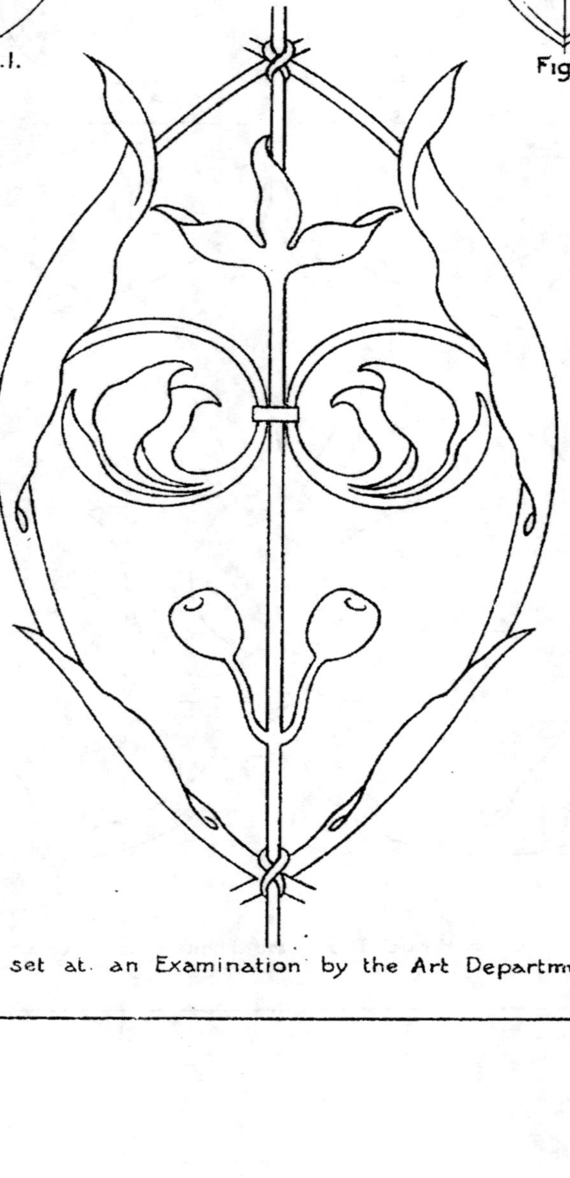

Copy set at an Examination by the Art Department.

PLATE 97.

Fig. 1.

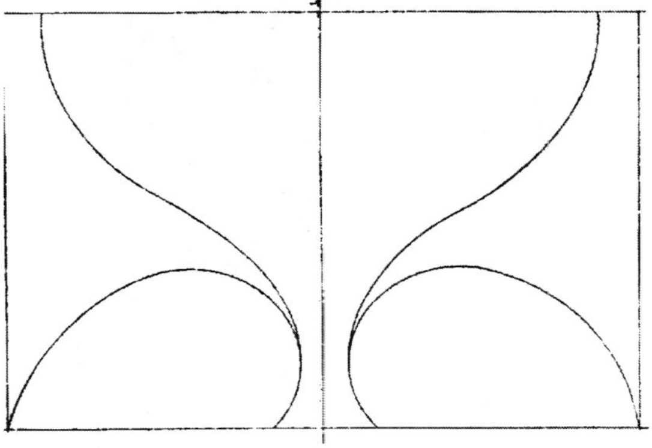

Fig. 2.

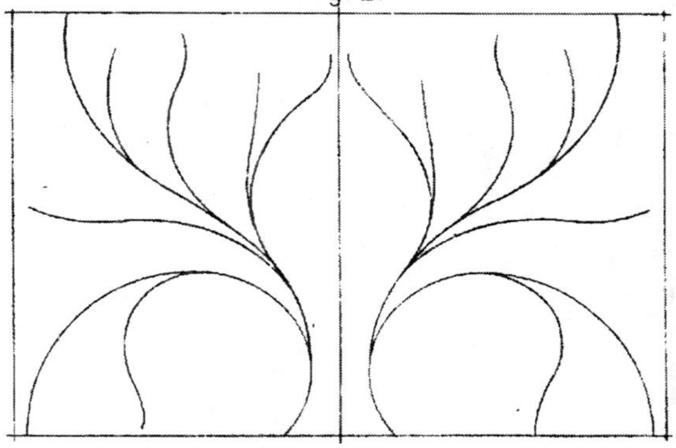

from a 13th Century Capital, in the Trocadero, Paris.

PLATE 98.

PLATE 99.

Nest of
Acanthus Leaves.

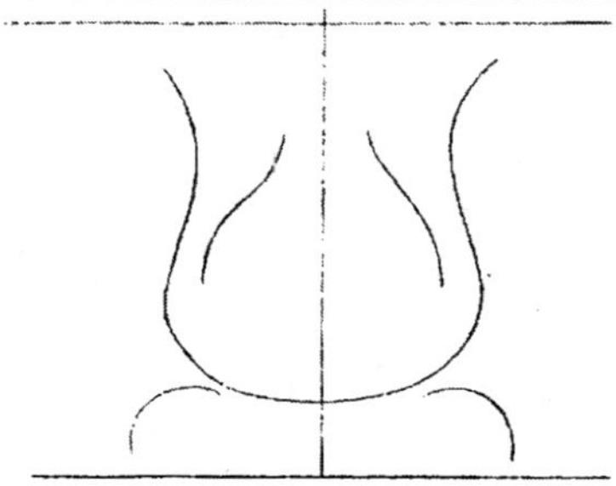

Fig. 1

Fig. 2.

PLATE 100.

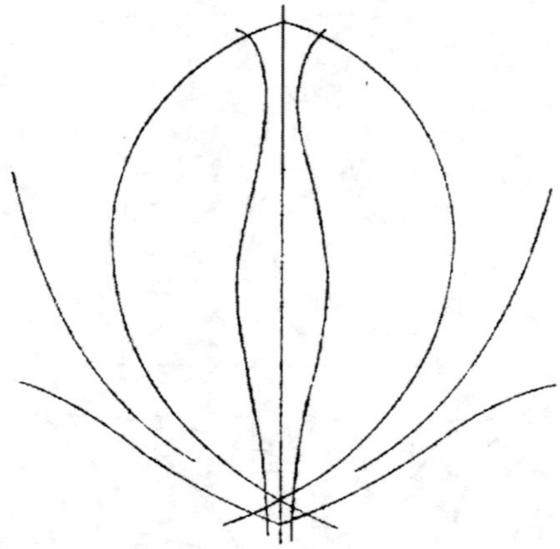

Fig. 1.

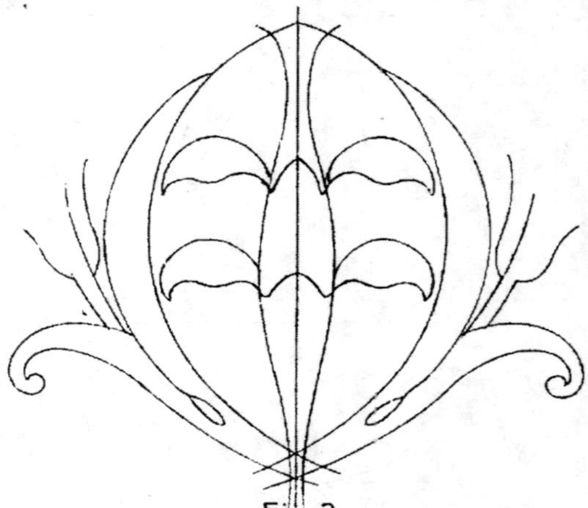

Fig. 2.

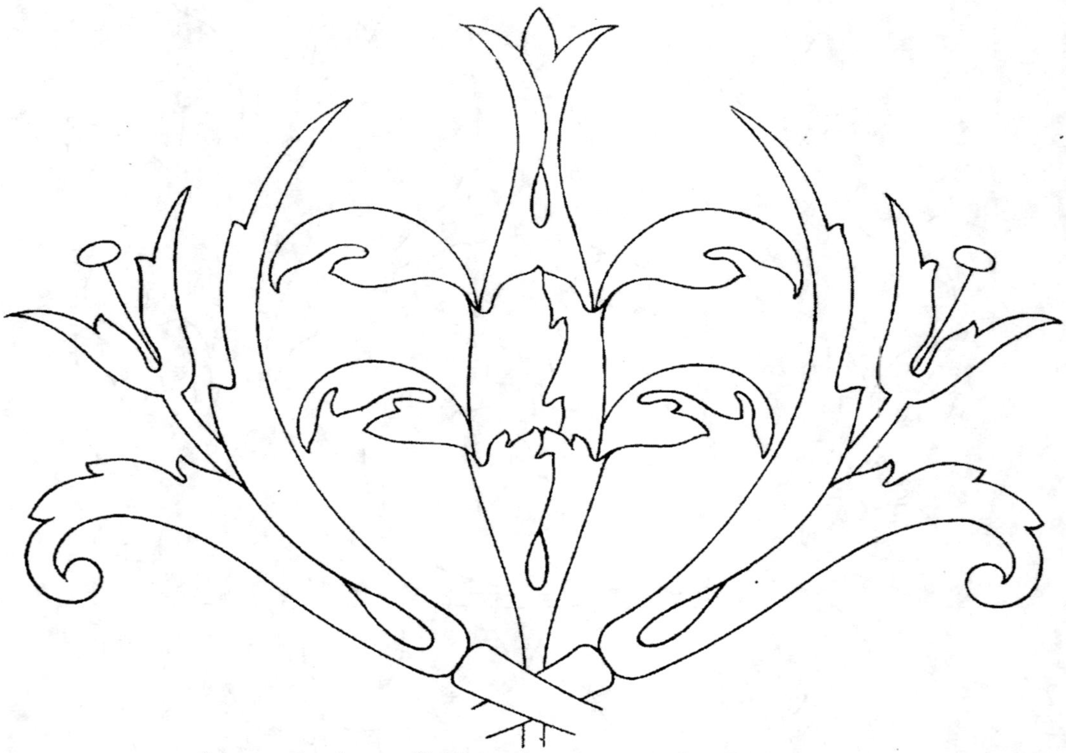

Copy set at an Examination by the Art Department.

PLATE 101.

from a 4th Century B.C
Greek Vase in the
S. Kensington Museum.

Fig. 1.

Fig. 2.

PLATE 102.

Fig. 1.

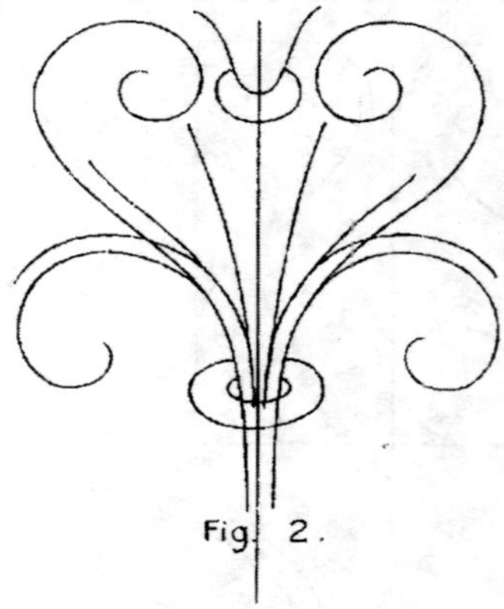

Fig. 2.

Copy set at the May Examination 1889 by the Art Department.

PLATE 103.

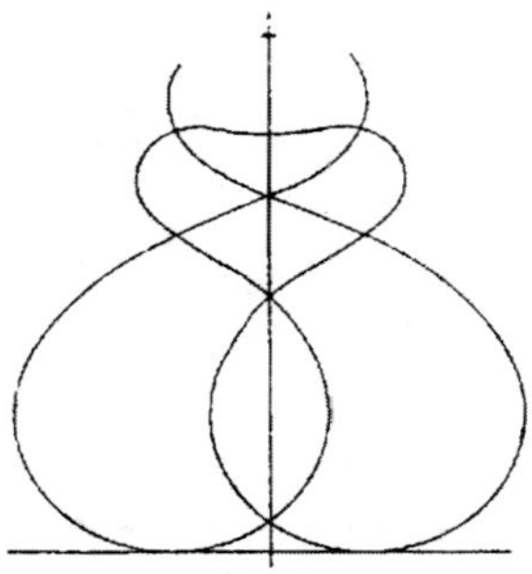

Fig. 1.

Fig. 2.

PLATE 104.

Design for an Iron Door-knocker.

PLATE 105.

Fig. 2.
Fig. 1.
From a 16th Century Italian Majolica Vase in the
S. Kensington Museum.

PLATE 106

PLATE 107.

PLATE 108.

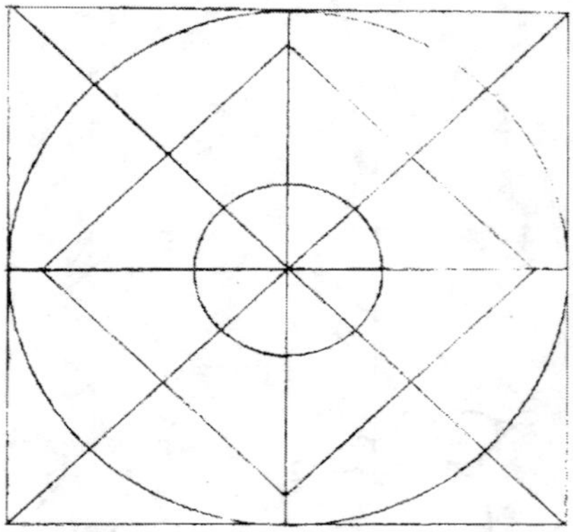

Fig. 1.

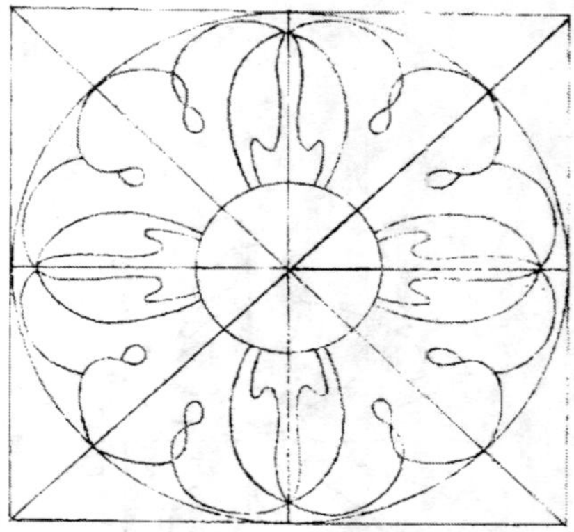

Fig 2

From a Rosette in the Trocadero, Paris

PLATE 109.

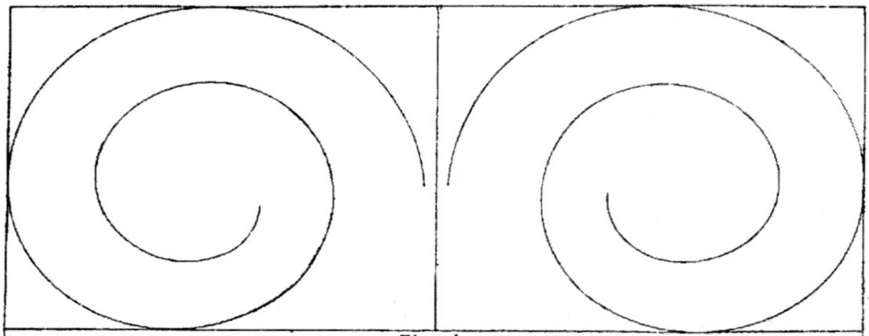

Fig. 1.

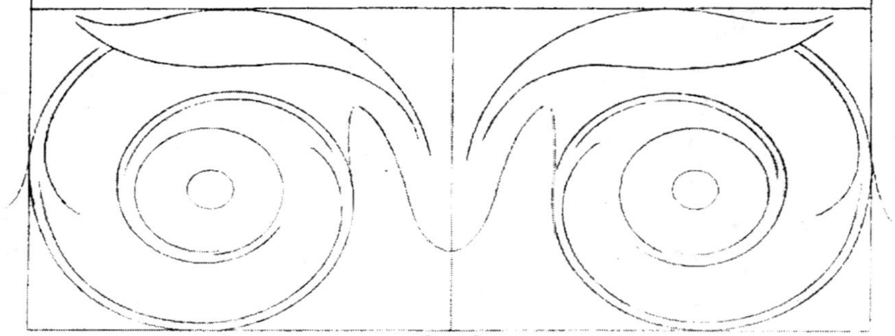

Fig. 2.

Copy set at an Art Department's Exam. in October 1894.

PLATE 110.

Exercise given at the Oxford Local Senior Examination 1894.

PLATE 111.

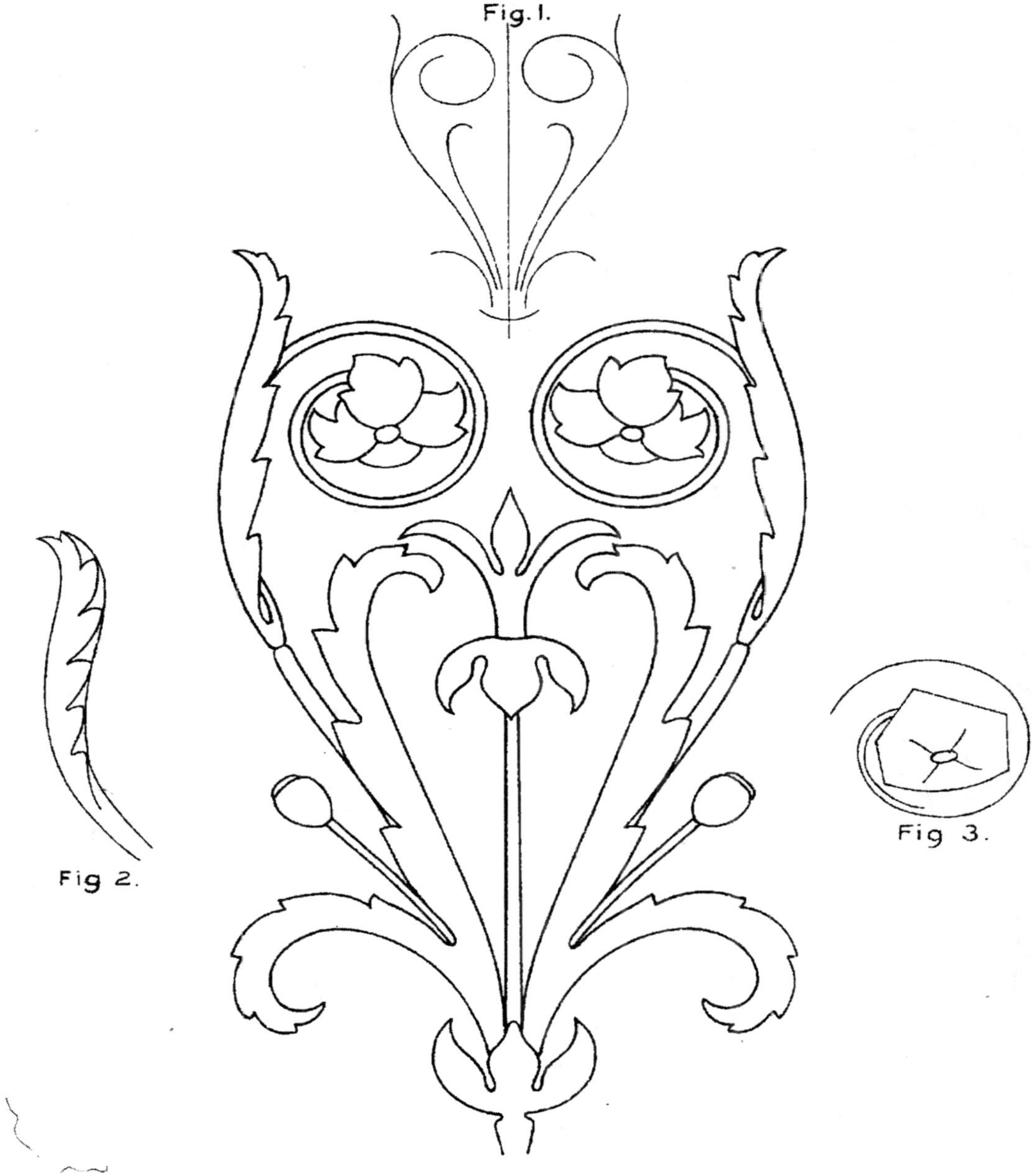

Copy set at an Examination by the Art Department

PLATE 112.

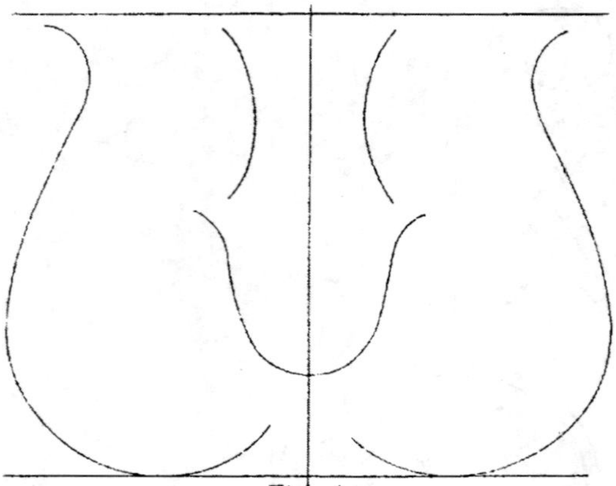

Fig. 1.

Fig. 2.

from a Majolica Vase in the S. Kensington Museum.

PLATE 113.

PLATE 114.

PLATE 115.

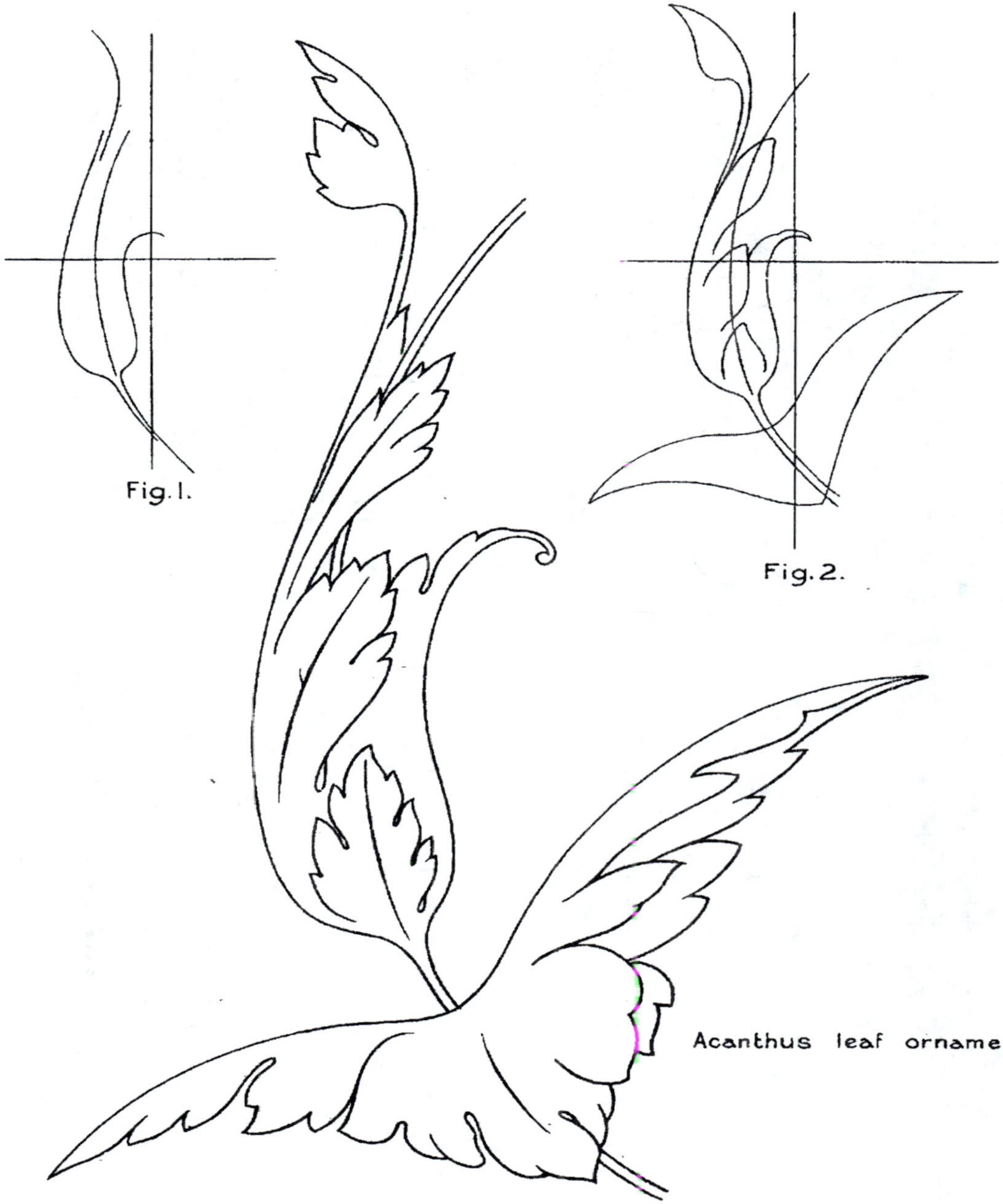

Fig. 1.

Fig. 2.

Acanthus leaf ornament.

PLATE 116.

Fig. 2.

Fig. 1.

From a plate border, — 16th Century French, — Limoges Enamel, — in the S. Kensington Museum.

PLATE 117.

CUSACK'S "FREEHAND ORNAMENT"

By CHARLES ARMSTRONG.

PLATE 118.

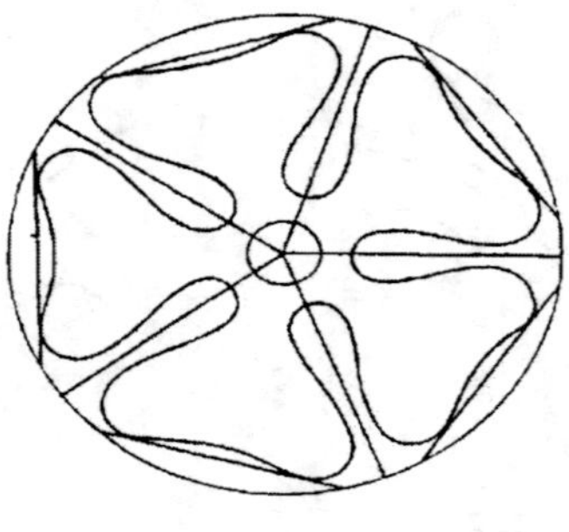

Fig. 2.

Fig. 1

17th Century English, from an inlaid wood table top in the S. Kensington Museum.

PLATE 119.

16th Century Italian Ornament, from a distemper painted frieze _ in the S. Kensington Museum.

PLATE 120.

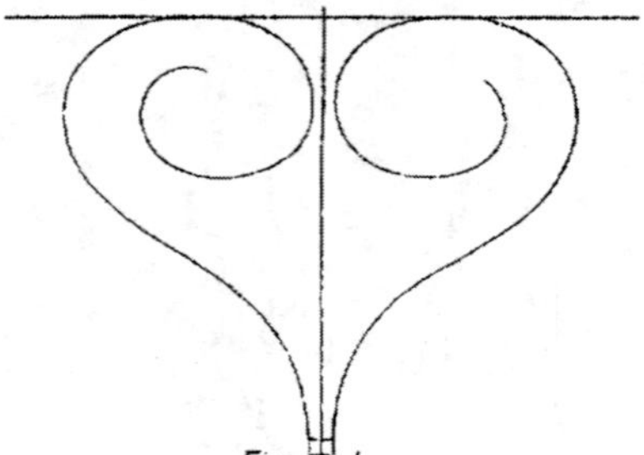

Fig. 1.

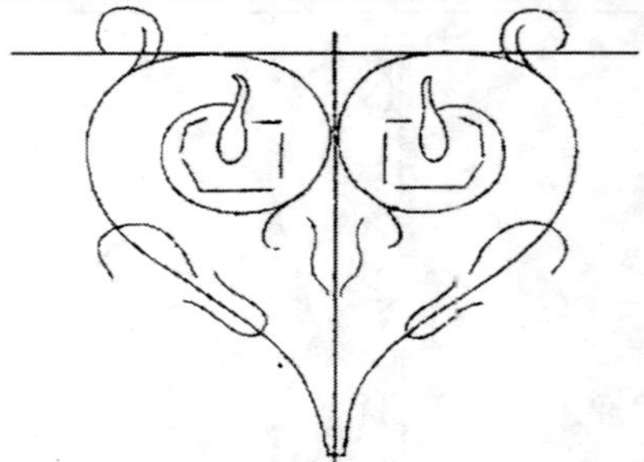

Fig. 2.

Copy set at an Examination by the Art Department.

PLATE 121.

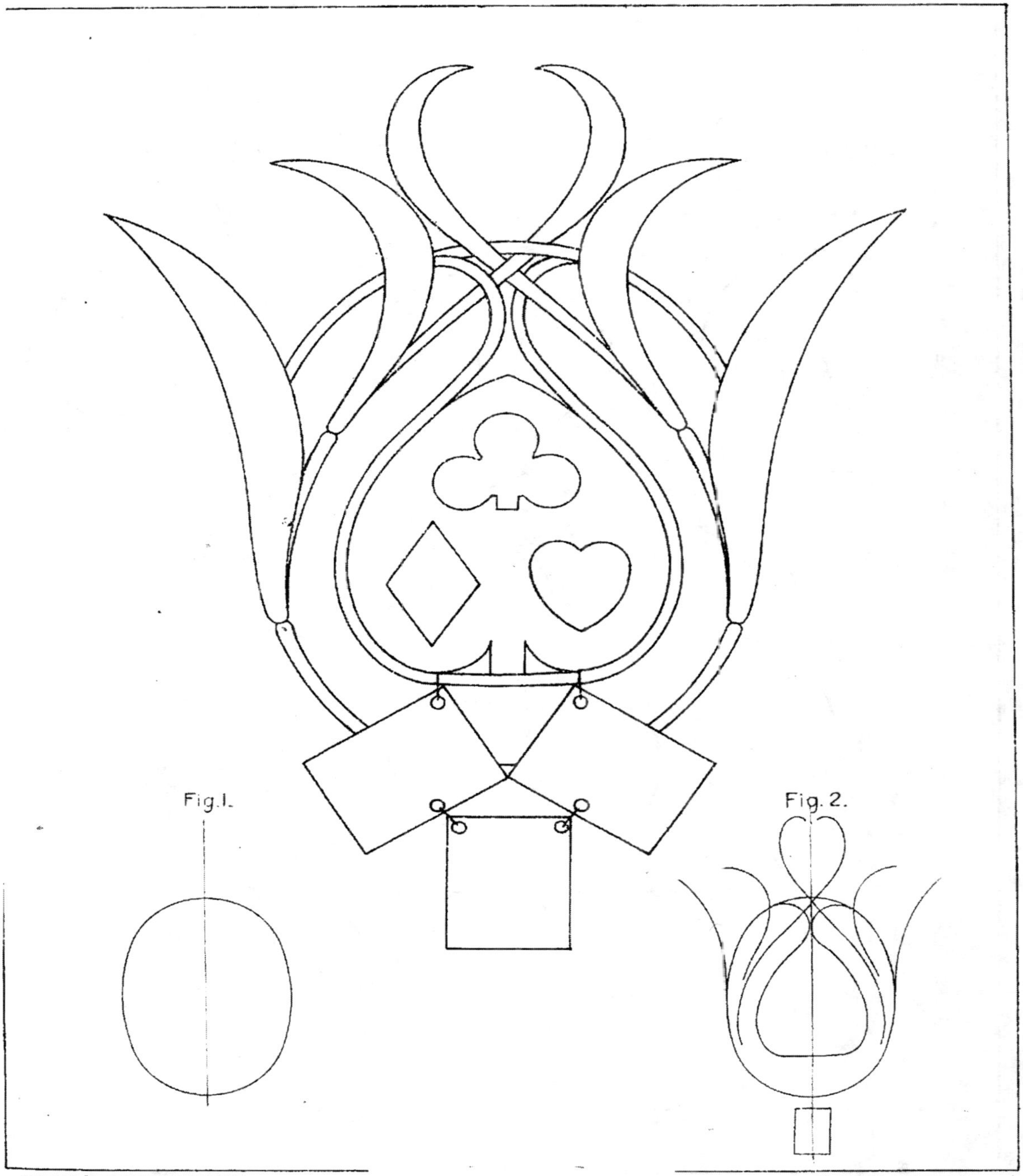

CUSACK'S "FREEHAND ORNAMENT" By CHARLES ARMSTRONG.

PLATE 122

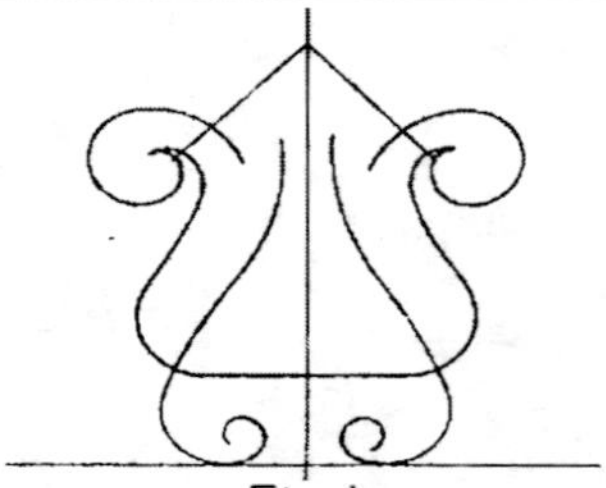

Fig. 1.

Fig. 2.

CUSACK'S "FREEHAND ORNAMENT"

By CHARLES ARMSTRONG.

PLATE 123.

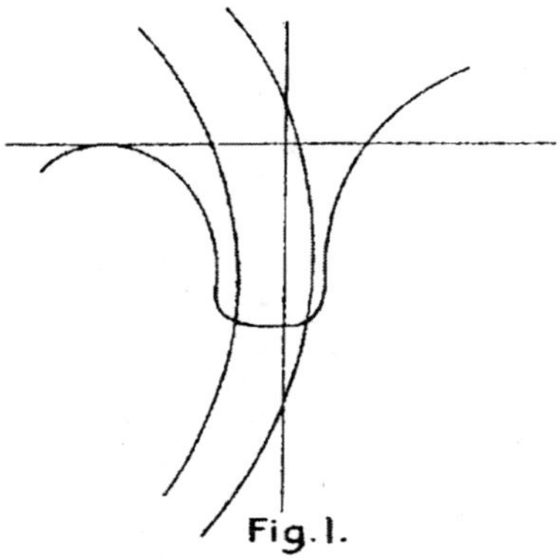

Fig. 1.

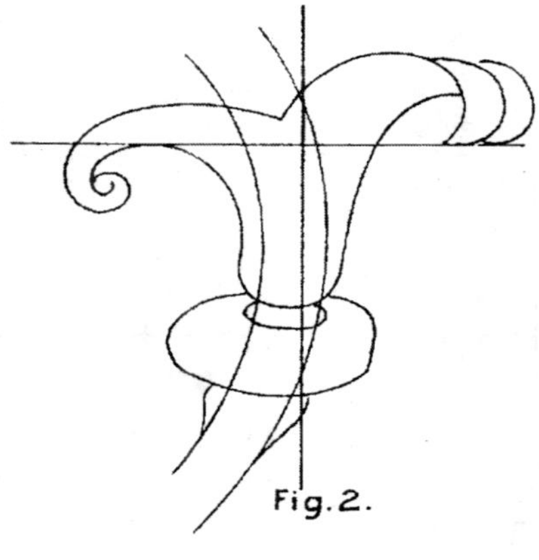

Fig. 2.

PLATE 124.

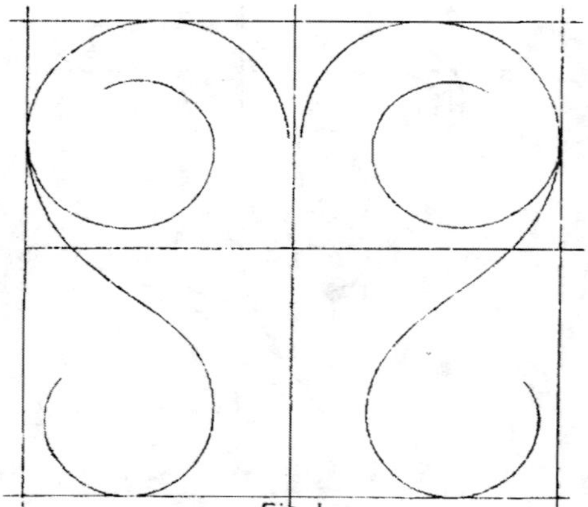

Fig. 1.

Fig. 2.

Copy set at an Examination by the Art Department.

PLATE 125.

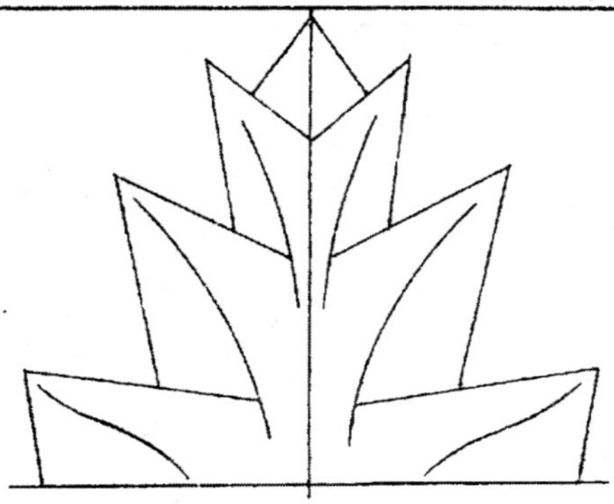

Fig. 1.

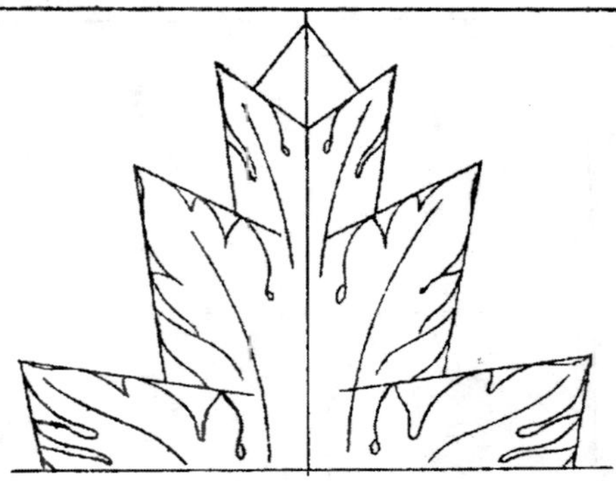

Fig. 2.

Acanthus Leaf

PLATE 126.

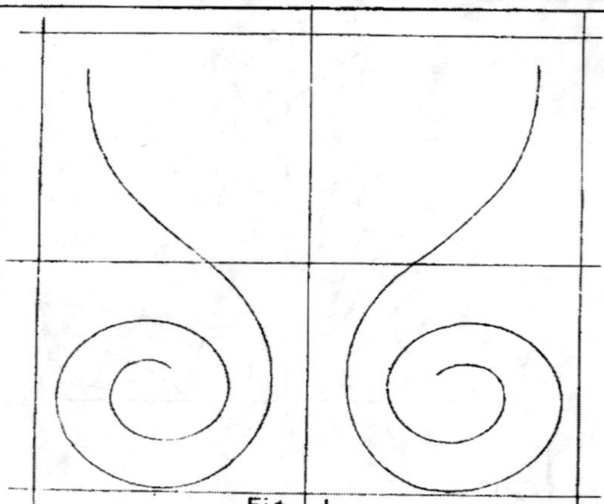

Fig 1.

Fig 2.

From a wall tile in the Entrance Hall, Cusack Institute.

PLATE 127.

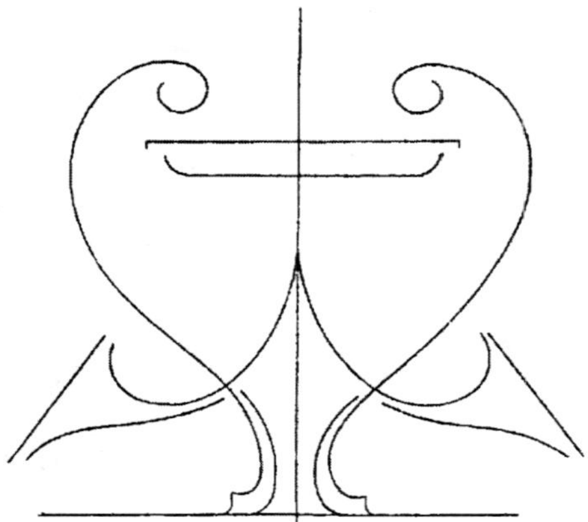

Fig. 1.

Fig. 2.

From a majolica plate border, Faenza Italian. in the S. Kensington Museum.

By CHARLES ARMSTRONG.

PLATE 128.

Fig 1.

Fig 2

Copy set at the May Examination 1895 by
The Art Department

PLATE 129.

Fig. 1.

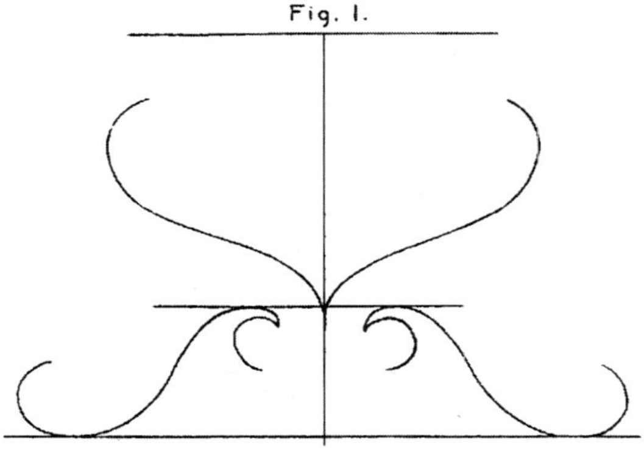

Fig. 2

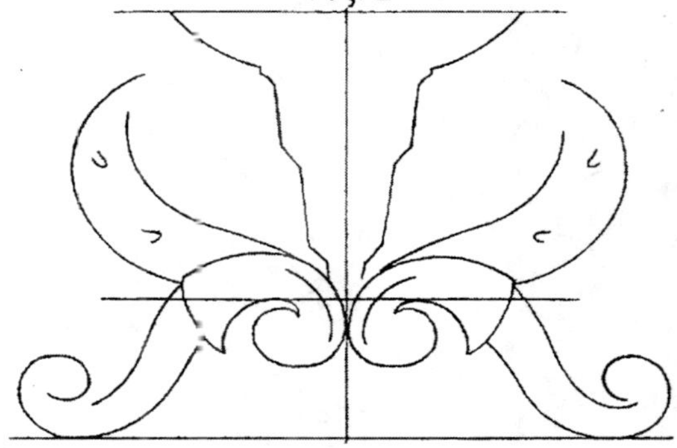

from a 16th Century Toledo Sparish tile
in the S. Kensington Museum.

PLATE 130.

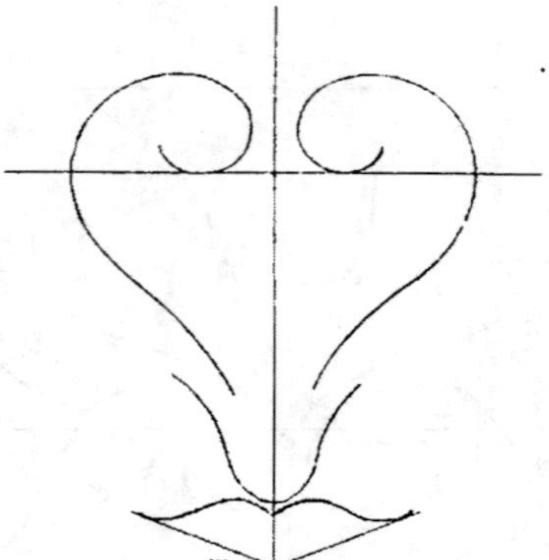

Fig 1.

Fig 2.

Copy set at one of the Art Department's May Examinations.

PLATE 131.

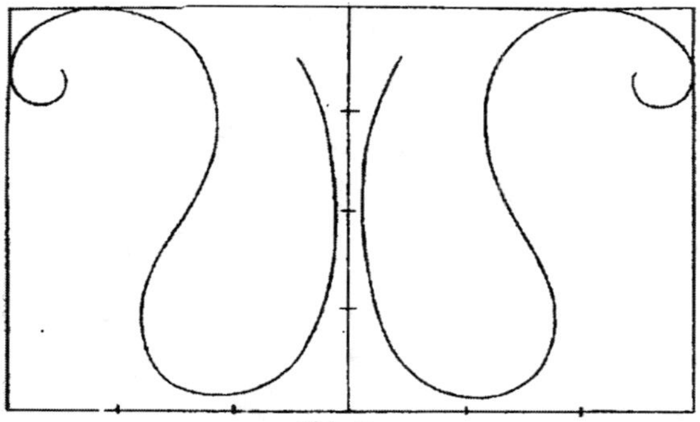

Fig. 1.

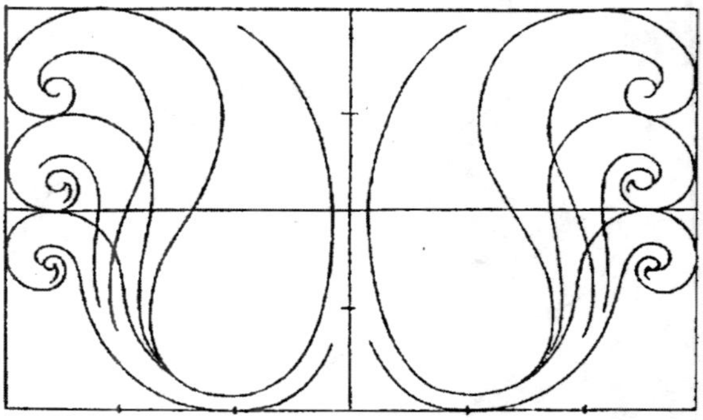

Fig. 2.

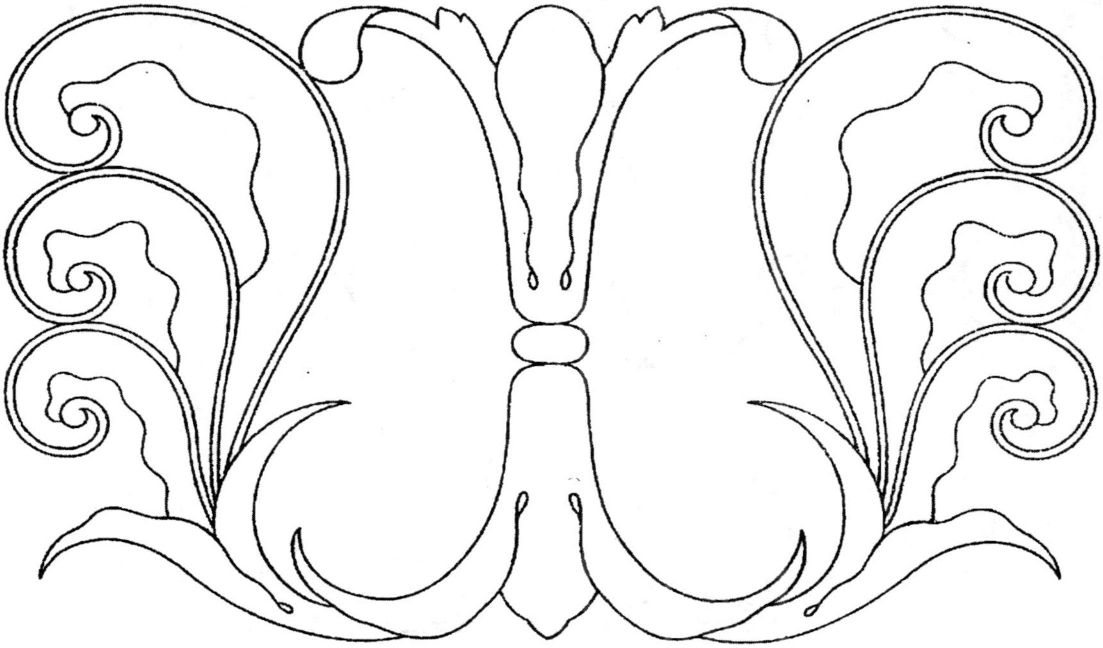

16th Century Italian. from a cast in the Trocadero, Paris.

PLATE 132.

Fig 1.

Fig 2

From a piece of 16th Century Ornament in the Trocadero Museum, Paris.

PLATE 133.

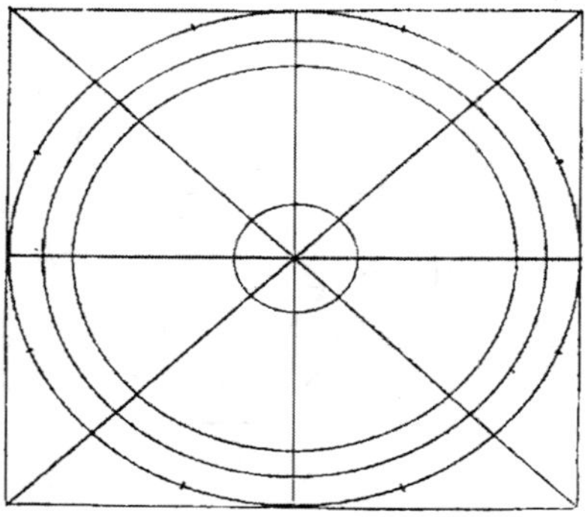

Fig. 1.

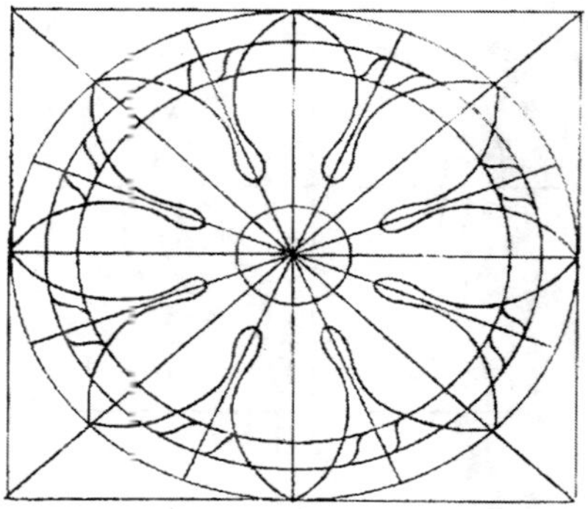

Fig. 2.

Rosette, from a cast in the Trocadero, Paris.

PLATE 134.

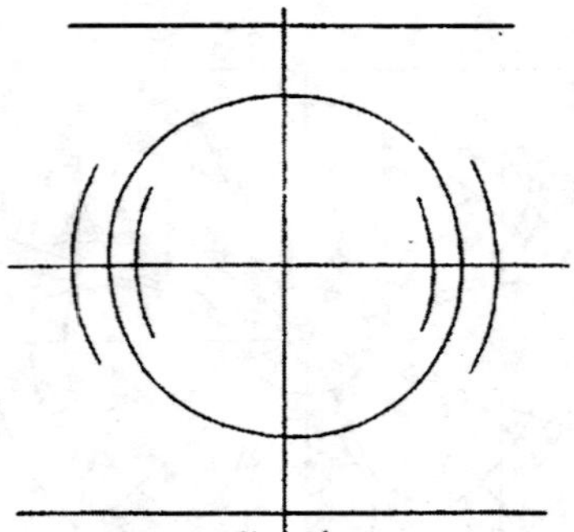

Fig. 1.

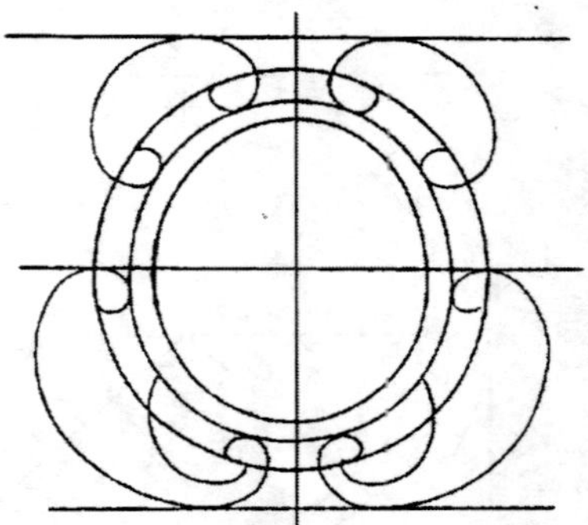

Fig. 2.

PLATE 135.

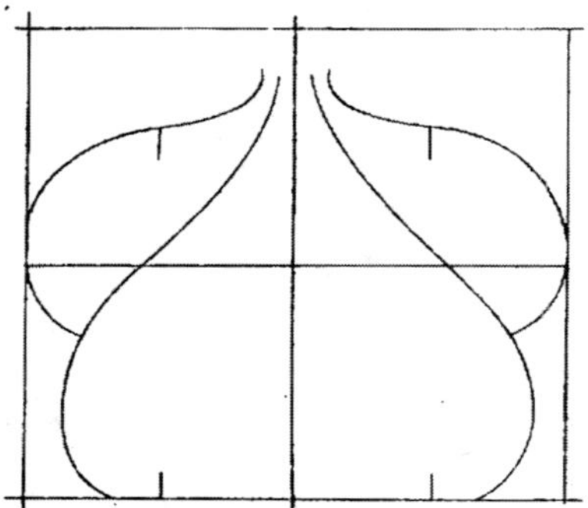

Fig. 1.

Fig. 2.

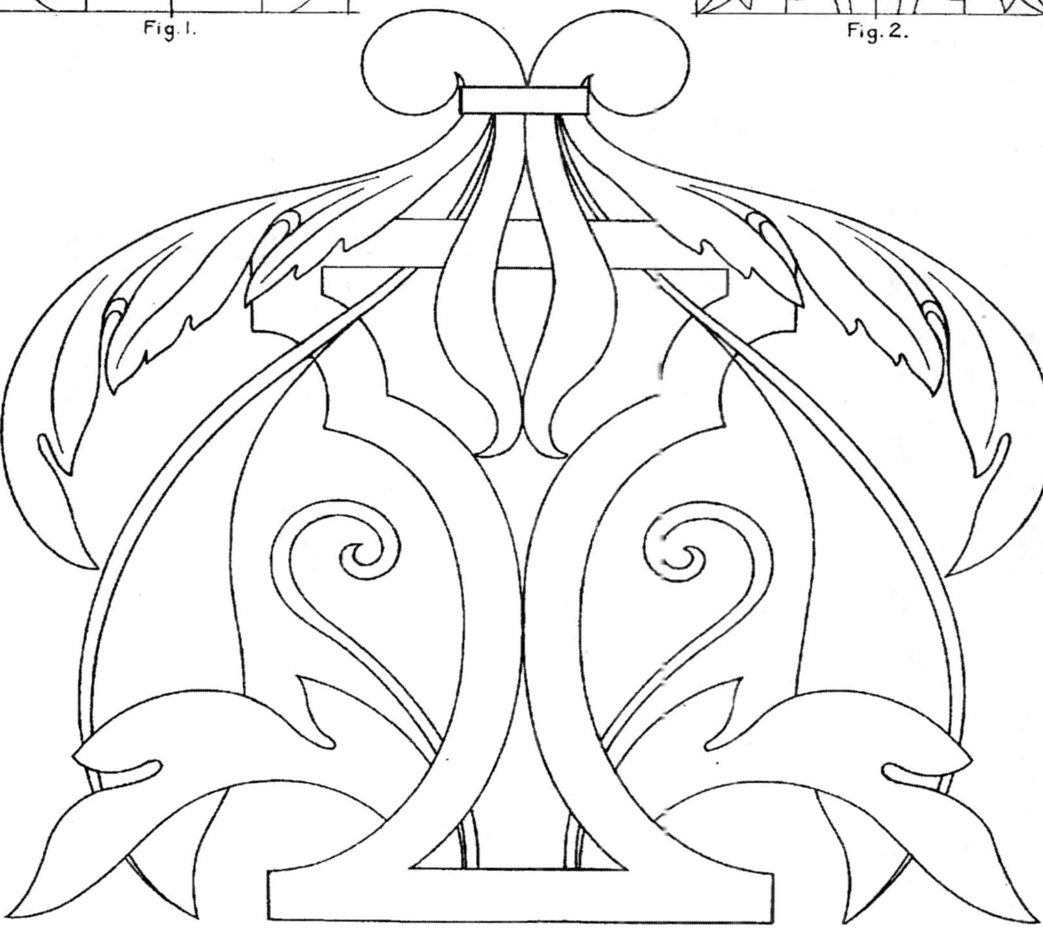

PLATE 136.

From a French 16th Century Limoges Enamel plate border._ in S.Kensington Museum.

PLATE 137.

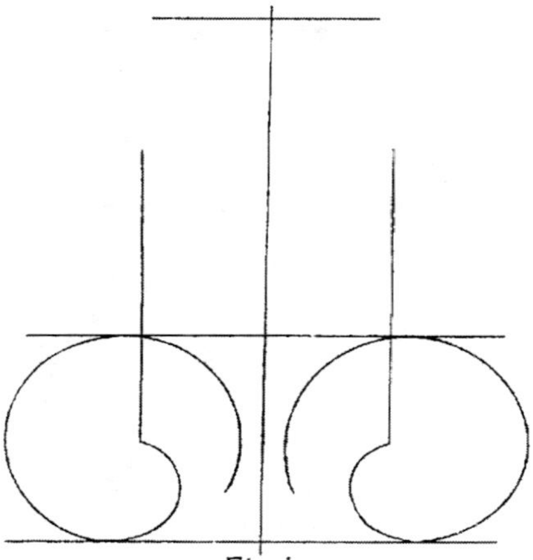

Fig. 1.

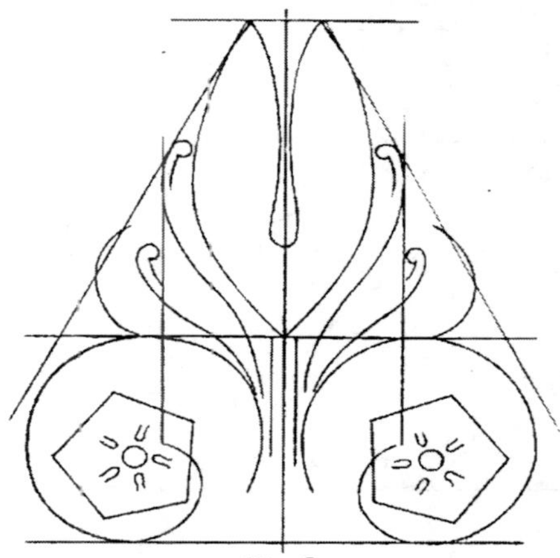

Fig. 2.

Example set at the May Examination of the Art Department. 1895.

PLATE 138.

Fig. 1.

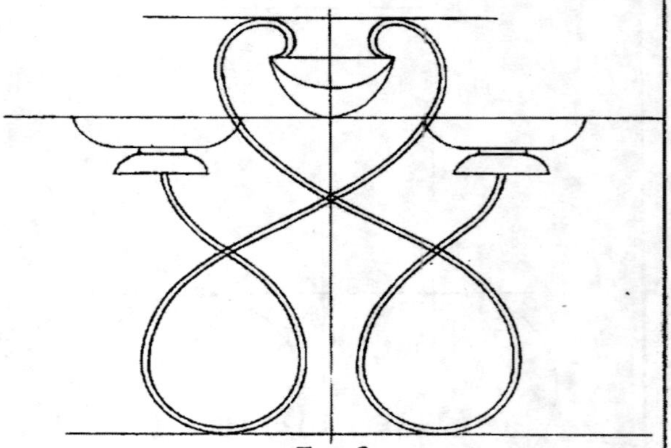

Fig. 2.

By CHARLES ARMSTRONG.

PLATE 139.

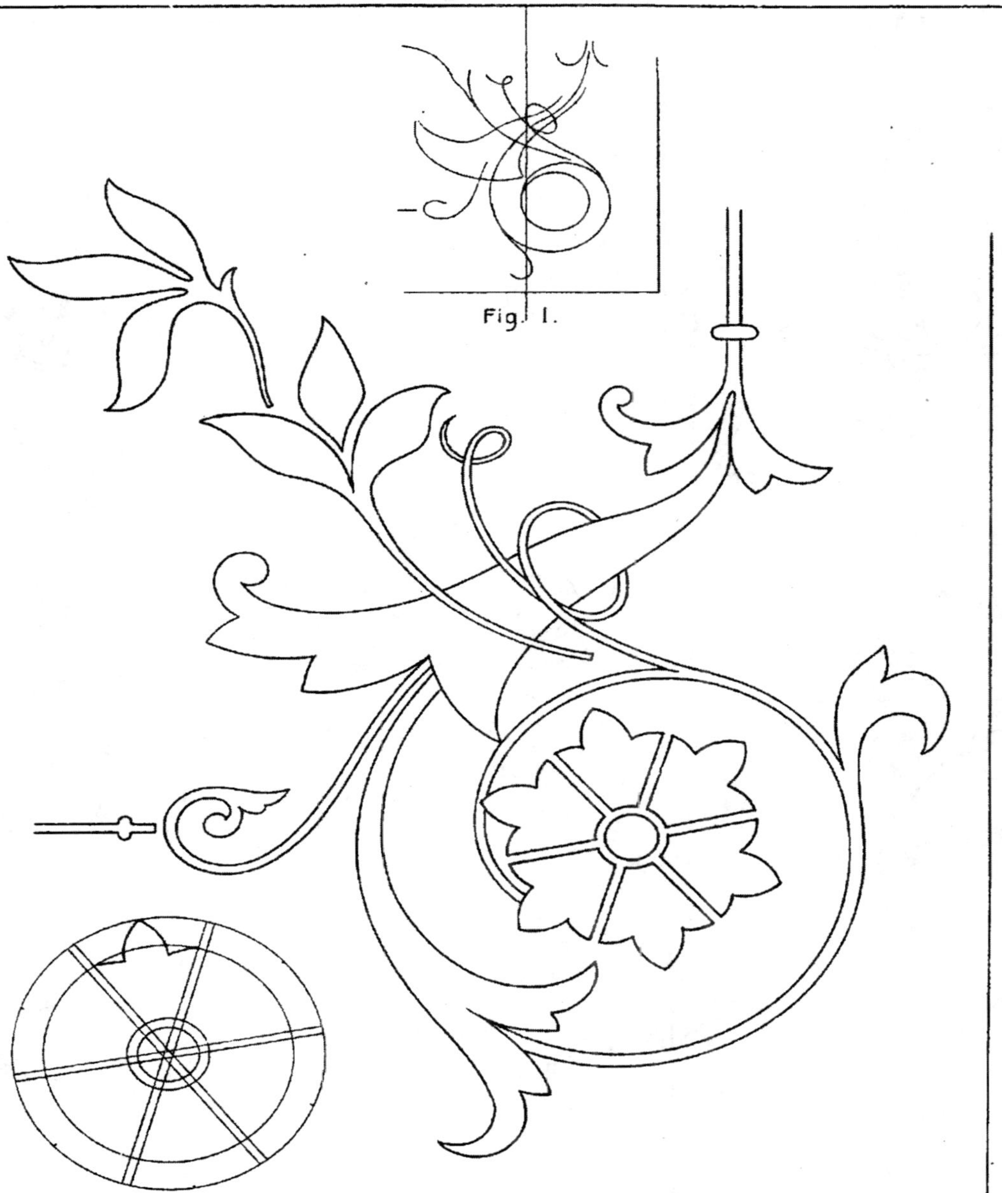

Fig. 1.

From a Mosaic Pavement in the Cusack Institute Entrance Hall.

PLATE 140.

Fig. 1.

Fig. 2.

From a Roman Terra Cotta in the British Museum.

PLATE 141.

from a cast in the Trocadero, Paris.

Fig. I.

Fig. 2.

PLATE 142.

By CHARLES ARMSTRONG.

PLATE 143.

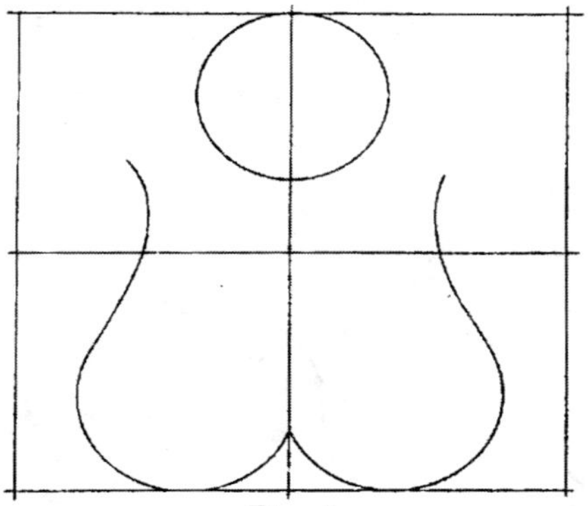

Fig. 1.

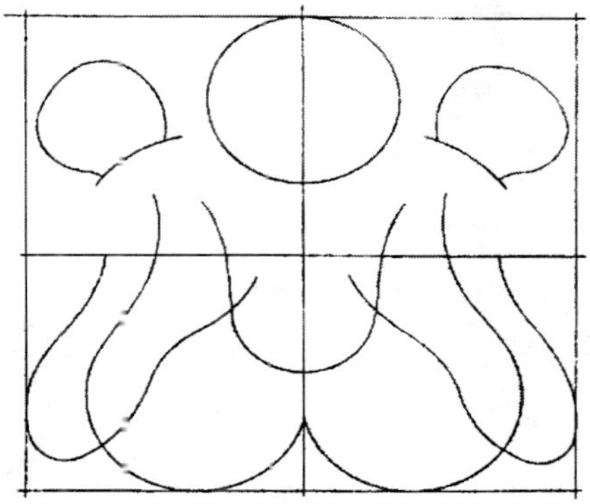

Fig. 2.

PLATE 144.

Copy set at an Examination by the Art Department.

Fig. 1.

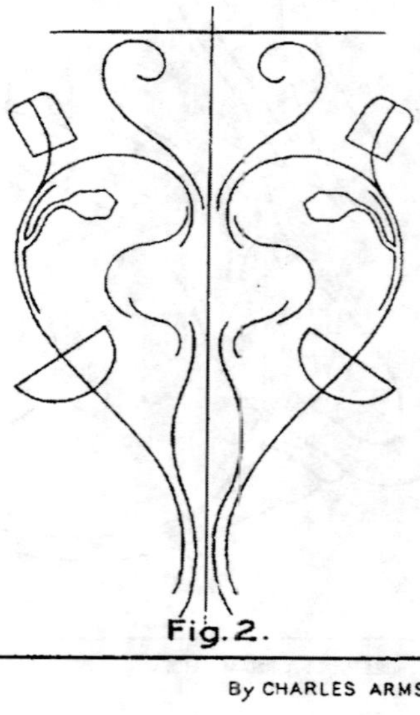

Fig. 2.

PLATE 145.

CUSACK'S "FREEHAND ORNAMENT." By CHARLES ARMSTRONG.

PLATE 146.

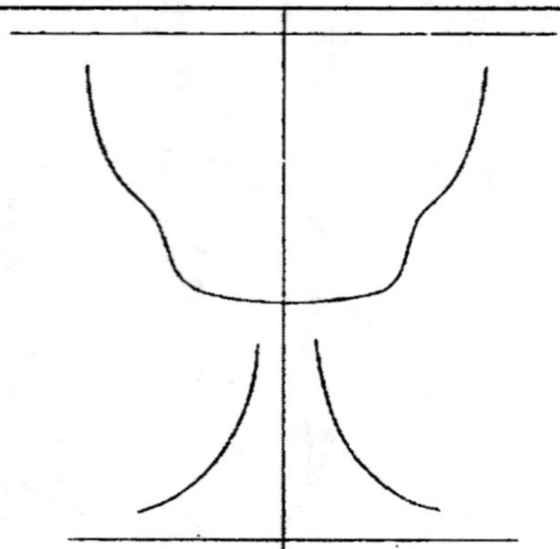

Fig. 1.

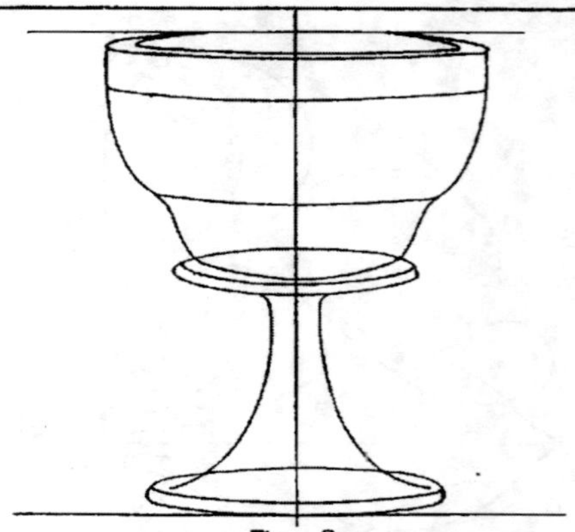

Fig. 2.

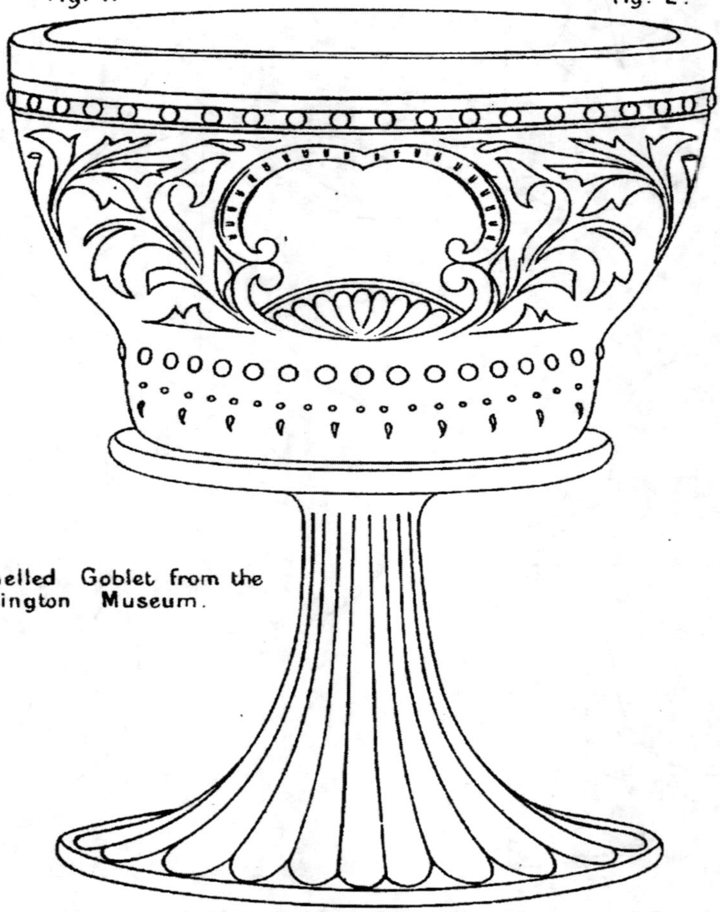

Venetian Enamelled Goblet from the S. Kensington Museum.

PLATE 147.

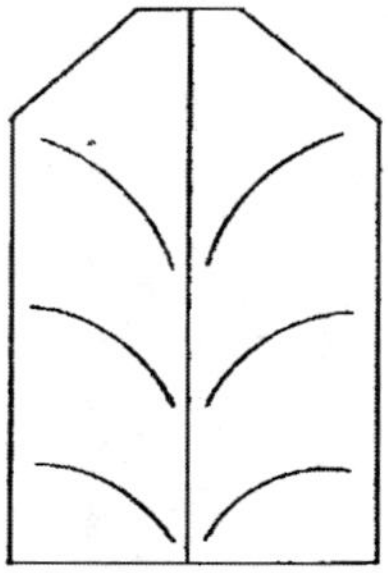

Fig. 1.

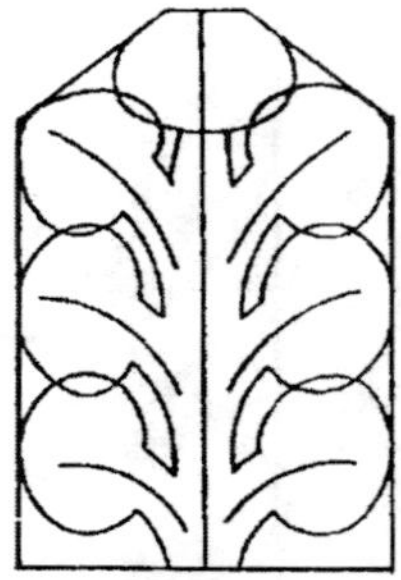

Fig. 2.

from a 13th Century capital in the Trocadero. Paris.

PLATE 148.

Fig. 1.

Fig. 2.

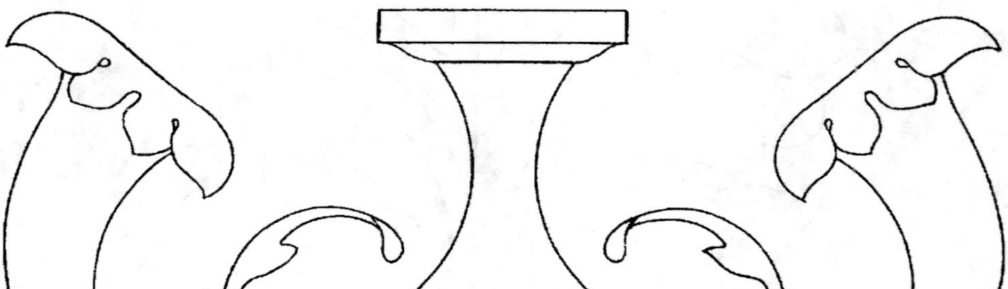

16th Century Ornament - from a cast in the Trocadero Paris.

PLATE 149.

Fig. 1.

Fig. 2.

Copy set at an Examination by the Art Department.

PLATE 150.

Fig. 1.

Fig. 2.

From a cabinet, Italian, ivory inlaid with ebony, in the Cluny Museum, Paris.

PLATE 151

PLATE 152.

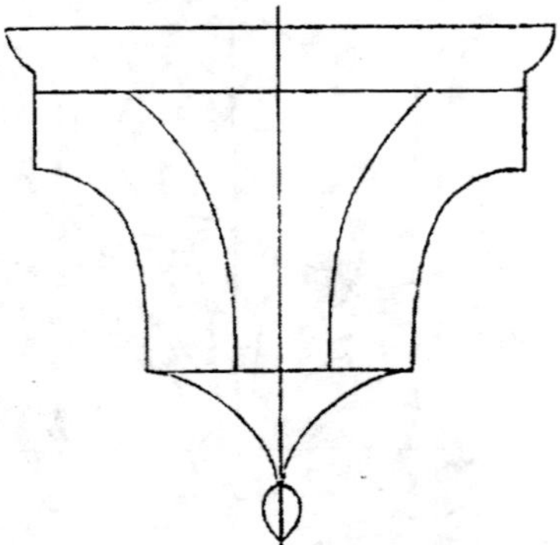

Fig. 1.

Fig. 2.

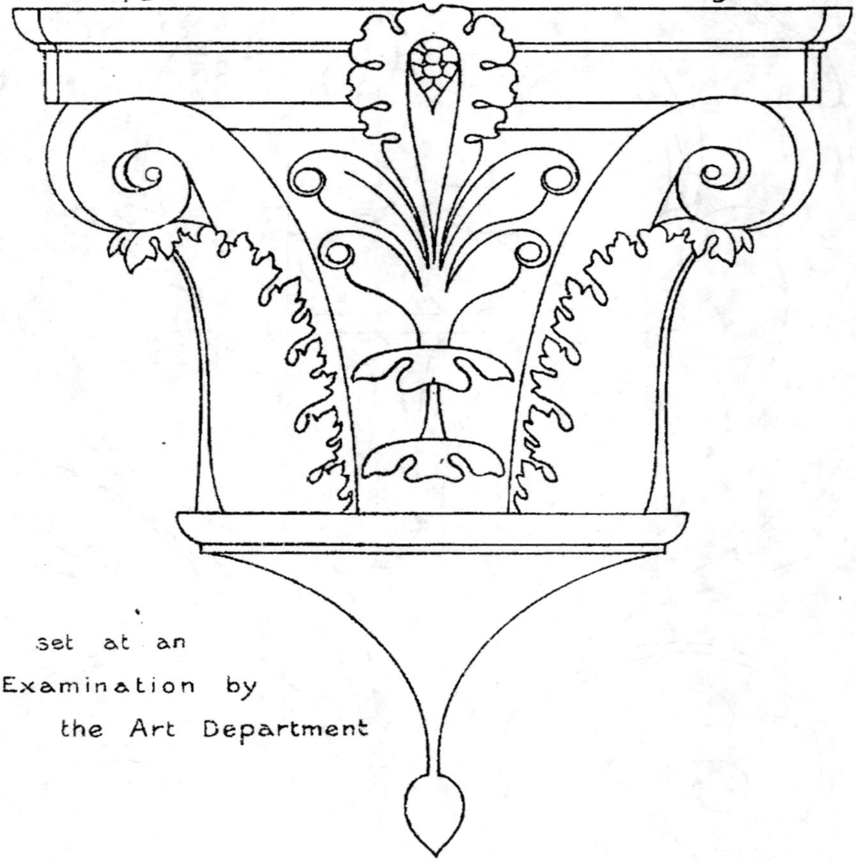

Copy set at an Examination by the Art Department

CUSACK'S "FREEHAND ORNAMENT"

By CHARLES ARMSTRONG.

PLATE 153.

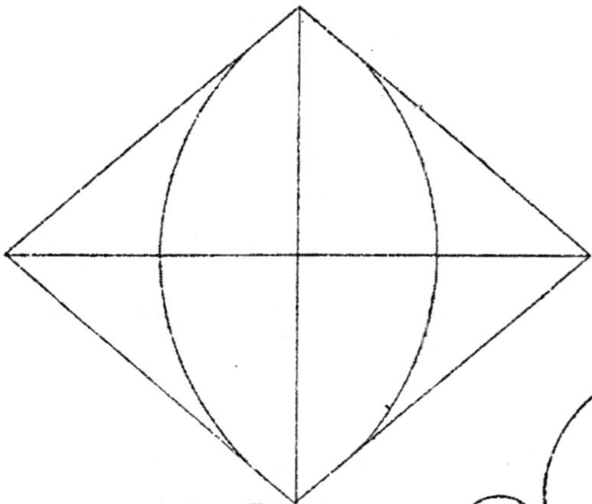

Fig. 1.

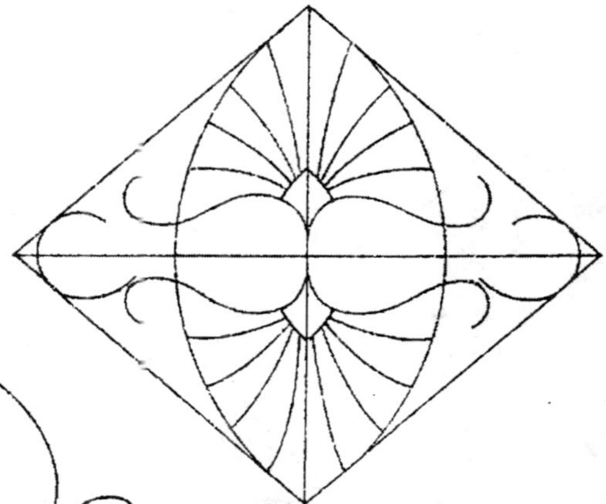

Fig. 2.

from an Egyptian Cornice decoration in the British Museum.

PLATE 154.

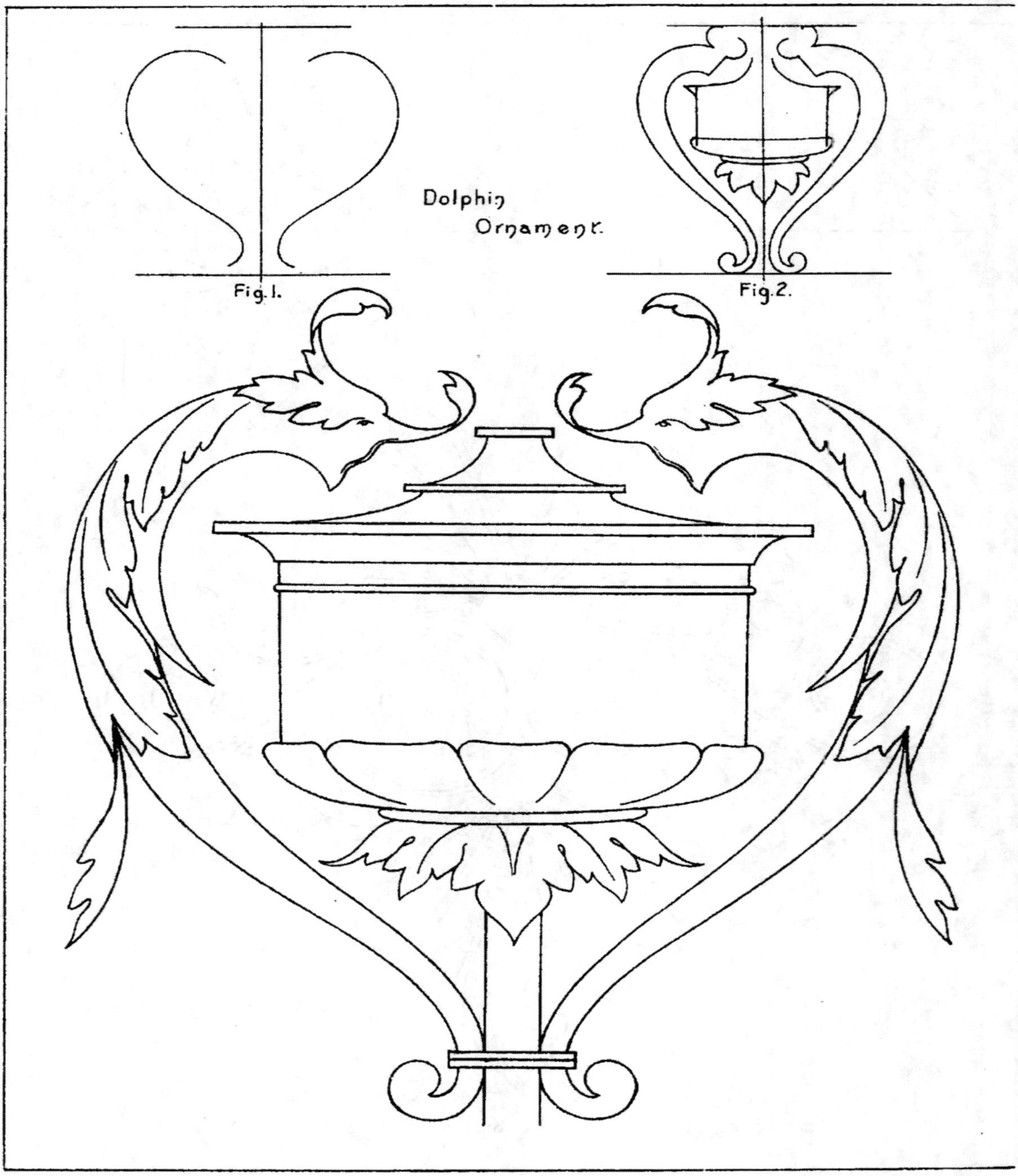

By CHARLES ARMSTRONG.

PLATE 155.

Fig. 1.

Fig. 2.

Copy set at one of the May Examinations of the Art Department.

PLATE 156.

Angle of a Scroll border:- -Ornament in Gold on leather.

German 1572.
South Kensington Museum.

PLATE 157.

PLATE 158.

Copy set at an Examination by the Art Department.

PLATE 159.

PLATE 160.

Fig. 1.

Fig 2.

Example set at a May Examination of the Art Department.

PLATE 161.

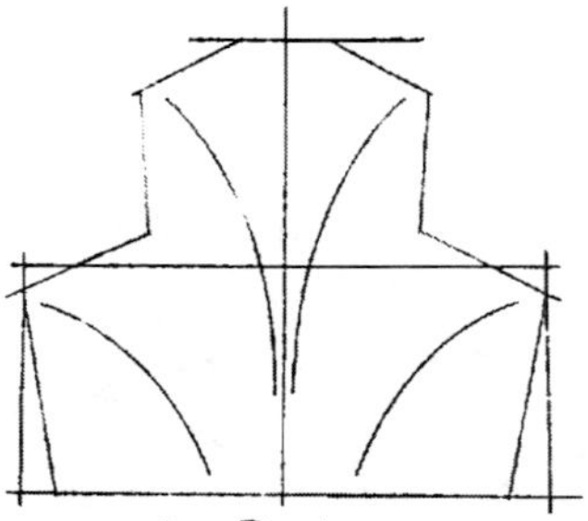

Fig. 1.

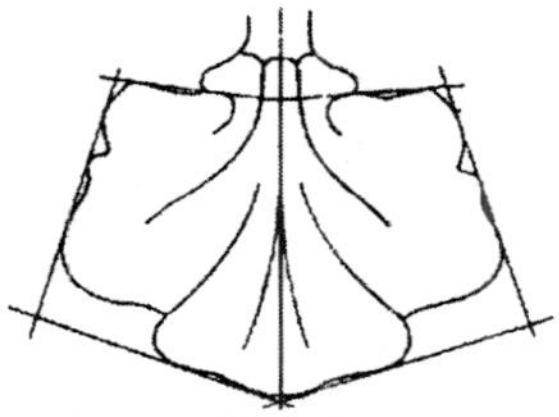

Fig. 3.

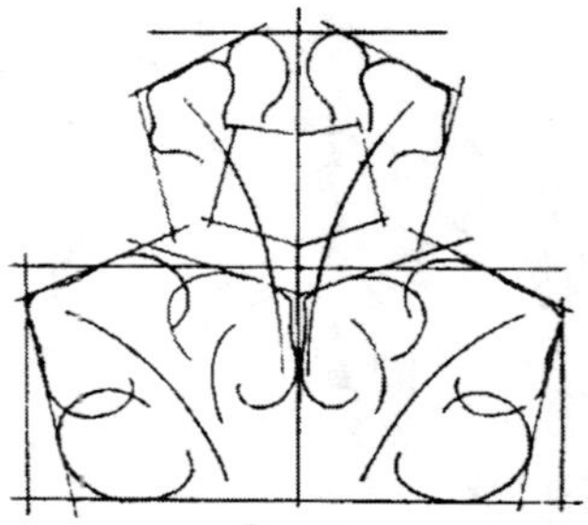

Fig. 2.

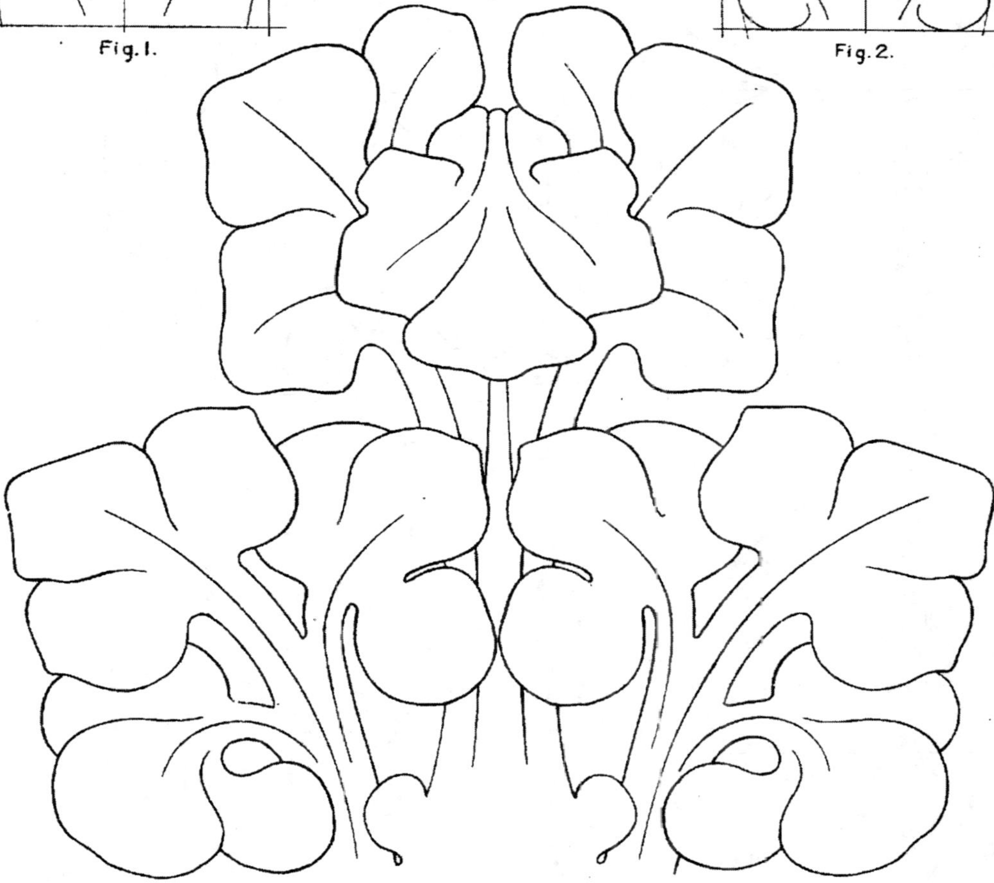

from a cast . in the Trocadero, Paris,

PLATE 162.

PLATE 163.

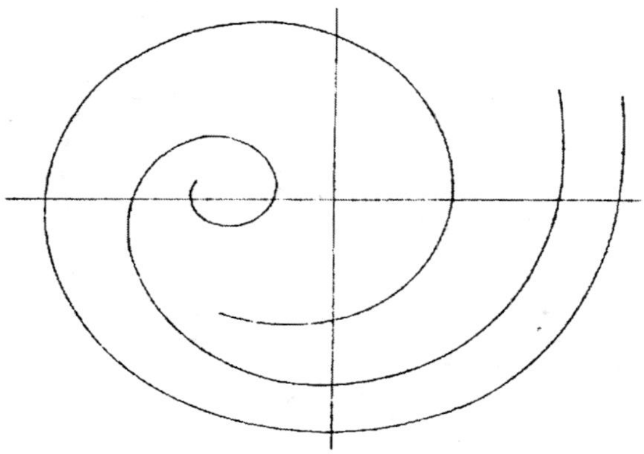

Fig. 1.

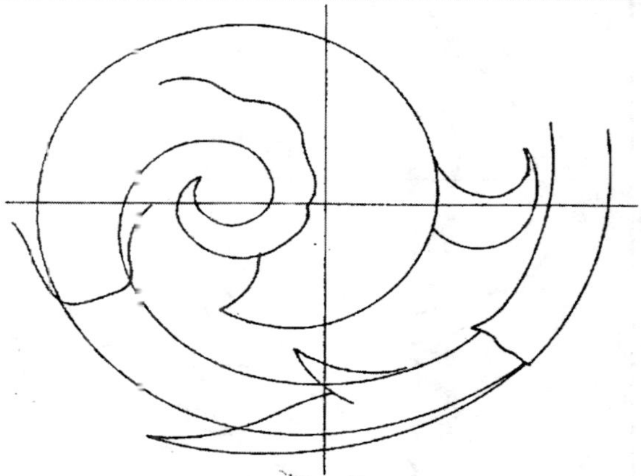

Fig. 2.

PLATE 164.

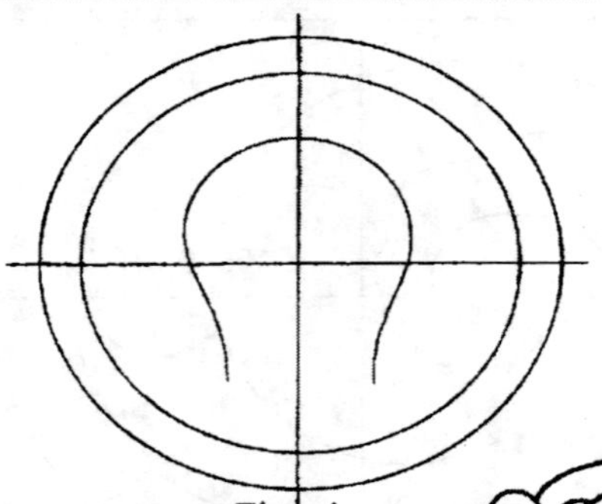

Fig. 1.

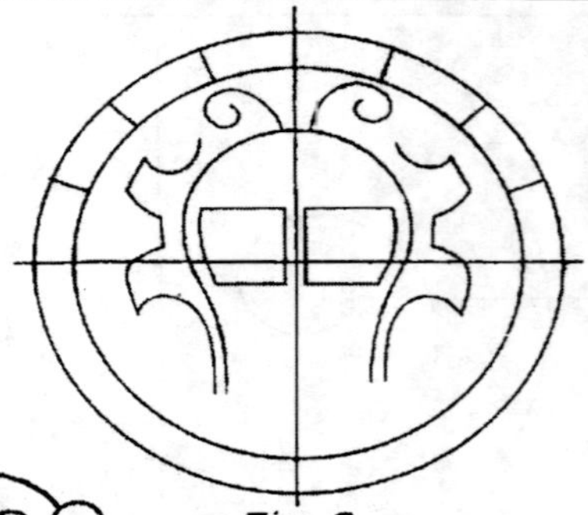

Fig. 2.

16th Century Italian,-from the centre of a carved Stone Chimney piece, now in the S. Kensington Museum.

PLATE 165.

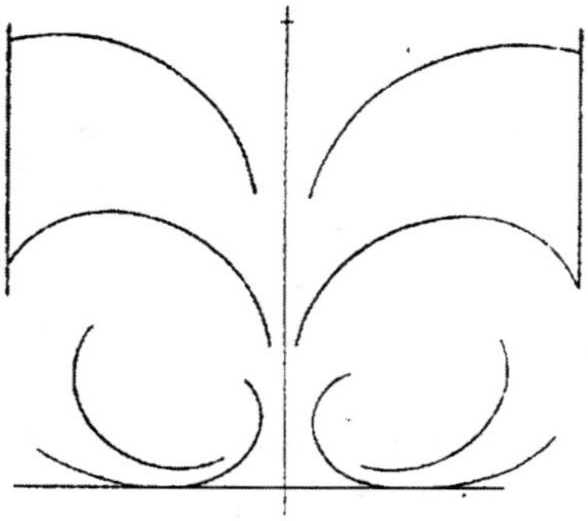

Fig 1.

Fig 2

PLATE 166.

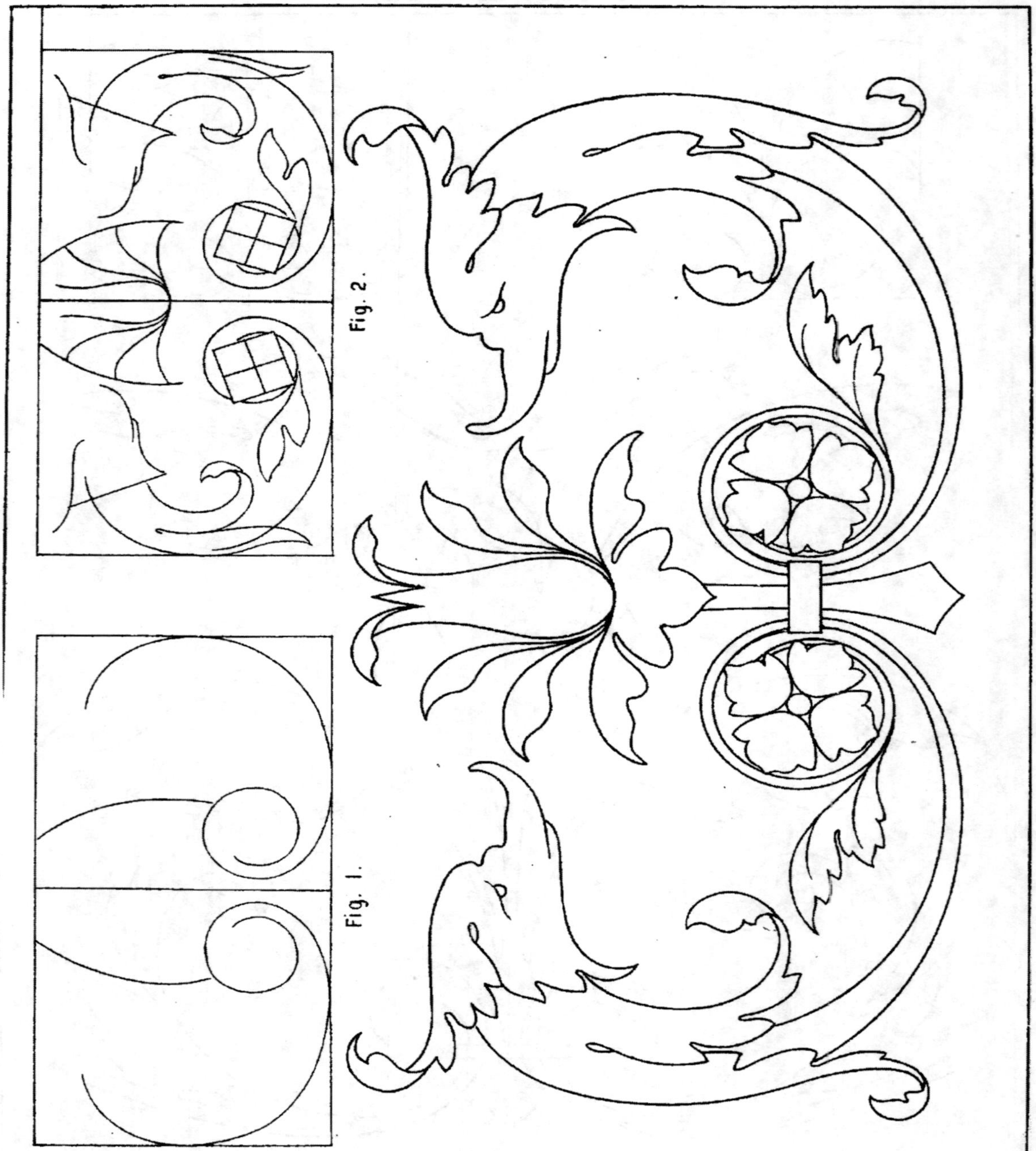

PLATE 167.

Design for an Iron Baluster.

Fig. 1.   Fig. 2

PLATE 168.

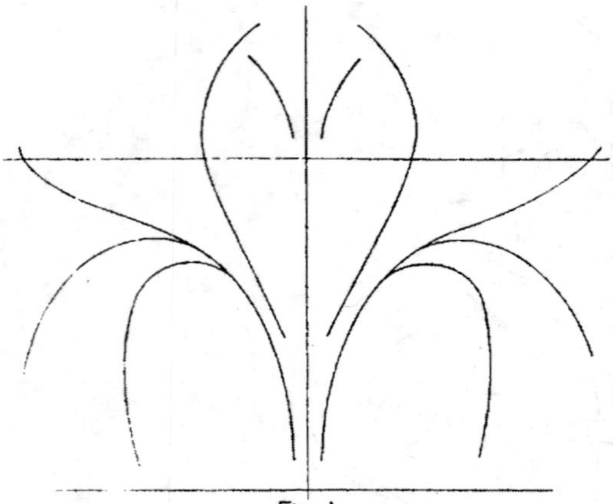

Fig. 1.

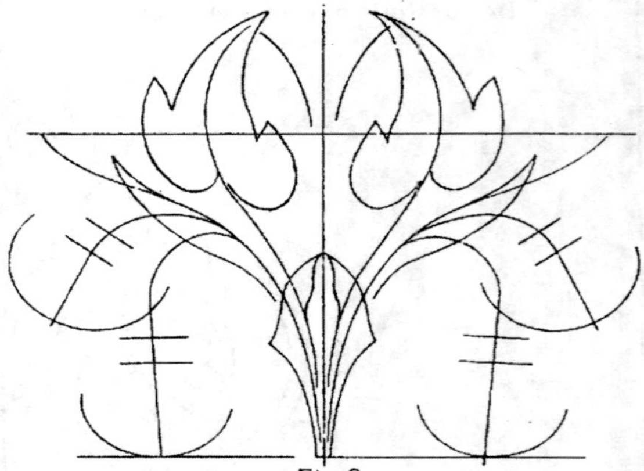

Fig. 2.

Symmetrical design based on the Abutillon flower.

PLATE 169.

from a 15th Century Italian wall fountain in the S. Kensington Museum.

PLATE 170

PLATE 171.

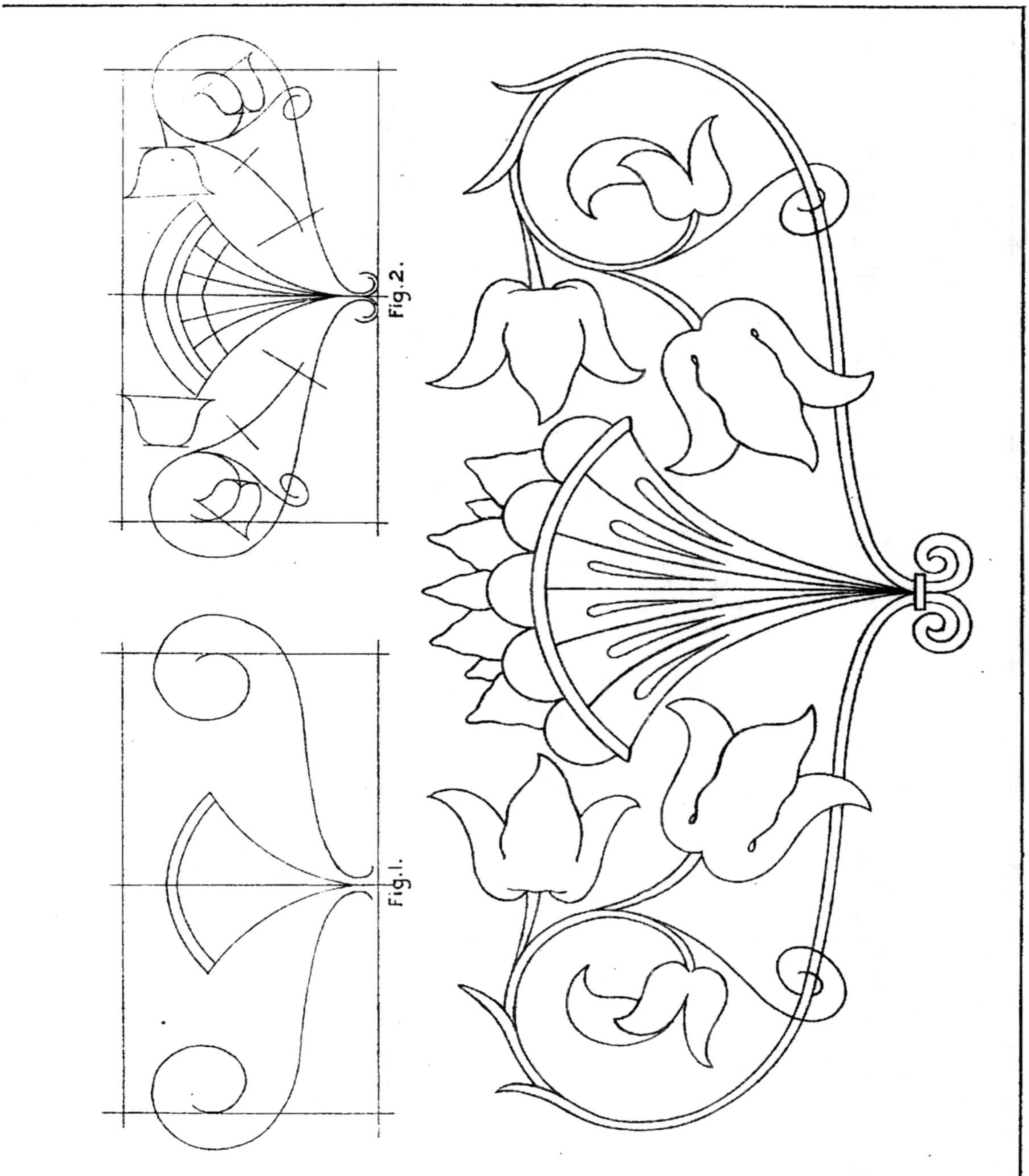

PLATE 172.

Fig 2
Fig. I.
Copy given at a College of Preceptors Examination in Drawing

PLATE 173.

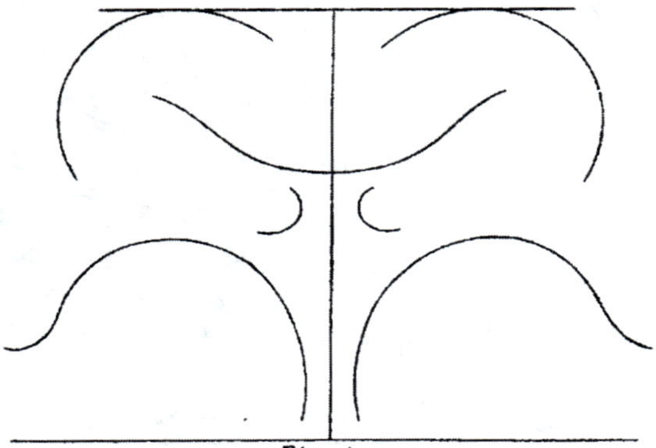

Fig. 1.

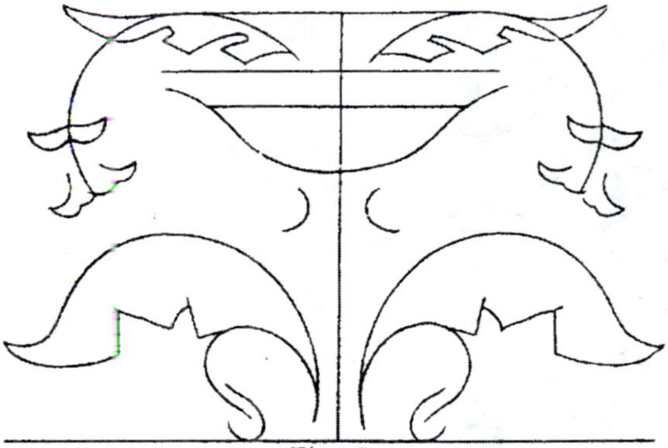

Fig. 2.

From a piece of 16th Century Ornament in the Trocadero. Paris.

PLATE 174.

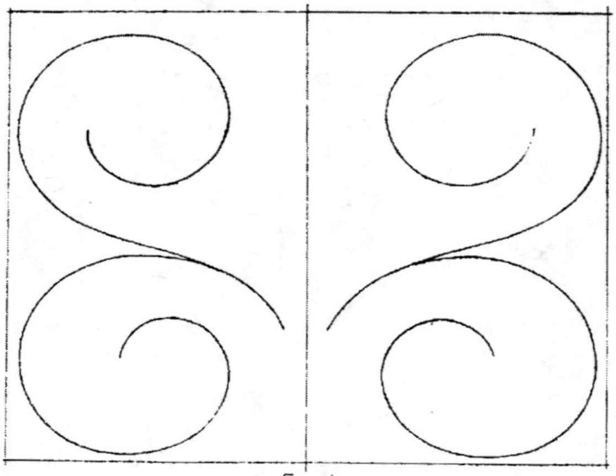

Fig. 1.

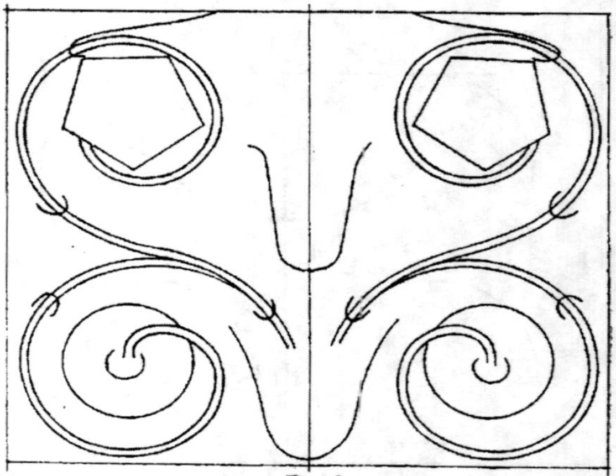

Fig. 2.

Example set at the May Examination of the Art Department. 1893.

PLATE 175.

Copy set at one of the May Examinations of the Art Department.

PLATE 176.

PLATE 177.

PLATE 178.

Fig. 1.

Fig. 3.

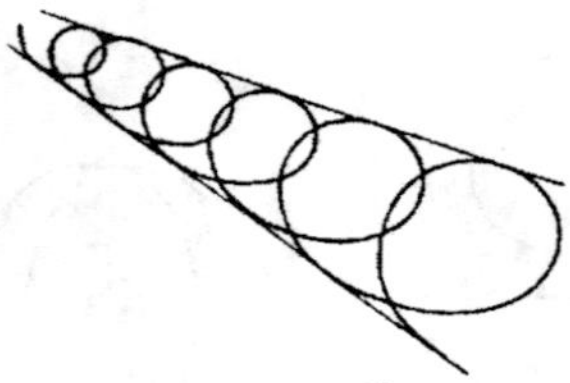

Fig. 4.

Fig. 2.

PLATE 179

Fig. 2.

Fig. 1.

Example of Elizabethan Ornament.

PLATE 180.

Ornament from
an Italian 15th Centy Wall Fountain
in the S. Kensington Museum.
Fig. 1.
Fig. 2.

PLATE 181.

From a 16th Century Capital in the Trocadero Museum Paris
Fig.1.
Fig.2.

PLATE 182.

16th Century Ornament from a Cast in the Trocadero, Paris.

PLATE 183.

By CHARLES ARMSTRONG.

PLATE 184.

By CHARLES ARMSTRONG.

PLATE 185.

Fig. 1. Fig. 2.

PLATE 186.

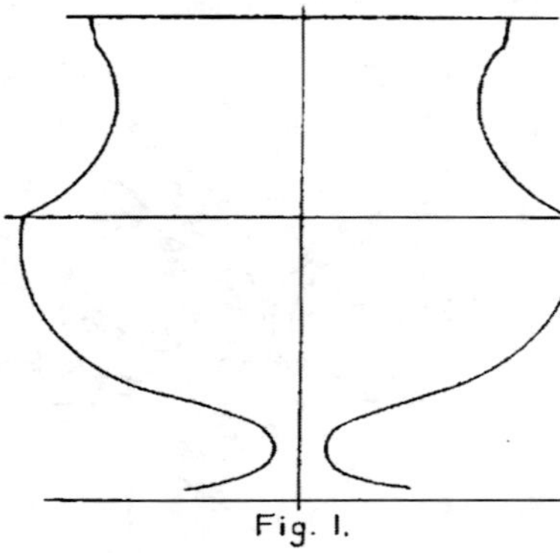

Fig. 1.

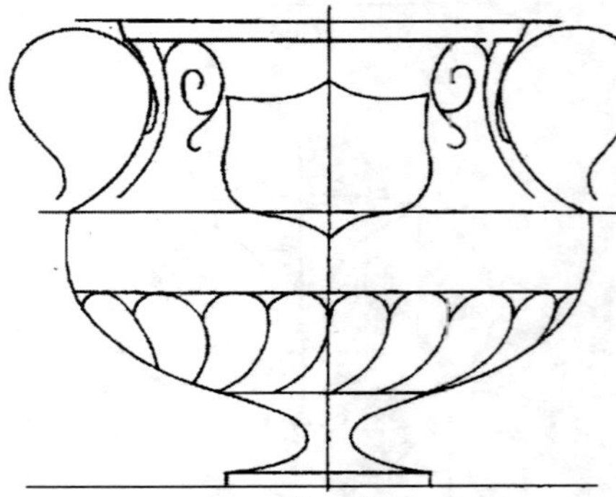

Fig. 2.

From a Majolica Vase in the S. Kensington Museum.

PLATE 187.

PLATE 188.

16th Century Ornament from a Cast in the Trocadero, Paris.

PLATE 189.

16th Century Ornament
From a Cast in the Trocadero, Paris.

PLATE 190.

From 16th Century Ornament in the Trocadero Museum, Paris.

PLATE 191.

Fig. 1.

Fig. 2.

From a piece of 16th Century Ornament in the Trocadero Museum, Paris.

PLATE 192.

Design for a circle based on the Abutillon flower.

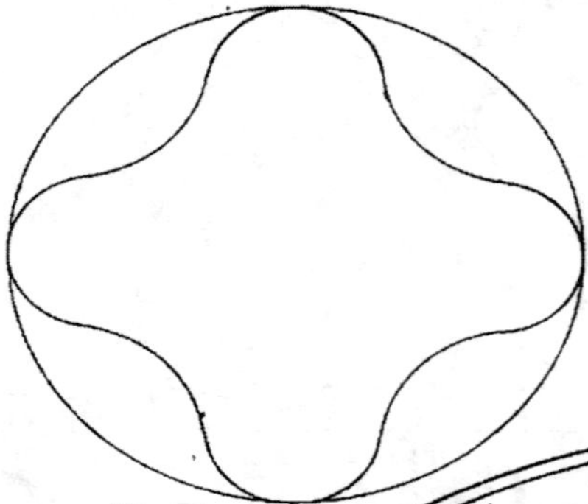

Fig. 1.

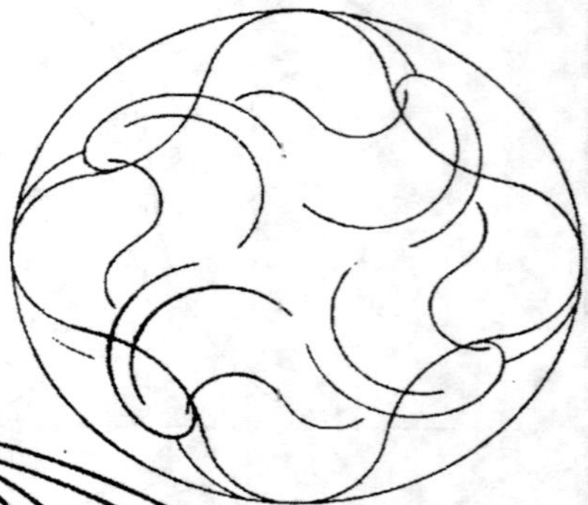

Fig. 2.